THINE IS
THE KINGDOM:

The Trial for Treason of Thomas Wentworth,
Earl of Strafford, First Minister to
King Charles I,
and Last Hope of the English Crown

———

John H. Timmis III

———

The University of Alabama Press
University, Alabama

This book is dedicated to
John H. Timmis II
and
Carolyn E. Timmis

941.0620924
T58   # CONTENTS

52789

ACKNOWLEDGMENTS

I wish to acknowledge the invaluable assistance of Prof. Iline Fife, who read through this book at a primitive stage and made many valuable suggestions and criticisms throughout its development; Prof. Carroll C. Arnold for his advice on critical methodology and who has given encouragement during its lengthy preparation; Prof. Eugene White read and commented on the first draft; Prof. Ronald Linker for his advice concerning Stuart documents; Mr. Maurice Bond, Clerk of Records, H.L.R.O. and his staff for the kindness and efficiency which make working in the records office so easy and pleasant. My thanks are also due to the Librarian and staff of the Sheffield Central Library, the Bodleian Library, and the British Museum. I also thank Mr. Cobb of the H.L.R.O. for his help in deciphering some particularly awkward pieces of the Braye Mss, and Mr. Charles Mann of the Penn State archives for his assistance in locating some rare sources. I am grateful to Miss Anne Steinkamp for her assistance with a voluminous trans-Atlantic correspondence and to Dr. Jessica Haigney Timmis for invaluable criticism, encouragement, and editorial suggestions.

John H. Timmis III

INTRODUCTION

Thomas Wentworth, Earl of Strafford, was the first Royalist hero of the English Civil War. His battlefield was the highest court of the land. His weapons, a brilliant mind and a formidable eloquence. His foe, the combined might of the remorseless Parliamentarians.

The fight began in earnest on November 11, 1640, when the Parliamentary leaders John Pym and John Hampden, attended by 300 members of the English House of Commons, delivered to the House of Lords charges of High Treason against Lord Strafford, pillar to the throne and First Minister to King Charles I. With Strafford's impeachment, the struggle between Crown and Parliament for supremacy in the English government reached that final and crucial stage which led to the Civil War. On May 12, 1641, Strafford was executed. During these six months, from November to May, took place one of the most important trials in the political, social, and legal history of England, and hence of all countries whose institutions derive from England.

Strafford's trial was a great test of strength between Crown and Parliament. The stakes were ultimate control of the government. At the time, Strafford had become the strong right arm of King Charles, the primary support to a tottering throne. If the House of Commons could bring Strafford down, then the final victory would be nearly within their grasp. Strafford's acquittal, on the other hand, would smash the budding revolution of Parliament. His trial became, in the end, one of a few agate points on which turned the final success of Parliament in its struggle for control of the State. Once Strafford was convicted and executed, the Crown was never again the strongest branch of the English government. In every sense, therefore, Strafford's trial was the first major battle of the English Civil War.

As a major event in the struggle between Parliament and the Crown, Strafford's trial has received the attention of historians from Clarendon to

Gardiner to Wedgwood. Their excellent work, unfortunately, has been limited by the early and deliberate destruction of official records of the case. Furthermore, little attempt has been made to interpret the rhetorical, forensic, and legal dimensions of the day-to-day strategic and tactical conduct of the trial.

Upon his restoration, Charles II ordered the proceedings of Strafford's impeachment and attainder to be expunged from the Journals of the House of Lords. Consequently, all historians of the Stuart period and of the trial have had to depend primarily upon John Rushworth for their interpretation of the case. Rushworth's account, though excellent so far as it goes, has two shortcomings: It is not an official record, and Rushworth was absent from the trial at its climax, with the result that the most important days of the trial have had to be reconstructed, heretofore, from very fragmentary sources.

The discovery of the *Braye Manuscripts* now allows the record to be corrected and extended. The *Braye Mss* are a nearly complete set of notes taken down at the trial by the official secretaries and stenographers of the House of Lords. From these minutes, the Journal of the Lords was written. Thus, we have the very source of the record which Charles II ordered blacked out of the Lords' Journals. On many significant points, the *Braye Mss* not only give new evidence but also extend the scope of inference beyond that permitted by Rushworth and by such other documents as were previously depended upon. Discovery of the *Braye Mss* is, by itself, sufficient reason to undertake a new history of Strafford's trial.

These manuscripts underscore and heighten the perennially fascinating circumstances which have always lifted the trial and execution of Strafford to the level of epic drama. And they make nearly inescapable the conclusion that Parliament, under color of law, murdered a brilliant and dangerous, but *innocent* foe, and that King Charles I, to save his own head, acquiesced in the slaughter of his best, most dedicated minister.

It is conceived that, in order to understand why Strafford lost at his trial—why, in effect, he won all the battles but lost the war—our concerns must go beyond a solely historical analysis of the data, to a close analysis of the forensic, rhetorical, and juridical aspects. For it was through his failure to maneuvre quite brilliantly enough in these sectors that Strafford lost his life. In this failure lay the fatal flaw that sealed the fate of one who henceforth must be seen as, in the fullest sense, a tragic hero.

1

The Nation Divides
Strafford and Kings James and Charles: 1603-1629

On the morning of March 24, 1603, Queen Elizabeth died and the Tudor dynasty came to an end. The Tudors had maintained their sovereignty for over a hundred years and the English government was on its way toward becoming an effective structure based upon a working relationship between Crown, Lords, and Commons. After the Tudors (a Welsh line), the throne passed to the Stuarts (a Scottish line), who were now to bear the brunt of a Parliament grown restive under the heavy guidance of the Tudors. The understanding between Parliament and Crown came to a violent close as the Commons grasped for sovereign power. The new Stuart kings soon clashed with these revolutionary forces; out of the conflict came Strafford's trial, the Civil War, Cromwell's Republic, the Restoration, and the Revolution of 1688.

At the beginning of the seventeenth century, the mainstay of English government was the gentry, untitled owners of estates who ranked between the nobility and the yeomanry. These men provided the membership of the House of Commons. Many privileges of the Commons had been established in Tudor times; by James I's accession, it was the right of members to vote taxes, make laws, and, within limits, discuss grievances.[1]

But England was changing. The habit of obedience to the Crown died with the last of the Tudors. During the reign of Queen Elizabeth, the Commons became restless under a civil and political code which had been cast in a feudal mold. The country gentlemen on whom the Tudors relied to maintain a balance against the old nobility, and on whom they had placed the responsibility for local government, were beginning to feel their strength; they began to work towards a government submissive to themselves. They became more forceful in their trespass upon the preserves of the Crown. Members frankly stated that only out of respect for the prestige, age, and sex of Good Queen Bess did they not push to the limit their constitutional demands. These hesitations vanished during the reign of James I: the Stuart Prerogative itself came under fire and his kingship ushered in a full-blown contest between Parliament and the Crown for preeminence in the government.

James' first Parliament at once raised the question of Parliamentary Privilege and Royal Prerogative. In dutiful but firm language the Commons reminded the king that their liberties included free elections, free speech, and freedom from arrest. James indulged his taste for lecturing, brushed contemptuously aside these expressions of national grievance, and reminded the Commons of his Divine Right to rule and their solemn duty to supply his needs.

When James began his reign, he inherited an English constitution which still rested firmly upon the old Tudor structure. Tudor power, however, had never depended upon force. The Tudors never had a standing army or paid bureaucracy and therefore obedience to their will could not be commanded from a country of five million people. Rather, these monarchs appealed sometimes to the love and always to the loyalty and "free awe" of their subjects. At the start of Stuart times, broad discretionary and emergency powers still belonged unquestionably to the Crown. King James spoke grandly of "divine right," but he was too canny, unlike his son, to push Parliament too hard or too far. In the political struggle that lay ahead, it was Parliament, not Kings James and Charles, who upset the Tudor political inheritance and demanded that the sovereign should submit to their modification of his traditional rights. Thus James was always on the defensive against a growing opposition always on the attack.

James and his Parliaments grew more and more out of sympathy as the years went by. Because the spirit of the members moved against the letter of the law, all of his Parliaments were generally unsuccessful. James asked his Commons to make themselves "Parliaments of love," but instead they tried to direct him and his Council in nearly every matter. As a result, James tried as much as possible to live of his own and call Parliament as infrequently as possible; in twenty-one years on the throne, he called but four.

The subsequent conflict argued the powers of the Royal Prerogative versus the powers of an Act of Parliament. James had no sympathy with these agitations. He did not care for compromise; but, unlike his son and like Strafford, he saw when compromise was necessary. It was only the need for money that forced him to deal with Parliament at all. He once told the Spanish ambassador that:

> The House of Commons is a body without a head. The Members give their opinions in a disorderly manner. At their meetings nothing is heard but cries, shouts and confusion. I am surprised that my ancestors should ever have permitted such an institution to come into existence. I am a stranger, and found it here when I arrived, so that I am obliged to put up with what I cannot get rid of.

On the defensive throughout his reign, James maintained the rights of the executive against the encroachments of an independently-minded House of Commons. By infrequently calling Parliament, by juggling the finances, and by usually staying out of Continental wars, he kept the Crown from becoming too dependent upon the purse of the Commons—their prime weapon with which to lever back the reach of the executive. Consequently, by the end of King James' time, Parliament had not been able to improve its constitutional position in relation to that of the Crown. But the king foresaw the coming danger and warned Prince Charles that someday he too would have his "belly full of grievances and impeachments."

Thomas Wentworth, the First Earl of Strafford, was born on Good Friday, April 13, 1593, in the thirty-fifth year of Queen Elizabeth's forty-five year reign. King James of Scotland, coveting the throne of England from his northern kingdom, was then twenty-seven years of age. Thomas was the eldest son of Sir William Wentworth of Wentworth-Woodhouse and his wife Anne, a daughter of Sir Robert Atkinson of Stowell, Gloucestershire. He lived forty-eight years, until May 12, 1641.

Young Wentworth was educated at St. John's College, Cambridge, and in November 1607, he was admitted to study law at the Inner Temple. At age eighteen, he made an important marriage to Margaret, the eldest daughter of the Earl of Cumberland. He was knighted by King James in the same year. After the fashion of the time, Thomas took the Grand Tour of Europe, returning home after fourteen months. At the age of twenty-one, in 1614, he sat for Yorkshire in King James' Addled

Parliament, and in the same year, he became second baronet and head of the family upon his father's death. In 1615, he was appointed to the local office of *custos rotulorum* in Yorkshire, succeeding Sir John Savile, who had resigned from the office in order to avoid dismissal by the royal favorite, the Duke of Buckingham. A lifelong quarrel between Savile and Wentworth was the result. Wentworth again successfully opposed Savile in 1621, this time as a candidate for the Yorkshire seat in the Parliament of that year. Since he stood for Parliament along with the Secretary of State, Lord Calvert, Wentworth was at that time prepared to support King James' government.

The main question before the Parliament of 1621 was military aid to Frederick, Protestant Elector Palatine, after his loss of Bohemia in the Thirty Years War. In this issue, Wentworth took a stand which he was consistently to follow throughout his career: avoid entanglement in Continental politics and give first place to domestic reform.

In the early part of the session, Wentworth (now twenty-eight) spoke only occasionally, and it was not until after the summer adjournment that he took any prominent part in the debates. The government proposed a vote of supplies to enable James to maintain a force in the Lower Palatinate during the winter, and left it up to the king whether to declare war the following summer. The opposition wanted an immediate and direct confrontation with Spain, more vigorously to uphold the Protestant cause. To give James time to come to an understanding with the House, Wentworth proposed on November 26 an adjournment. When this motion was lost, he supported the government in its demand for supplies and the choice of when to declare war. Later in the session, when a constitutional question was raised by the king's declaration that the privileges of Parliament were a grant of the Crown, and not the "ancient and undoubted right" of the House, Wentworth stated on December 15 that he was opposed to the position of the king. He recommended that the avowed privileges of Parliament be set down in a protestation which would make the members' position clear, but which need not be formally communicated to the king, thus maintaining the ground taken by the House but avoiding a direct collision with James. Wentworth's proposal was adopted (thus anticipating by many years the strategy of the Petition of Right), but James took the protestation as an affront, dissolved Parliament, and personally tore the offending page from the Commons' Journal. Only twenty-nine years of age, Wentworth had at the same time angered the king and displayed during the session statesmanlike qualities, marking him as a young man on the rise who might some day perform noteworthy service to his country.

In the spring of 1622, Wentworth had a serious fever. Shortly thereafter, his young wife died, leaving no children. After her death, Thomas returned to Wentworth-Woodhouse, again seriously ill, showing a weakness of health that was to serve him poorly years later at his trial.

In the last Parliament of King James in 1624, Wentworth sat for Pontefract. From scattered hints in his letters, it appears that he had no sympathy with the eagerness of Parliament and the Duke of Buckingham to rush into a war with Spain. The whole tone of Wentworth's conduct at this time indicates a man who has ranged himself on the anti-Puritan side, but who is outraged by the mismanagement of the government and is irritated by his own exclusion from the conduct of affairs of state.

Wentworth remarried on February 24, 1625, at the age of thirty-two. His second wife was Arabella, second daughter of John Holles, the powerful Earl of Clare, and sister of that Denzil Holles who was to hold the Speaker in his chair during the reading of John Eliot's Protestation. King James died on March 27. James' death and the accession of Charles I made it necessary to summon a new Parliament. Wentworth, ready and willing to extend his power and influence beyond Yorkshire, doubtlessly hoped that the new king would appreciate his abilities.

Of the many descriptions of Charles I at the beginning of his reign, none is more attractive than the cameo which we owe to the studies of Will Durant. He says:

Before the storm soured the milk of human kindness in him, he was a reasonably good man—a loving son, an unusually faithful husband, a loyal friend, a father idolized by his children. He had begun the struggle of life by fighting a congenital weakness of physique; he could not walk until he was seven. He overcame this defect by resolute pursuit of vigorous sports, until in maturity he could ride and hunt with the best. He suffered from an impediment of speech; until ten he could hardly speak intelligibly; his father thought of having an operation performed on the boy's tongue. Charles gradually improved but to the end of his life he stammered and had to counter his difficulty by speaking slowly. When his popular brother Henry died, leaving him heir apparent, Charles was suspected of complicity in the death; the charge was unjust, but it shared in darkening the Prince's mood. He preferred a studious solitude to the bibulous hilarity of his father's court. He became proficient in mathematics, music, and theology, learned something of Greek and Latin, spoke French, Italian, and a little Spanish. He loved art; he cherished and expanded the collection left by his brother; he became a discriminating collector, and a generous patron of artists, poets, and musicians. He invited the Italian painter Orazio Gentileschi to his court, then Rubens, Van Dyck, and Frans Hals. Hals declined and Rubens came chiefly as ambassador; but all the world knows Charles as the proud and handsome king, with Van Dyck beard, repeatedly painted by Van Dyck.[2]

To this must be added the king's lack of insight and humor, his customary silence, and his intellectual shortcomings—all of which were poor protection against rough going. He was guided by his emotions and prejudices; he was shifty and unstable; and he usually submitted to advisers of second-rate ability.

Charles' marriage and parentage also contributed to his downfall. From James I, he inherited his conception of the absolute royal prerogative, with power to make law, to rule without Parliament, and to override laws enacted by Parliament. His view was justified by English precedent and taken for granted in France and Spain; it was encouraged in Charles by his favorite, the Duke of Buckingham, the Court, and Queen Henrietta Maria. England's queen was a devout Roman Catholic; she had been brought up at the French court during the period when Richelieu was making her brother Louis XIII absolute in France.

The bishops who took the king's fancy were all High Churchmen. For primate of England, Charles selected William Laud, Bishop of London and an avowed enemy of the Puritans. Laud upheld a new movement in the English Church which opposed Puritanism, laid stress upon the beauty of holiness, and questioned the doctrine of predestination. In the Netherlands, a theologian named Arminius had concurrently attacked predestination; consequently Laud and his friends were nicknamed "Arminians" and because they refused to deny that Roman Catholics were true Christians, they were also assailed as "spawn of the papists." The king favored Laud's religious point of view and was later to use the Archbishop as a chief adviser.[3] But at the outset of the reign, he had nobody in Laud's, or Wentworth's, class for a minister; affairs were in the hands of the incompetent Duke of Buckingham.

Charles had not simply inherited the reckless duke from his father: he had grown up with him, forming a life-long friendship which made it impossible for the king to see Buckingham as the disastrous counselor that he was. Buckingham, with the support of Parliament, had led James into a war with Spain, aiming to restore the king's son-in-law, Frederick the Winter King, to the Palatinate. The war chest voted by James' fourth Parliament was quickly spent, partly on equipment for an English expeditionary force commanded by the German soldier Mansfield. Charles, immediately upon becoming king, therefore summoned his first Parliament and in his opening speech, after thanking God that the business in hand did not need much explaining "for I am neither able to do it, nor doth it stand with my nature to spend much time in words,"[4] called upon the members to vote more taxes for the war which they had encouraged the Crown to start. Charles fully expected a liberal grant. He was, after all, championing the Protestant cause, and was planning with the duke operations against Spain that would rival the glories of Drake.

Charles I's first Parliament met on June 18, 1625. One hundred Lords sat in the Upper House; five hundred men, three-fourths of them Puritan, had been elected to the Lower House. The House of Commons was not a democratic house: they represented the economic wealth of the realm, not its population, and had been elected through the political and financial influence of lords or of the gentry. This House had ability and ambition; in it were Coke, Selden, John Pym, Sir John Eliot, and others marked for history, including Sir Thomas Wentworth, later to be Earl of Strafford and chief minister to the king. The total wealth of the Commons exceeded threefold the wealth of the Lords. The Commons showed its temper early: the king asked for an appropriation for governmental expenses and the war with Spain, but the Commons voted him 140,000 pounds, which was purposely inadequate to fight the war that they had advocated; the fleet alone required twice that sum. The Commons even tried to cut the Crown's regular and traditional income: for two centuries, English monarchs had been granted for the duration of their reign the right to levy customs duties (tonnage and poundage); now Parliament's tonnage and poundage Bill would give Charles this right for one year only. The members distrusted Buckingham and believed that no matter how much money they voted, the favorite would waste most of it. Also suspicious of Arminians at Court and papists in the country, they demanded stringent enforcement of the anti-Catholic laws.

In the first Parliament of King Charles, Wentworth again sat for Yorkshire, but he was immediately unseated on the charges that the sheriff had prematurely closed the poll in the faces of supporters of his old rival Savile. In the proceedings which followed in the House, Wentworth, contrary to the rules of order, tried to speak in his own defense while the case was under investigation. This brought on a fierce attack by John Eliot, who compared him to Catiline, coming into the Senate to destroy it.[5]

Wentworth was reelected to his disputed seat on August 1, in time for him to join Parliament when it met that summer in Oxford, a change of site made on account of a London plague. During this session, Buckingham conveyed to him an offer of favor, to which Wentworth replied that he "was ready to serve him as an honest man and a gentleman."[6] Wentworth, however, was not in favor of a war with Spain, whether it was promoted by Buckingham or else by Eliot; for he said in the House:

> Let us do first the business of the Commonwealth, appoint a committee for petitions, and afterwards, for my part, I will consent to do as much for the King as any other.[7]

This speech clearly stated the main principle of Wentworth's political conduct: avoid external complications; pursue internal reforms. In 1625, this view put him in opposition to the policy of both the duke and popular sentiment.

At the close of the session, Wentworth's sense of independence was affronted by the threat of a dissolution by Charles. To a proposal that the Commons should cease its stubborn opposition to Buckingham, he replied:

> We are under the rod, and we cannot with credit or safety yield. Since we sat here, the subjects have lost a subsidy at sea.[8]

The Commons were resolved to compel thereafter an annual summoning of Parliament and an annual examination by Parliament of governmental expenditures. Charles took offense at these economies and encroachments, and when plague threatened London, he used it as an excuse to dissolve the Parliament (August 12, 1625).

Buckingham went ahead with his plans for an operation against Cadiz, arguing that victory would unite the country behind the Crown and encourage the Commons to loosen their purse strings. The duke's expedition went badly, and Charles, desperate for funds, resigned himself to calling his second Parliament.

In November 1625, when a new Parliament was in the making, Wentworth was made sheriff of Yorkshire to prevent his sitting in the House. Yet, Wentworth's approach to the relations between Crown and Parliament was markedly different from other members who were disabled by royal appointments. Charles himself was aware of this when he looked down the list and remarked: "Wentworth is an honest Gentleman."[9] The important difference between Wentworth and other opponents of the Crown was clearly shown by his own words not long after he had been excluded from Parliament:

> My rule which I will never transgress is never to contend with the Prerogative out of Parliament, nor yet to contest with a King but when I am constrained thereunto, or else make shipwreck of my peace of conscience, which I trust God will ever bless me with, and with courage, too, to preserve it.[10]

It was the misfortune of Charles and Buckingham that they did not know how to turn a half-hearted opponent into a friend. Wentworth was far from associating himself at this time with the attack on the favorite: indeed, on the basis of a rumor that the Presidency of the Council of the North was vacant, he wrote and asked for the appointment.[11] There was no vacancy, but at Easter he came to London, still hopeful of preference, and was civilly received by the duke. Scarcely a month later, however, he felt the weight of the king's displeasure. His name was listed among the opponents of the royal party, and he was dismissed from his offices of justice of the peace and *custos rotulorum*, which latter office was at last given back to Sir John Savile.[12] The order for his dismissal from the Custoship was handed to him while he was presiding at a session, but he showed a dignity equal to this intentional public affront.[13]

From the language used by Wentworth when he announced his loss of place, it appears that he had refused to perform some particular service to the king—probably failure to support the royal demand for free benevolences. Subsequently, when the benevolence reappeared without its disguise, a forced loan this time, Wentworth refused to pay his quota and was locked up in the Marshalsea in May 1627. After six weeks' imprisonment, he was paroled to Dartford, obliged to stay within two miles of the place.[14] At this time, Wentworth seems to have had as a rule on the one hand, that Parliament had no right to encroach upon the royal prerogative by usurping executive functions; and, on the other hand, that the king had no right to levy taxes without the consent of Parliament. It is probable that his support of Parliament was strengthened by his sense of personal wrong, and partly by his dislike of the favorite's reckless foreign policy, which had involved the country in wars with both France and Spain.

Upon Buckingham's less than triumphal return from the expedition against Cadiz, John Eliot, once a friend of the duke, led the House in an attack upon the mismanagement of the war. "Our honor is ruined!" he thundered. "Our ships are sunk. Our men perished. Not by the sword, not by the enemy, not by chance, but...by those we trust!"[15] He called on the Commons to follow the example set in James' reign by impeaching the hated favorite. Charles rebuked the Commons, saying, "I would not have the House to question my servants, much less one that is so near me."

But Parliament was resolved to unseat the glittering, incompetent minister. The Commons told Charles:

> We protest that until this great person be removed from inter-meddling with the great affairs of State, any money we shall or can give will through his misemployment be turned rather to the hurt and prejudice of this your Kingdom than otherwise.[16]

Charles angrily reminded Parliament that he could at anytime dismiss them: "Remember that Parliaments are altogether in my power for their calling, sitting, and dissolution. Therefore, as I find the fruits of them good or evil, they are to continue or not to be." The Commons replied by sending Eliot to the Lords with an impeachment against Buckingham. The king struck back by throwing Eliot in the Tower and ordered the case against the duke to be heard in the prerogative court, the Star Chamber, where he was acquitted. The Commons were unfrightened, denied the Crown their money, and were dissolved. The issue of ministerial responsibility was left to the future.

Charles was again destitute. A large quantity of royal plate was sold. "Free benevolences" were asked of the country, but the yield was slight since English money was pro-Parliament. Charles ordered his officials to collect tonnage and poundage, without parliamentary consent; he commanded the ports to maintain the fleet; he allowed his agents to impress men into military service. English and Danish troops, fighting for

Protestantism in Germany, were being overwhelmed by Imperial troops; Denmark demanded the subsidy that Charles had promised.

Then, a new complication was added. Charles had hoped to conclude an alliance with France against the Hapsburg rulers of Spain and the Empire. But France showed no desire to shed blood in England's behalf for the recovery of the Palatinate. Too, disputes arose over the fulfilment of Charles' marriage contract with Henrietta Maria, and the breach was widened by the cause of the Huguenots. Englishmen delivered arms at Bordeaux and La Rochelle to Huguenots fighting Richelieu. France declared war (1627). Charles ordered a forced loan: every taxpayer was to lend the government one percent of the value of his real property, and five percent of the value of his personal property. In 1627, a large force was dispatched under Buckingham to help the Huguenots besieged at La Rochelle. It landed off the coast on the Ille de Rhe, failed to storm the citadel manned by an inferior force, and withdrew in disorder. Thus, Buckingham's military efforts were again marked by waste and failure. The 200,000 pounds raised by the loan were gone, and Charles, at his money's end, summoned his third Parliament.[17]

The whole country was now in a ferment against Charles and the duke. The election returned men who had resisted payment of the recent forced loan, pledging them to resist arbitrary exactions. Charles managed to secure a promise that the impeachment of Buckingham would not be pursued, but the failure at La Rochelle left Parliament eager to condemn and protest. The Parliament which assembled in March 1628 embodied the will of the natural leaders of the nation. Coke, Eliot, Sir Thomas Wentworth, and John Hampden were returned, and Huntingdon Borough sent up a squire named Oliver Cromwell. Parliament wished to support the war, but it would grant no more money to a king and a minister that it distrusted. The nobility and gentry, Lords and Commons alike, were united in defense of property.

The king instructed the two Houses to provide means for meeting the common danger. He used the threat of arbitrary action. The Crown must have

. . .such supply as to secure ourselves and save our friends from imminent ruin. . . . Every man must now do according to his conscience, wherefore if you, which God forbid, should not do your duties in contributing what this State at this time needs, I must use those other means which God hath put into my hands to save that which the follies of other men may otherwise hazard to lose. Take this not as threatening, for I scorn to threaten any but my equals...but as an admonition.[18]

It must not be supposed that all the hard dealing was on one side. Parliament had approved the wars and now, intent on pushing back the prerogative, played a hard game with the king, confronting him with the shame of deserting the Huguenots, or else yielding the prerogative of his predecessors. Their tactics were clever: they offered five subsidies, amounting to 300,000 pounds sterling, all to be paid within a year, but before they would vote the bill, they insisted on voicing their grievances.

Wentworth joined the Parliamentary leaders in their agreement to drop the attack on the duke and to concentrate on the violated rights of the subject. Whatever Wentworth felt about the duke, however great his distrust, he regarded the first duty of Parliament as something more statesmanlike than the impeachment of individual ministers. In Wentworth's opinion, the misdeeds of Buckingham were chiefly that he had encouraged the king to override the law. On the 22nd, he spoke to this point, especially on the

> illegality of the raising of loans strengthened by commissions with unheard of instructions and oaths, the billeting of soldiers by the lieutenants and deputy lieutenants.

He argued in the same speech that the fault was in the king's instruments, not in the king himself. A secret council, a privy council, which was not responsible to the constitutional council of the king, had been utilized, "ravishing at once the spheres of all ancient government; imprisoning us without banks or bonds or bounds." In the speech, Wentworth complained specifically against: imprisonment without cause and forced loans. He then recommended a clearcut remedy: The House should vindicate the

> ancient, sober, and vital liberties by reenforcing of the ancient laws of our ancestors, by setting such a stamp upon them as no licentious spirit shall dare hereafter to enter upon them.[19]

After this speech, Wentworth was accepted by the Commons for the next weeks as the architect of their policy. Excepting a demand for the abolition of martial law, his address contained the substance of the future Petition of Right, with one important difference: The Petition declared the law to have been broken; Wentworth asked that the long-existing law should be clearly explained.

In the following weeks, the Commons debated mainly the issue of imprisonment without cause shown. On April 2, there was a debate upon supplies for the war. But Wentworth refused to discuss foreign affairs, giving his ground as: "Unless we be secured in our liberties, we cannot give," he said. "I speak not this to make diversions but to the end that giving I may give cheerfully."[20] He carried an adjournment of the debate until the 4th, in order to learn unofficially whether the king was prepared to give ground on the question of imprisonment. The adjournment brought only vague assurances from the king that the liberties of his subjects were not in danger.

Wentworth was now known as the man "who hath the greatest sway in Parliament." He represented the general temper of the times in favor of an accommodation with Charles, if the king would drop his so-called unconstitutional claims. On April 4, Wentworth reported to the assembly a motion that five subsidies should be granted. He followed up this success by carrying another motion that no report of the grant should be made to the House. Hence, the king could not, as he had done after the last session, demand payment on the ground that the House had approved a grant, though no bill had been passed. The present offer was to be contingent upon settling the scope of the liberties of the subject. Wentworth asked, therefore, that a subcommittee be appointed to draw up a bill setting forth these liberties.[21]

At this time, Wentworth—as far as was possible in those days—stood forth as the leader of the House of Commons. But the motion to avoid reporting out the grant had offended the king, and when the four resolutions had passed the House, the Lords struck out the section on imprisonment, thus allowing the king to continue to commit without showing cause.

In these debates of 1628, Wentworth stated his view of the prerogative; he was to state it many times thereafter; he was to state it again at his trial; he was to state it on the scaffold. It was this: Let the law be declared, with provisions to enforce it. If some necessity arose, the king could use his prerogative and go beyond the law for the safety of the State. The weakness of Wentworth's position[22] lay in the difficulty of making sure that the executive would not use the extraordinary powers of the Constitution on routine business—a problem unsolved even today.

Wentworth's proposal was, however, adopted, and on April 28, a bill was brought into the Commons by the subcommittee. No reference was made to the past conduct of the government, and the following were declared to be the existing law: every freeman committed by the king's sole command shall be bailed or delivered; no tax, tallage, or other imposition shall be levied; no soldier shall be billeted. The question of martial law was passed over. On May 1, Wentworth proposed to soften down the bill. It would be enough to confirm the old laws, without denying the king's emergency powers of commitment; but whenever he did commit without showing cause for trial, the judges would be required to bail the prisoner.[23]

Wentworth had the House with him, but he could not depend upon the king. At the same time, the Commons ignored the king's demand for supplies, hoping by equal stubbornness to force Charles from his position. On the 28th, the king once again sent a message reiterating his intention to respect all existing laws, so that new legislation or confirmation of old laws were in no way necessary. Concurrently the Secretary of State stated that whatever laws Parliament might make, he was duty-bound to commit without showing cause to anybody but the king. The ground was thus cut from under Wentworth's feet.

The king would offer only to confirm the old laws "without additions, paraphrases, or explanations." He would accept only a reenactment of Magna Carta and a few other ancient statutes. For the rest, Parliament must be content with his royal word.[24] Wentworth's mediation between Crown and Parliament had broken down, and it was not for him to lead the Commons further. The Petition of Right—not a piece of legislation but a petition for the maintenance of the laws as elucidated by the present Parliament—took the place of his bill, but it was drawn by other hands. Wentworth concurred with the Petition as it stood, for it adapted to public use the private procedure of petitioning the Crown:

> To the King's Most Excellent Majesty:
> We humbly show unto our sovereign Lord the King . . . that whereas it is declared and enacted by a statute...of Edward I...that no tallage or aid shall be laid or levied by the King...without the good will and assent of the archbishops, bishops, earls, barons, knights, burgesses, and other the freemen of the commonalty...your subjects have inherited this freedom, that they should not be compelled to contribute to any tax, tallage, aid, or other like charge not set by consent in Parliament.

The Petition went on to protest against forced loans and the king's violation of the rights of *habeas corpus* and trial by jury as embodied in Magna Carta, and asked that in the future the law should be obeyed. "We shall know by this [petition] if Parliaments live or die," said Coke. Charles gave to it an ambiguous consent, whereupon Parliament sat on their purse. Finally, Charles assented to the Petition of Right in a form acceptable to Commons. There broke out in London such ringing of bells as had not been heard in the city for years.[25]

Parliament, moving forward still, next requested the king to dismiss Buckingham. Suddenly, both sides were astonished to find the issue taken out of their hands, John Felton, a former army officer with a grudge against the duke, walked sixty miles to Portsmouth and stabbed Buckingham to death.

The months following Buckingham's assassination were a turning point for the reign, for Charles was now less than ever ready for compromise. He regarded the inflammatory speeches of Eliot and his followers as the cause of Felton's act. He no longer felt it necessary to tone down his religious policy, so Laud and Montague, both Arminians, were moved up in the hierarchy of the Church. He also continued to collect tonnage and poundage, although his grant had lapsed. He sent another ill-fated expedition to La Rochelle, the failure of which doomed the Huguenots to surrender to the kings of France.

As the parliamentary session of 1628 drew to a close, Wentworth received an overture from the Court through the Treasurer, Lord Weston. The move was not surprising, for:

> Wentworth had given proof of energy, abilities and judgment of a kind that the King and his advisers would be unwilling to lose. It was not until they saw him in opposition that they took the full measure of the man whose efforts to serve the Crown had, for the past ten years, met chiefly with rebuffs.[26]

On the following July 22nd, Wentworth was created a baron, and on December 10, a viscount. On December 25th, he was appointed President of the Council of the North. Thus, what is usually hailed as "Wentworth's Apostasy" was accomplished before the end of the year. A courtier, sneering at the lot of new creations, described him as "a northern lad, Thomas Wentworth, Baron of I know not where."[27]

Wentworth's colleagues in the Parliament of 1628 must have reacted with surprise and cynicism to his elevation and return to favor. But the hatred of the "Grand Apostate" did not develop until later, "when his defeated, silenced, or imprisoned colleagues saw him mounting to ever greater and more formidable power as the pillar of a sovereign authority that they hated and feared."[28]

Wentworth's move was usual—commonplace, a shifting of opinion, a move away from the Court and back again. He had ratted, and re-ratted. The day of fixed party allegiances lay far in the future; indeed, the operation of English politics until the late nineteenth century allowed such shifts. As Wedgwood rightly points out, what made Wentworth's shift memorable and dramatic was that which came after it:

> He had been, briefly, the tacitly acknowledged leader of the "country" party, the principal pilot who steered the Petition of Right to success. He was to become the chief minister of King Charles...and to be prosecuted to death by some of the same men whom he had led in the Commons in 1628. But at the time of the change no one could have foreseen this. He had a peerage; he was back in favor and might expect—at long last—that some important position would be conferred on him. But he was not yet even a member of the Privy Council, and his future...was still doubtful.[29]

Because the drama of Wentworth's so-called apostasy was exploited to a degree at his trial, it has become one of the more dramatic myths of English history. Macaulay, for one, sounded it like a clarion call:

> He was the first Englishman to whom a peerage was a sacrament of infamy, a baptism into the communion of corruption. As he was the earliest of that hateful list, so was he also by far the greatest; eloquent, immutable of purpose, in every talent which exalts or destroys nations pre-eminent, the lost Archangel, the Satan of the Apostasy.

It is indeed a come-down from Archangel of the Apostasy to the "northern lad" who became "baron of I know not where." But the truth is less dramatic: Wentworth's move from "country" to "court" in the summer of 1628 provoked little more than a few mutterings.

Nor was there in him any real change of principle. Wentworth had sought to limit the royal powers for the sake of both king and subject. But he had never tried to move control of the executive from the king to Parliament, nor had he favored the growth of Puritanism in the church.

Yet, a change of position often brings with it a change of perspective. Few men could be expected to see things in the same way after a change in role from critic to actor. Wielding the executive powers of the Crown in the North, Wentworth would come more and more to regard the Crown as the sole upholder of the rights of the State and most opponents of the Crown as subverting the authority without which the State would dissolve in anarchy. In a speech which he delivered on December 30 to the Council of the North, Wentworth stated his conception of the unity of interest which ought to prevail between king and subject:

> To the joint individual well-being of sovereignty and subjection, do I here vow all my cares and diligences through the whole course of my ministry. I confess I am not ignorant how some distempered minds have of late very often endeavored to divide the consider-ations of the two, as if their end were distinct, not the same—nay, in opposition; a monstrous, a prodigious birth of a licentious conception, for so we would become all head or all members.
>
> Princes are to be the indulgent nursing fathers to their people; their modest liberties, their sober rights ought to be precious in their eyes, the branches of their government to be for shadow, for habitation, the comfort of life. [The people] repose safe and still under the protection of their sceptres. Subjects . . . ought, with solicitous eyes of jealousy, to watch over the Prerogatives of a Crown. The authority of a King is the keystone which closeth up the arch of order and government, which contains each part in due relation to the whole, and which once shaken, infirmed, all the frame falls together into a confused heap of foundation and battlement. . . . Verily, these are those mutual intelligences of love and protection descending, of obedience and loyalty ascending, which should pass . . . between a King and his people. Their faithful servants must look equally on both, weave, twist these two together in all their counsels; study, labour, to preserve each without diminishing or enlarging either, and by running in the worn, wonted channels, treading the ancient bounds, cut off early all disputes from betwixt them. . . .
>
> I do here offer myself an instrument for good in every man's hand; he that thus useth me most hath the most of my heart, even to the meanest man within the whole jurisdiction.[30]

Thus, Strafford's conception of government was not similar—as he has been accused—to what was to prevail in Imperial Germany under

Bismarck and the Wilhelmian Emperors. It was similar to what was practiced in England from the Tudors to the Reform Act of 1832—a theory of "mixed government."

The early-Stuart Royalists held the law to be voluntaristic in character: law derives its force not from any inner merit but from the will of the sovereign power. In the 1620s, Parliament argued the pre-existent, non-voluntaristic nature of law. By the 1640s, they had shifted to a voluntaristic stand, adding that the sovereign power resided in Parliament. The Parliamentary view was, therefore, jural: government derives its authority from national law. By now, however, the extreme Royalists (like Charles and not like Strafford) held to a naturalistic monarchy: monarchy is a natural institution; law is derivative from monarchy. The legalistic school of the time believed that the king derived his authority from the laws.

Law, then, to both views is derivative. But, what agency sustains the sovereign power? To Strafford, the operation (not the source) of the law depended upon the will of the king, the force which sustained the sovereign power. To Parliament, the source and the operation of the law depended upon the will of Parliament, the force which sustained the sovereign power.

The first overt appearance of this controversy was the trial of Strafford. He was impeached for treason against the nation, for attempting to subvert the fundamental laws.

Parliament believed that it too represented the kingdom, that it was charged with a trust by the kingdom, and that the king was also a trustee and if he failed in his duty, the law required Parliament to perform it for him. Strafford held the same view, only he felt that it was Parliament which had failed in its duty, and that the law required the Crown to perform it for them. Hence, the general view of government of both Strafford and Parliament was nearly identical.

The theory of "mixed government" or the "classical theory" of the English Constitution arose in Tudor England and achieved supremacy by the end of the 17th century. The major tenets of the classical theory held that the English government had achieved a blending, a combination and balancing of the three main types of government that political theorists derived from Aristotle—monarchy, aristocracy, and democracy. Monarchy was defined as the rule of one; aristocracy as the rule of the few; and democracy as the rule of the many. Each of these types in its pure form evinced virtues and vices. The virtue of monarchy was power; its vice, tyranny. The virtue of aristocracy was wisdom; its vice, faction. The virtue of democracy was goodness; its vice, tumult or violence.

It was their good fortune, Englishmen reasoned, to have developed a mixed government, in which the virtues of each form were given free rein while their vices were curbed. In the English style of mixed government, the monarchic form was embodied in the Crown; the aristocratic in the House of Lords; and the democratic in the House of Commons. In these three branches of government sovereignty was lodged, in the words of Sir William Blackstone, "as beneficially as is possible for society. For in no other shape could we be so certain of finding the three great qualities of government so well and so happily united. If the supreme power were lodged in any one of the three branches separately, we must be exposed to the inconveniences of either absolute monarchy, aristocracy, or democracy; and so want two of the three principal ingredients of good polity; either virtue, wisdom, or power."[31]

C. C. Weston succinctly explains why one branch of the government does not emerge supreme:

> This mixed government could continue to exist because of the presence of a system of checks and balances, by which each of the three branches of the government was armed with sufficient powers to repel the encroachments of the other branches, singly or together. The three branches were considered equal and thoroughly independent of one another. Each member of the trinity of king, lords, and commons possessed an independent veto upon legislation while at the same time each possessed powers peculiar to itself. The king, for example, named ministers, summoned and dissolved parliament, created peers, etc.; the House of Lords had the supreme judicial power; and the House of Commons possessed the powers of supply and impeachment.[32]

"The cardinal document in the history of the theory of mixed government in modern England," Miss Weston continues, "and a document of the first importance in the constitutional conflicts of the seventeenth century was the Answer to the Nineteen Propositions, issued by King Charles I in June 1642, on the very eve of the first Civil War. It was drafted by moderate Royalists whom the king had recently appointed to office but was issued in his name and given wide publicity by his order. In it Charles I completely abandoned the theory of the divine right of kings, with which his name is nowadays commonly associated, and declared that the English government was a mixture of monarchy, aristocracy, and democracy, with political power divided among king, lords, and commons."[33] Charles' comments on the English government were widely known during the Civil War and during the Restoration were referred to as the "King's Constitution."

The Nineteen Propositions, in which the Long Parliament presented their ultimatum to the king, is a very well-known document, usually discussed by Stuart historians. The Answer to the Nineteen Propositions, on the other hand, has been generally neglected. Weston has rightly given it the attention which Gardiner, Firth, Davies, Wedgwood, Trevelyan, Clark, and Ogg did not. Hitting upon the Answer in a footnote of Hume's, she investigated the pamphlet literature aroused by the impeachment of the Earl of Danby and the Exclusion Crisis and also by the Glorious Revolution in order to learn to what degree English politicians made use of the Answer to the Nineteen Propositions in their political theory and in their limitation of the power of the Stuarts. Her conclusion, for which the evidence is given in Chapter III of her book, is that "Charles I must be placed side-by-side with John Locke in any account of the constitution that underlay the Glorious Revolution."[34]

Now the Earl of Strafford fits into the picture: While King Charles still spoke grandly of divine right and ruled without Parliament, Strafford was speaking in the mixed-government tones of his speech of December 1628. Hence, the genesis of the Answer can be traced back further—to Strafford. During the years that Strafford thought of mixed government—as he tried to pick up the pieces left by Buckingham, Laud, and Charles; as he called and manipulated Parliaments in Ireland; as he persuaded Charles to end the Personal Rule; as he did all this and practiced in an imperfect manner a mixed government—those who later wrote the Answer for Charles, Hyde and Falkland, ranged themselves against him. It was a time when the vices of each form of government had their season: tyranny, faction, and violence. The sides differed not mainly in principle, but application, as each sought to "check and balance" the excesses of the other. That they could not come to an understanding is what provides the tragedy of the Earl of Strafford with its moving force.

The cardinal document of the theory of mixed government may be the Answer to the Nineteen Propositions. And Charles I may deserve to be ranked with Locke. But the antecedents of the Answer can be traced to Strafford.

During the short session of 1629, Parliament admonished the king that his continued collection of tonnage and poundage violated the Petition of Right; hence, Parliament encouraged merchants to refuse to pay the duties. It was on religion that the main attack began. Reasserting their right to legislate on religion, despite the ecclesiastical supremacy of the Crown, the House of Commons proclaimed a strictly Calvinist, anti-Arminian interpretation of the Thirty-Nine Articles of Faith. They proposed to enforce religious conformity on this basis, and to deal out penalties to Catholics and Arminians alike. Religion brought the Commons together, joining religious zealots with politicians who were trying to establish Parliamentary supremacy. The Parliamentarians found in the religious prejudices of England a bond of union.

Whether Lord Wentworth took any part in the debates of the upper House during the short session of 1629 is not known. But it is extremely probable that he regarded the Commons as at fault on the occasion of the early dissolution.

Late in the year, Wentworth learned of a paper written in 1614 by Sir Robert Dudley which had advised King James to establish a military dictatorship in England. Wentworth took this information to Charles. Since it was suspected that the paper was being circulated by the opposition as a sign of Charles' true intentions, he made Wentworth a Privy Councilor as a reward for his loyalty. Later Wentworth spoke strongly in Star Chamber against Alexander Leighton, and it is said that a common feeling against militant Puritanism drew him on that occasion into an intimate friendship with Archbishop Laud, which continued to his death.[35] There exists little information on Wentworth's action during these years on the Privy Council, but it is certain that he did not have at this time the predominant influence over affairs which has been subsequently attributed to him. He would have been more effective if only the king had trusted him. But Charles feared Wentworth's domineering personality and sent him first to the North, and then, as Lord Deputy, to Ireland.

During the short parliamentary session of 1629, the major grievances of the Commons were embodied by Eliot in a Remonstrance. The Speaker, who had been gained to the king's side, tried to muzzle debate on the Remonstrance and announced on March 2 that the king adjourned the House until March 10. A wave of wrath swept through the assembly. Two strong young members, Denzil Holles and Benjamin Valentine, thrust the Speaker back into his seat and held him there. "God's wounds!" cried Holles. "You shall sit until we please to rise!" Never before had the king's right to adjourn Parliament at his pleasure been questioned. To prevent the seizure of the mace, the doors were barred against the Sergeant-at-Arms and Black Rod. The Remonstrance on religion and taxes, recited from memory by Holles, was carried by acclamation, and the House voted its adjournment. Parliament was not to meet again for eleven years.

The Lord Strafford (Van Dyck)

2
Strafford
and the Personal Rule of King Charles: 1629-1640

The personal rule of the king was not set up covertly or by degrees. Charles openly proclaimed his intention:

> We have showed by our frequent meeting our people our love to the use of Parliaments; yet, the late abuse having for the present driven us unwillingly out of that course, we shall account it presumption for any to prescribe any time unto us for Parliaments, the calling, continuing, and dissolving of which is always in our own power, and shall be more inclinable to meet in Parliament again, when our people shall see more clearly into our interests and actions and when such as have bred this interruption shall have received their condign punishment. [1]

Charles' basic mistake, of course, was his failure to realize that the wealth now represented by the House of Commons was much greater than that loyal to, or wielded by the Crown, and that its control over affairs of Parliament must accordingly be increased.

King Charles' policy of personal rule required large measures. First, he had to have peace between England and the Continent; hence, the struggles with France and Spain were brought to a close. Charles did try to maintain England's voice in the councils of Europe and tried to maintain the fleet, but while Europe was savagely fighting the Thirty Years War, England, generally speaking, enjoyed the pleasure and profit of neutrality.

The second condition of personal rule was to win over some of the Parliamentary leaders. In those days, there were few men who did not seek the favor of the Crown; some sought it by subservience, others by opposition. Eliot was regarded as incorrigible; Pym and Cromwell were not yet prominent; but Sir Henry Savile, Thomas Digges, and Sir Thomas Wentworth were viewed as possible and valuable acquisitions. Wentworth, above all, was a man worth winning. In the debates on the Petition of Right, he had followed a line which had been highlighted by important restraints: he apparently meant to purge the evils from Buckingham's administration without prejudicing the real power of the royal government. His abilities were obviously of the first order, and so were his ambitions. Wentworth, Savile, and Digges accepted office.

The third condition of the personal rule was money: the king had to live of his own without summoning a Parliament. First, an extreme frugality must be practiced by the executive—"no wars, no adventures of any kind, no disturbances, all State action reduced to a minimum, quietness by all means." Second, the king supported by the judges, employed a number of financial devices to pay the costs of running his government. He continued to take tonnage and poundage. Freeholders owning land worth forty pounds or more a year were fined for not taking knighthoods at the Coronation. Grants by the Crown of Scottish lands were resumed. The royal forests were enlarged. Defective land titles were confirmed, for a price. Wardship over the estates of minors was exercised. The royal jewels were pawned. Monopolies were sold. Finally, "Ship Money," a direct tax on real property was revived and levied to pay for the fleet. On the question of ship money, Charles had first consulted the judges. Nevertheless, John Hampden, a Buckinghamshire squire, to test its legality refused to pay his assessment, and brought his case to court. Only two of twelve judges found for Hampden in principle, but the opinion of the majority made it appear that the prerogative was so far-reaching that no man was left with anything that he could safely call his own.[2]

The broad social and economic policy pursued by Charles during the eleven years of his personal rule was dictated primarily by the need for money. But the executive nevertheless was at its weakest. The king reigned on the smallest scale. He was a despot, but an unarmed despot. No standing army enforced his decrees. It would therefore be a travesty to represent the period of personal rule as a time of tyranny in any effective sense. Probably the mass of people were quite satisfied with the existing conditions, and there is little evidence that any widespread anxiety existed for the recall of Parliament. Churchill expresses very well the apathetic mood of the nation during most of the personal rule:

Hungry forces still lay in shadow. All the ideas which they cherished and championed stirred in the minds [of the Parliamentarians] but they had no focus, no expression. The difficulties of travel, the dangers of gathering at any point, the pleasant easy life of peaceful England, oppressed their movement. Many who would have been vehement if the chance had come their way were content to live their life from day to day. The land was good; springtime, summertime, autumn had their joys; in the winter there was the Yule log and new amusements. Agriculture and fox hunting cast their compulsive or soothing balms upon restless spirits. Harvests were now abundant and the rise in prices had almost ceased. There was no longer a working-class problem. The Poor Law was administered with exceptional humanity. Ordinary gentlefolk might have no share in national government but they were still lords on their own estates. In Quarter Sessions they ruled the shires, and as long as they kept clear of the law and paid their taxes with a grunt they were left in peace. It required an intense effort by the Parliamentary party to rouse under such conditions a national feeling and concern for the State. The malcontents looked about for points which would inflame the inert forces of the nation.[3]

While Charles organized in London the administrative details of a government without Parliament, Wentworth served as his Lord Deputy to the North. In October 1631, Wentworth lost his second wife, the mother of his children. At York there was a strong feeling of sympathy with the Lord President in his trouble. In October 1632, Wentworth married his third wife, Elizabeth, daughter of Sir Godfrey and granddaughter of Francis Rhodes.[4]

Wentworth's main difficulties in governing the North arose from the spirit of independence of the nobility and gentry of a district where the idea of the predominance of the state had made less progress than in the more thickly populated and wealthier South. His first conflict was with Henry Bellasys, the son of Lord Fauconberg, who, coming into Wentworth's presence in Council, neglected to make the customary reverence. Bellasys was sent before the Privy Council at Westminster, and agreed, after a month's imprisonment, to make due submission both there and at York.[5] More important was the struggle with Sir David Foulis, a Scot who had received a grant of lands from James I. Foulis not only impugned Wentworth's personal honesty, but later urged the county sheriff to refuse obedience to the Council's summons to York, on the ground that it had been founded by the king's commission and not by act of Parliament.[6] Wentworth stood in defense of the prerogative. In a letter to Carlisle, he stood firm on the need to prevent subjects from imposing conditions upon the Crown, in his eyes the chief cause of irritation in the last Parliament after the acceptance of the Petition of Right.[7] When Foulis attempted to bargain with Charles by offering to win for him the affections of the gentry, if he were himself taken into favor, Wentworth's wrath blazed higher. His Majesty, he said, should make Foulis an example of his justice; ordinary men were not to bargain with the king. To Wentworth, the king was the head of the state, executor of justice without fear of personalities or parties. In the end, Foulis was sentenced in Star Chamber to fine and imprisonment.

Lord Eure, also, resisted an order in Chancery until Wentworth ordered up guns from Scarborough Castle, and had them fired at Eure's house in Malton. Sir Thomas Gower insulted the king's attorney at York, took refuge in London, and, since he was out of the jurisdiction of the northern circuit, drove off Wentworth's officers when they attempted to arrest him in Holburn. Charles took the Lord President's part, and on March 21, 1633, a new set of instructions were issued, giving the fullest possible powers to the Council of the North.

On January 12, 1632, Wentworth was transferred to a wider sphere of action: he was appointed Lord Deputy of Ireland. In Ireland, the new Deputy's problems were likely to arise, not from the native Irish, but from the English settlers, who occupied all posts in Dublin, were seated in Council, and had the ear of influential luminaries at the Court of Charles. Because of the settlers' strong position, Wentworth, while still in England, drew up regulations to protect the Irish revenue against encroachments and his powers as Deputy against the granting of writs by the king behind his back. His proposals were, by Charles' order, registered in the Council Book, so that they might not be disregarded.[8] Wentworth intended to run his government according to the motto frequently found in his correspondence with Laud: "Thorough," that is to say, according to a complete disregard for private interests and upon the establishment, for the good of the whole community, of the royal power as the executor of the state.

Upon his arrival in Dublin, Wentworth found that a recent grant of money by an informal Irish assembly—a grant made in return for certain

graces by the king—was coming to an end. By mingling hopes of a
Parliament with hints that he could exact money by force, the Deputy
obtained a year's renewal of funds. Thus able to pay his soldiers, he began
to rebuild his small army to secure his power; but he hoped rather to build
upon good government and the creation of economic prosperity in the
country. The piracy which was rife in St. George's Channel was put down.
Schemes were developed for opening commerce with Spain. The growth
of flax was introduced, and industry of nearly every kind was encouraged,
except those which kept Ireland dependent on England. Wentworth's
policy was to make Irishmen as prosperous as Englishmen, but at the same
time to make them as much like Englishmen as possible, with the aim that
they might be equally loyal to the English Crown.

The aim of Irish dependence instigated Wentworth's reforms of the
Protestant church in Ireland, which was in no state to win the hearts of
Irishmen. The ecclesiastical courts were nothing but machines for
extortion. Scarcely a minister was able to address an Irishman in Gaelic.
Churches were in ruin, the clergy impoverished and ignorant, and their
revenues often in the hands of the laity. For example, by an annual
payment of twenty pounds, the Earl of Cork had secured the revenues of
the bishopric of Linsmore, worth 1,000 pounds a year. Wentworth
brought a suit against Cork in the Castle Chamber and compelled him to
give up the bishopric. Wentworth tried to enforce Anglican uniformity,
though far short of what Laud was enforcing in England. In November
1634, he forced the Irish convocation to adopt the articles of the Church
of England, in place of the Calvinistic ones, drawn by Ussher, which they
previously had adopted. He also tried to suppress the Puritan practices of
the Ulster Scots. But his main efforts in church reform were toward the
recovery of the property of the church, to be used as an inducement to
men of ability to accept appointment in Ireland.

To secure enough money to enable him to carry out his program, until
such time as an expanding economy would give him a consistent revenue,
Wentworth convinced Charles to summon a Parliament. This Irish
Parliament did not, like an English Parliament, represent a fairly united
nation. Rather, it had been manipulated to contain (1) a large minority of
representatives of the English and Scottish settlers; (2) another large
minority of representatives of the Roman Catholics of Anglo-Norman
descent; and (3) a small number of officials who could form a majority by
throwing their votes to one side or the other. Such an assembly easily lent

itself to manipulation, and Wentworth intended it to be manipulated. Parliament met on July 14, 1634. In his opening speech, the Lord Deputy frankly declared that the king looked to the Members to pay off his debts, and to make good the annual deficit of 20,000 pounds. He said:

> It is beneath the Crown's dignity to come at every year's end, with his hat in his hand, to entreat that you would be pleased to preserve yourselves.

They should trust the king and vote supplies in this session; in return, the king would grant another session for redress of grievances. Let them not make factions, dividing Catholic and Protestant, English and Irish; above all, let them make no division between king and people:

> Most certain is it that their well-being is individually one and the same, their interests woven up together with so tender and close threads as cannot be pulled asunder without a rent in the commonwealth.[9]

The Protestant members, reinforced by the officials, were in a majority of eight, and on July 18, six subsidies were voted; on August 2, Parliament was prorouged.[10] On September 20, Wentworth asked the king for an earldom as a sign of the royal support in the Irish struggle, but Charles, who liked to originate his own favors, turned him down.[11]

The second session of the Irish Parliament met on November 4th. The Catholic members expected that Wentworth would introduce bills to confirm the "graces" to which the king had given his word. When he announced that he did not intend to submit all of these to legislation, the Roman Catholic members broke out into open opposition to the Lord Deputy. The Catholic members of Parliament, under the leadership of Sir Piers Crosby and being through the absence of some Protestant members in a temporary majority, urged the rejection of all bills before them. Wentworth treated their conduct as obstructionism, arising not from anger at the king's broken promise, but from a desire to prevent effective English Government:

> The friars and jesuits fear that these laws would conform them here to the manners of England and in time be a means to lead them on to a conformity in religion and faith also; they catholicly oppose and fence up every path leading to so good a purpose; and indeed I plainly see that so long as this Kingdom [Ireland] continues popish, they are not a people for the Crown of England to be confident of;

whereas if they were not still distempered by the infusion of these friars and jesuits, I am of belief they would be as good and loyal to their King as any other subjects.[12]

Herein lay the driving force behind Wentworth's Irish policy: He would do his best to raise Ireland to a higher standard of well-being—so long as the Irishmen in the end looked and acted like Englishmen. The customs, feelings, and religion of the Irish might meet with contemptuous toleration for a time, but it was the Crown's policy to sweep them away.

Wentworth recovered his majority when the Protestant absentees returned. He removed Crosby from the Privy Council and, in three short sessions in 1635, he obtained the passage of legislation carrying into effect the greater number of the "graces." He wished to keep this Parliament in existence, but Charles insisted on a dissolution.

There were two graces refused by Wentworth: (1) to confirm defective land titles, and (2) to promise the landowners of Connaught that their right to their estates should never again be questioned. The Lord Deputy did not want to seize lands from owners whose titles had been lost or destroyed in the wars of Ireland: he merely meant to make the concession profitable to the state. Therefore, he appointed commissioners to negotiate with each landowner, requiring them to set aside a permanent rent to the Crown in return for a confirmation of their titles. The land titles of Connaught were part of a larger policy. Wentworth had decided to carry on the plantation policy of James I, whereby English colonists were to be settled in the purely Celtic regions to teach the natives the advantage of English civilization, and to be a bulwark against rebellion and foreign invasion. In order to plant Connaught with Englishmen, the Lord Deputy grounded England's claim on the technicality that the lands had been granted in the 14th century to Lionel, Duke of Clarence, and that the lands belonged to the Crown because King Charles was the duke's heir. In Roscommon, Sligo, and Mayo, Wentworth got juries to pass verdicts in favor of this view of the case. In Galway he came up against a recalcitrant jury, fined the sheriff for returning a prejudiced jury, sent the jurymen before a prerogative court to account for their prejudice, and procured a decree from the Court of Exchequer to set aside the original verdict. His methods in this case showed his impetuous character at its worst. In pursuit of a politically expedient policy, he not only coldly ignored the wishes and feelings of the people with whom he was dealing, but then justified his action by the employment of legal chicanery. He could not know that in a few short years, he was to be prosecuted to the death by men who also could turn the letter of the law to their own political ends.

Uncaring for the sensibilities of entire regions, Wentworth was not likely to avoid giving offense to private persons, and many in Ireland and England were to come to know his impatience with contradiction. Many of these personages who had their feathers ruffled by the Lord Deputy in the name of progress, were to return to haunt him at his trial; especially Lord Mountnorris. Wentworth's eagerness to secure from English officials at Dublin the same devotion to the public interest and service that he himself displayed brought him into conflict with Lord Mountnorris, then the Vice-Treasurer for Ireland and a member of the Council. During 1634 and 1635, Wentworth constantly complained of irregular practices by Mountnorris in the execution of his office. Mountnorris, knowing that the Deputy was building a case against him, placed his case in the hands of the king. He probably made this move because there was a party at Court hostile to Wentworth and supported by the queen, who disliked Wentworth's resistance to her wish to grant rich posts in Ireland to her favorites. Mountnorris, believing himself secure under the smile of the court party, was quick to take offense with Wentworth, and at a dinner at the Lord Chancellor's, he dropped a thinly veiled threat against him. But the king supported his Lord Deputy and, on July 31, he gave Wentworth authority to inquire into Mountnorris' malpractices.[13] and subsequently empowered him to bring Mountnorris before a court martial.[14] An inquiry was held which turned out badly for Mountnorris, and on December 12, Wentworth summoned him before a Council of War. Being a captain in the army, Mountnorris was condemned to death for inciting another officer, his brother, to mutiny and revenge against the Deputy. Wentworth, however, only wanted to frighten Mountnorris into resigning his office, and when that was obtained, he was set free.[15] So much hostility had been generated by Mountnorris' case that Wentworth thought it wise to make sure of his position at Court. Consequently, on June 21, 1636, he reviewed before the Council at Westminster his entire Irish policy. He returned to Dublin with the king's continued favor.

Up to this time, so far as is known, Wentworth's opinion had never been asked regarding affairs of state outside of Ireland. However, on February 28, 1637, Charles, who had just received the judges' favorable decision on the ship money levy, asked his advice on England's taking part at sea in the war which France and other states were waging against the Hapsburg Empire. Apart from his dislike of a war with Spain, and a clear view of the difficulties in any attempt to recover the Palatinate, Wentworth argued that the king was not strong enough to go to war at all. It was true that the opinion of the judges in favor of the legality of ship money was "the greatest service that that profession hath done the Crown at any time," but unless the king "were declared to have the like power to raise a land army upon the same exigent of state," the Crown stood upon "one leg at home" and was "considerable but by halves to foreign princes abroad." To "fortify this piece" would forever vindicate "the royalty at home from under the conditions and restraints of subjects." This far had Wentworth traveled from the day when he had been known as the man "who hath the greatest sway in Parliament." In the Commons, it is true, he had never done more than support the House in refusing supplies required to carry out what he judged to be a false policy; yet, he had never before so distinctly sided with the tendency towards a strong monarch.

At the close of the summer of 1637, Wentworth boasted of the prospects for the economic development of Ireland: from Limerick he wrote:

> Hither we are come through a country, by my faith, if as well husbanded, built, and peopled as are you in England, would show itself not much inferior to the very best you have there.

Two more districts, Ormonde and Clare, had been secured for English settlement, "which beauties and seasons the work exceedingly well with all possible contentment and satisfaction of the people." But despite his rosy projections into the future, Wentworth's attempts to build up the economy of Ireland, and his attempts to Anglicize the country, came to nothing. Englishmen had too much to do at home, and the expected settlers for Ireland did not materialize.

Then, Strafford's administrative work was becoming more and more interrupted by the unrest in Scotland, which finally led to revolution.

The factor which finally inflamed "the inert forces of the nation" and brought the peaceful years to a close was religion. Here emerges the figure of the man who of all others was Charles' evil genius—William Laud, Archbishop of Canterbury. With the elevation of Laud to the Primacy, control of the Church passed to the High-Church-Arminian group, who were definitely a minority. James I, who was more of a politician than his son, had recognized that Laud was a born meddler. "The plain truth is," he said, "that I keep Laud back from all place of rule and authority because I find he hath a restless spirit, and cannot see when matters are well, but loves to toss and change."[16] This was exactly what Laud did. As soon as he reached Canterbury, he began imposing uniformity and purging the country of Puritan manifestations. Altars were moved; vestments were required; the Book of Common Prayer was required; Puritanism was suppressed; prosecutions before Prerogative Courts began, and some sentences were savage. And all over England men and women found themselves haled before Justices of the Peace and fined one shilling for each absence from church. Here indeed was something that ordinary men and women could understand.[17]

Yet, it is by no means certain that, if left alone, England would have revolted. It was instead in Scotland, home of the Stuarts, that the spark was ignited which started the conflagration. Laud prevailed upon the king to set the spiritual house of Scotland in order. They shocked the Scots by extending the authority of the bishops over the presbyteries of the Kirk. They recklessly alienated the Scottish nobility by an Act of Revocation which rescinded all grants of Church or Crown lands made to Scottish families since the accession of Mary Stuart. They appointed to the Privy Council of Scotland five bishops and an archbishop. Laud insisted that worship be carried out with the almost Catholic ceremonial of the high-Anglican church, including vestments, candles, altar, and crucifix. In an effort to impose their authority over the presbyteries, the bishops drew up liturgical rules which gave to the king full jurisdiction over all ecclesiastical matters in Scotland. The ministers of the Kirk argued that the Reformation was thereby undone, and feared that Charles was about to resubmit to the Pope. When an attempt was made in St. Giles' Church, Edinburgh, to conduct a service according to the new liturgy, a riot broke out. Petitions from all over Scotland from all classes were sent to Charles—pleading, demanding revocation of the new formulae.[18]

At the beginning of February 1638, representatives of the Scottish ministry and laity gathered to draft and sign a National Covenant, a solemn bond of the whole nation pledging themselves to defend the "true religion," and to reject all religious alterations not approved by a free assembly of the Kirk. The Earl of Sutherland was the first to sign his name, followed by a long list of notables. Many signed in blood, and copies were taken for signature to every village in Scotland. The Covenant embodied the resolve of a whole people to die rather than submit to popery. Zealots of all classes came to church for guidance armed with claymore and dirk; even women took up pistols or carried stone and earth for the frontier fortifications. Nothing of this sort had ever been intended or dreamed of by the king, but such was the storm that he had aroused.

Generally aware of the course of events in England and Scotland, Wentworth began to send advice to the king, but Charles, in return, kept him poorly informed. Being distracted from his work in Ireland, Wentworth harshly judged the men whom he felt were responsible. Writing to Archbishop Laud on April 10, 1638, he expressed his desire that Hampden and his ilk could be "whipped into their right minds." In July, he expressed himself just as strongly on the Scottish Covenanters, and recommended that Berwick and Carlisle should be manned and English troops prepared during the winter for a summer invasion of Scotland, when the ports could be blockaded. He also recommended that a strong hand against the Scottish nation should be accompanied by magnanimity in victory towards individuals: no blood was to be shed upon the scaffold; conquered Scotland was to be governed by a council subordinate to the English Privy Council; the English Common Prayer Book was to be substituted for the "Laudian" one against which the Scots had so strongly protested.

As the king prepared for war, Wentworth protested against attempting an offensive campaign with a raw army, and urged Charles to be content with a blockade of the Scottish ports until he had fully trained his army. Such a recommendation indicates how long Wentworth had been absent from England, for he clearly did not grasp the change of feeling there towards the Crown, and he thought that English soldiers would still serve five or six months at their own expense, and that Parliament would be willing to grant supplies for a Scottish campaign.

In spite of elaborate negotiations by the Duke of Hamilton, friend of the king, the Covenanters were adamant and raised a force of 26,000 men aflame with patriotic and religious fervor. The king mustered an unenthusiastic army of 21,000 men and marched north. When the two forces came face to face at Berwick, Charles agreed to allow the disputed matters to be settled by a new Scottish Parliament and Assembly of the Kirk, thus ending without bloodshed the First Bishop's War. When the Assembly and Parliament met, they declared bishops in Scotland to be abolished and ordered every Scot to sign the Covenant. Thus, Charles was asked to accept the overthrow of his authority in his northern kingdom. "No bishop, no king," muttered the ghost of his father. Charles rejected the resolutions and both sides prepared for war.

The king became at last aware of a desperate situation which needed a desperate remedy: Wentworth! In 1649, during the last days of his own life, King Charles reflected upon the career and fall of Lord Strafford and wrote:

> I looked upon my Lord of Strafford as a gentleman, whose great abilities might make a Prince rather afraid, than ashamed to employ him in the greatest affairs of the royal State.[19]

Now, faced with rebellion in Scotland and obstructionism in England, Charles was prepared to put away his fears of Wentworth's domineering personality. Only at the dark and extreme eleventh hour did the king turn away from Hamilton, Holland, and their like and look, at last, towards the most able and devoted of his servants. Charles wrote privately, in his own hand, consulting no one. He wrote little, but trusted the Bishop of Raphoe to carry to Ireland what could not be put on paper.

On August 5, 1639, nine days after leaving the camp near Berwick, the Bishop of Raphoe reached the little town of Naas in Wicklow, where Wentworth was supervising the building of his great house. Here he gave him the letter from the king. "Come when you will," the brief message ended, "ye shall be welcome to your assured friend, Charles R."[20]

In his new position as the king's chief councilor, Wentworth suggested that an English Parliament be summoned after eleven long years. Consistent with his view of mixed government, he felt this to be necessary; besides, he thought he could manage Parliament. The king needed money to pay for the Second Bishop's War against the Scots. In this unforeseen way, the personal rule came to an abrupt end.

Before the English Parliament met, Wentworth returned to Ireland to summon a parliament in Dublin to show the path of wisdom and loyalty to the one at Westminster. On January 12, 1640, he was created Baron of Raby and Earl of Strafford. The assumption of the title of Raby gave deep offense to the elder Sir Harry Vane, who had a long and sincere attachment to the locale and coveted the name for his house. This shows again a lack of sensitivity on Strafford's part which did him ill service in his relations with other people. Clarendon says of the Raby incident:

> It was an act of the most unnecessary provocation that I have ever

known, and I believe was the chief occasion of the loss of his head.

Clarendon states his point so strongly because later Vane was to be the chief witness of the prosecution for their strongest charge against Strafford.

Shortly after Strafford had been raised to an earldom, he was made Lord Lieutenant of Ireland. Next, he was named Lieutenant General under the Commander-in-Chief, Northumberland, and was to bring with him from Ireland a thousand men to serve against the Scots.

On March 23, an Irish Parliament composed of officials and Roman Catholics, under the eye of Strafford, voted four subsidies, or about 18,000 pounds. The Catholics hoped, by supporting Charles against the Covenanters, to obtain toleration for their own religion. Armed with these subsidies, Strafford believed that he could bring an army of nine thousand men from Ireland, if shipping were provided.[21] As soon as the Irish parliamentary session was ended, he returned to Westminster to take his place in the House of Lords in the Short Parliament. There he found everything in confusion and going against the king:

> The Parliamentary forces, though without public expression, had been neither impotent nor idle. Under a mild despotism they had established a strong control of local government in many parts of the country. When suddenly elections were held they were immediately able to secure a Parliament which began where its predecessor had left off. More than this, they presented the issues of 1629 with the pent-up anger and embitterment of eleven years of gag and muzzle. Charles had now to come back cap in hand to those very forces which he had disdainfully dismissed. The membership had been slightly changed by time and fortune.[22]

The Commons were resolved not to vote supplies until their grievances had been redressed. Thereupon, Lord Strafford boldy advised Charles to go in person to the House of Lords to ask the Peers to declare that the king should be supplied before grievances were taken up. Charles was supported on this point in the Lords by a majority of sixty-one to twenty-five. With this tactical victory, Strafford gained both the support of the Lords and the favor of the queen, who in the final days of peril now perceived his value. The Commons, however, declared the intervention of the Lords to be a breach of privilege.

On May 2, 1640, the king asked for an answer to his request for money;

Strafford followed up the king's request with a threat that a refusal would bring a dissolution. On the 3rd, Strafford talked Charles into a concession whereby he would give up his right to ship money without benefit of Act of Parliament, and at the same time, the earl urged him not to require all of the twelve subsidies which Sir Harry Vane had been authorized to demand, but simply to depend upon the affections of his subjects. Charles could not understand the wisdom of extending such concessions, but he agreed to settle for eight subsidies.

At this point, a crucial change occurred and it is uncertain whether Vane, who later danced to John Pym's tune, betrayed Charles or persuaded the vacillating king to return to his former ground. In any event, on the 4th Vane announced to the House that if the king was to give up ship money, then all twelve subsidies must be granted. This broke up the Commons for the day without any decision. That night, the Court got the word that John Pym intended to move in the next meeting of the House a petition asking the king to come to terms with the Scots. Charles at once summoned the Privy Council to meet at the unusual hour of 6 a.m. When Vane declared that there was no hope that the Commons "would give one penny," Strafford voted with the majority for a dissolution, bringing the Short Parliament to an end. Strafford would have accepted whatever reasonable sums the House was inclined to give, so long as they supported the war; he refused to go along with them if they made it a condition that the war was to be stopped—thus, in his eyes, condoning rebellion.

Later that morning, a meeting of the Committee of Eight, appointed to give advice on Scottish affairs and of which Strafford was a member, was held to discuss future plans. Vane and others wanted the king to fight a defensive war to protect England against invasion. Strafford, believing that it would be impossible to procure supplies for protracted defensive operations, wanted to take the offensive against Scotland, which he thought would be decisive in a short time. He urged that the City should be required to lend 100,000 pounds for the war, and that ship money be collected. Northumberland hesitated to begin a war with such slender means. Strafford replied, at least so far as Vane's hurried notes show:

> Go on vigorously or let them alone. No defensive war; loss of honor and reputation. The quiet of England will hold out long. . . .Go on with a vigorous war, as you first designed, loose and absolved from all rules of government. But reduced to extreme necessity,

everything is to be done that power might admit, and that you are to do. They [Commons] refusing [all aid], you are acquitted before God and man. You have an army in Ireland you may employ here to reduce this Kingdom. Confident as anything under heaven, Scotland shall not hold out five months. One summer well employed will do it. Whether a defensive war is as impossible as an offensive, or whether to let them alone.[23]

The Irish army was to be brought over to fight against the Scots. Yet, within two days, it was rumored that the king was considering the use of the Irish army against his English subjects as well as against the Scots. From that moment, a strong feeling of fierce indignation arose against Strafford among his countrymen. Henceforth, he was known as "Black Tom Tyrant."

The government's greatest need was to raise money. On May 10, the Lord Mayor of London refused to take any steps to raise a loan, and Strafford told the king that unless he hanged some of the aldermen, he would get nothing from the City. Frustrated by stubborn London, Strafford turned to the Spanish ambassadors, requesting a loan of 300,000 pounds from the King of Spain. In the midst of all these problems, Strafford was laid low by an attack of dysentery. During his convalescence, he was visited by Charles. To receive his king properly, Strafford threw off his warm covers, with the result that he caught a chill and for several days was on the brink of death. Strafford was not sufficiently recovered to take his seat in Council until July 5.

Meanwhile, the Irish Parliament had become agitated during Strafford's absence and voted a method of collecting its subsidies which would greatly reduce their amount. Nevertheless, the Irish army was scheduled to rendezvous toward the end of July at Carrickfergus, in readiness to cross the sea. In England, several expedients for raising money had been tried and failed, and the English forces were marching north in a dissatisfied, almost mutinous condition. On July 11, Strafford supported a money-raising scheme for the debasement of the coinage, threatening strong measures against anyone who opposed it. Later in the month, he pleaded again in vain with the Spanish ambassadors for a loan, this time offering his own personal property as collateral against the repayment of 100,000 pounds. When on July 30, a petition from Yorkshire was presented against the trespasses of the English soldiery, Strafford urged that it should be treated as an act of mutiny. At this stage of the game, it is clear that Strafford believed that, if Charles were to be saved at all, it could be done only through the ruthless use of the royal power, "loose and absolved from all rules of government."

The Irish army never crossed the sea. The English force broke down. On August 8, Strafford once more pleaded with the Spanish ambassadors for a loan, if only 50,000 pounds. This time the ambassadors recommended that the request be granted, but it was too late: Charles' military power had fallen into a condition beyond rescue. On August 20, the Scots crossed the Tweed. Strafford convinced himself that the disgrace of armed Scots on English soil would rally the country around the king. On the 27th, he told the gentry of his own country of Yorkshire that they were bound to resist the Scottish invasion "by the Common Law of England, by the law of nature, and by the law of reason."[24] Next day, the Scots defeated Conway at Newburn and the beaten troops retreated to York, where the main body of the English army was gathering.

The army was now virtually under Strafford's command, since Northumberland's health had failed him and the Commander-in-Chief had remained in the South. As he surveyed the military situation, Strafford was not optimistic at the prospects of victory. To the king he maintained a cheerful face, but to his close friend, Sir George Radcliffe, he admitted the near hopelessness of the situation:

> Pity me, for never came any man to so lost a business. The army altogether necessitous and unprovided of all necessaries. That part which I bring now with me from Durham, the worst I ever saw. Our horse all cowardly; the country from Berwick to York in the power of the Scots; an universal affright in all; a general disaffection to the King's service; none sensible of his dishonor....God of his goodness deliver me out of this the greatest evil of my life.[25]

To some extent, Strafford had been right when he thought that Englishmen would be aroused by a Scots' invasion. On September 13, he persuaded the Yorkshiremen to support their own trained bands, for which success he received the Garter from his grateful king. Other counties in the Northern Midlands seemed likely to follow Yorkshire's example, but the feelings stirred up by advancing Scots did not extend to the South, and London was clamoring for a redress of grievances by a new Parliament. On September 24, a Great Council of Peers, the first in two hundred years, met at York, where Charles told the Lords that he had issued writs for another English Parliament. Strafford at once stated the necessity of raising an immediate 200,000 pounds, and the Lords sent a deputation to London to ask the City for a loan. In vain on October 6, Strafford tried to convince the Great Council to resist the Scots any further. On the recommendation of the Peers, treaty negotiations were begun with the Scots, and after a preliminary agreement had been reached at Ripon in the last week of October, the Scots were asked to send Commissioners to London to ratify the terms with Parliament. Meanwhile, their army would occupy the Northern Counties at the expense of the English.

When the Great Council held its last session, Strafford did not again argue fighting the Scots. And of the newly elected Parliament, he foresaw enough of their bad temper to decide to remain up north in Yorkshire when they assembled. On November 3, 1640, the Long Parliament met. Lord Strafford had six months to live.

Strafford at his Trial (Hollar)

3

The Impeachment
of Strafford

On November 3, that famous assembly which was to be known for all time as the Long Parliament met at Westminster. The Members of Parliament were firmly convinced that their time had finally come. The future Cavalier and the future Roundhead were united on this, and they had resolved to reform the government, to purge it of years of accumulated evils.

The attempt of King Charles to place as many supporters as possible in the new Parliament had been a dismal failure, and the electoral tide ran strong against the Court. The new House of Commons was as stubborn in its composition as the voters could make it. Three-fifths of the Members of the Short Parliament, 294 of 493, had been returned, and nearly all the newcomers were opponents of the government. Of the members who had made a name in opposition, every single one was reelected. The king could count on less than a third of the House.

It was observed that the members had come together in a mood of grim purpose and strange exaltation: those who in the Short Parliament had talked of moderation had now thrown it to the winds. John Pym and John Hampden, the leading figures in the new House of Commons, were immediately in command of a large and acrimonious majority. Pym said that: "They must now be of another temper than they were during the last Parliament. They must not only sweep the House clean below but must pull down all cobwebs . . . by removing grievances, and pulling up the causes of them by the roots."[1]

The new Parliament believed that all their grievances resulted from a conspiracy to replace law and liberty at home with an absolute monarchy, which in turn was to be subjected to the ecclesiastical despotism of Rome. Such, they believed, was the premeditated and settled plan of Laud and Strafford. The Long Parliament derived its force from a blending of political and religious principles. It was moved by the need of a growing society to base itself upon a wider foundation than Tudor paternal rule. No Parliament had ever met with so great a strength of popular support. It used for tactical purposes the military threat of the invaders from Scotland, and the ever-present menace of the London mob to an unarmed government. By the combination of circumstances, it had become impossible for Charles to defy his Parliament without defying the Scottish army as well. Unless he could pay the agreed-upon 850 pounds a day for their maintenance, the Scots would declare the Treaty of Ripon to be violated, cross the Tees, and march southwards. There was no English force which could be counted upon to stop the Scots anywhere between Yorkshire and London. It was therefore absolutely necessary for Charles to find money which therefore made a dissolution of Parliament impossible.

As recent events had revealed, the London mob had become a menace too. Less than a fortnight before Parliament met, a group of ruffians sacked the Court of High Commission, and even Star Chamber dared not lift a finger to punish them. The Commons kept the mob simmering from day to day, so that at any required moment it could be brought howling into the streets.

The Speech from the Throne to open Parliament was coolly received, and the Commons proceeded to their own chamber to pursue an independent policy—a policy inspired and directed by John Pym. Pym had had his dress rehearsal as leader of the House the previous spring during the Short Parliament. The following summer he had been in the inner councils of the Opposition Peers. His abilities marked him out as the principal man of the Commons, while his relations with the Lords Warwick, Saye, Brooke, Mandeville and the rest linked him to the king's critics in the Lords. By virtue of his business connections, Pym occupied a stronger position than any political leader in the Commons had held before. He had connections with the City, the navy, and the Peerage, and he had the clear mind, the cool judgment, and the comprehensive grasp of an administrative genius. John Pym was the principal architect of the constitutional revolution of the next eighteen months in England, and therefore one of the most significant single figures, and one of the most remarkable intellects in the constitutional history of England.[2]

The initial debates of the Long Parliament showed unmistakably the way things were to go. Pym led a chorus of members in a preliminary catalogue of grievances, all competing with each other in denouncing the government; or, more ominously, calling for vengeance on the persons supposed to be responsible. There was not a dissenting, hardly a moderating voice. It soon became evident that a final reckoning was about to be demanded from the Crown.

No one knew better than Lord Strafford what danger was hanging over his own head. He had been marked to bear the offenses of all. To the mass of Englishmen, he was the blackest of hearts, the dark apostate who had forsaken the Constitution to build a tyranny. The Scots too held him as an enemy: of their church and country as well as the cause of the Bishops' Wars, which—unfortunately for Strafford—had been as obnoxious to Englishmen as to Scots. Courtiers, whose schemes for their own enrichment had wilted under his imperious frown, were eager to remove from their path this formidable obstacle. The Puritans regarded him as their deadliest foe. The City of London remembered how he had threatened its aldermen, and had endangered trade by the scheme to debase the coinage. The opposition in Parliament believed him to be the strongest support to the throne, without whom the king would be delivered into their power.

The new Parliament was hardly a week old when the decisive issue was joined. In the nearly helpless and powerless state to which he was reduced, the king still had, and clung to, the support of Strafford, now more than ever the dominating figure upon whose force of genius it seemed possible to rely to turn back the revolutionary flood. The king was unwilling to face the most critical Parliament of his reign without Strafford to uphold and guide him.

Strafford knew that the only place where he could be safe was in Yorkshire. When the king was ready to depart the north for London, Strafford asked to stay at his post as Commander-in-Chief of the English army. With his clear appreciation of the political situation, he knew that if he went to London he would be walking into a trap. He knew the men with whom he would have to contest. It had been plain for a long time that they meant to bring him down, to have his head if necessary; and once in their power there would be no escape. At York, he would be in the midst of his troops and free to flee to Ireland in a pinch.

But Charles felt the need to have Strafford in London by his side. And there were other voices whispering in Charles' ear. The belief of Strafford's family was that Hamilton and Vane, to make their peace with the Parliamentary leaders and save themselves, persuaded the king to send for Strafford. Charles himself was eager to lean on his strong shoulders and to consult his resourceful mind. The queen seconded her husband's request with declarations of her protection.

With Strafford there could be no question of refusal, no hesitation, only one possible answer: his king needed him and that was enough. Only recently he had brought himself to death's door, merely in order to greet his sovereign with due deference. Now there was, as he must have realized, the greatest possible danger if he went to London. But he was prepared to gamble. And he certainly knew that he was gambling with his life: his last request to the king was that he might have two or three days at Woodhouse to set his private affairs in order. Three days later, he set forth, sick and in pain, with a brave heart and against his own judgment. He knew that his enemies were ready and waiting as he wrote: "I am tomorrow to London, with more danger beset than ever any man went with out of Yorkshire. Yet my heart is good, and I find nothing cold in me. It is not to be believed how great the malice is, and how intent they are about it."[3]

Yet, Strafford went south in no fatalistic mood. He would try to dominate, whatever the odds. His behavior indicates that he had formulated a three-pronged plan of characteristic boldness for dealing with Parliament. He would not wait for Pym and his friends to act, but would seize the initiative and strike first.

First of all, Strafford believed that if Parliament and the country knew in full detail the humiliating and expensive terms exacted by the Scots in the Treaty of Ripon, they would turn against them and their parliamentary allies. Strafford, using the Lords and the courtroom as his forum, would broadcast the Scottish demands to the country.

Second, Strafford possessed proofs of the correspondence carried on by Pym and others with the invading Scots' army. This was plain treason, if the king's writ still ran. Strafford intended to expose, before the nation, the treason of which they were guilty by conspiring with the king's enemies to lay England under tribute.

Third, and if the other two failed, Strafford would actually go before the bar to vindicate the king and the government. Strafford believed that the Commons would try to bring him down with an impeachment. In his youth, he had seen three successive Parliaments waste their fury impeaching Buckingham. Now the same situation was about to arise in his own case, but the game had to go under different rules. The king had never allowed Buckingham to come to trial so that the favorite's guilt had never been proven legally. Now, however, if an impeachment were moved against Strafford, the king could not stop it because a dissolution of Parliament would bring the Scots marching down on London. Yet, if this Parliament were allowed to impeach Strafford, they would have to abandon general vilification for specific charges based upon statute law, and would have to prove them to the satisfaction of the judges. It was one thing to call a man the "source of all evils" or "tainted apostate" or "Black Tom Tyrant." It would be another to prove treason against him, especially since he had committed none by any English law.

This, then, was Strafford's last hope and final line of defense. If plans one and two failed, he would stand forth as the architect of the king's hated policy, face whatever charges Pym and the Commons brought against him, and he would refute them. That this was a firm plan is indicated by the fact that Charles did not order Strafford to be tried in a Prerogative Court like Star Chamber, but instead allowed the trial to proceed before the House of Lords. The reasons are plain: If Strafford won an acquittal in a Prerogative Court, the country would believe that he was acquitted through the king's influence upon a subservient judge. If, on the other hand, he was tried before the Lords, then the proceedings would be open to all London and there could be no doubt as to the justice of his case.

From past experience Strafford knew the volatile temperament of a Parliament. He knew that a good half of the discontented members, who presently held him alone to be responsible for the evils of the last twelve years, would be impressed when they saw the weakness of the legal case against him. In the calculations of the opposition, there could be no failure when they moved against Strafford: for failure would divide the Commons from the Lords, and divide the members among themselves. In any such moment of division, Strafford and the king could regain much ground, perhaps all.

In the end, the contest between Strafford and Pym was a close one; both antagonists calculated the odds very accurately. If the Earl of Strafford had been as intelligently supported by king and court as Pym was by Parliament, he would have won. Indeed, more than once during the trial, victory was almost in his grasp. In May, at the Great Council table he had said, "I would carry it or lose all." This was still his mood and the reason he came to London.

The destruction of Lord Strafford was the key to the political strategy of the opposition led by John Pym. The success of their whole attack upon the position of the Crown depended upon victory in the trial of the earl.[4] Years later, it seemed that Strafford had gone with open eyes to his death and contemporaries looking back to his trial called him a patriot or an idiot, according to their politics. The royalist Hamon Lestrange declared that "his repair to London was in effect a rendering up of himself captive to the will of his deadliest enemies."[5] Lord Clarendon, the historian, who was an active member of the Commons during the arraignment and trial, thought "that he had acted out of sheer contempt of the people's anger, of the machinations of his enemies."[6] One contemporary sympathetically observed that he was "under the same necessity that was enjoined upon our Savior: somebody must be sacrificed to appease the people and he is thought the fittest."[7]

Lord Strafford left Woodhouse for London on November 6, 1640, traveling slowly because of his poor health. By Sunday, November 8, he had reached Huntington, where he received news of the business which had occurred in Parliament subsequent to its convention on November 3. He learned that complaints about Ireland before the House of Commons had brought about a Committee of the Whole to discuss Irish affairs. There had been opposition to taking up the question of Ireland and the division on the question had been close: 165 to 150. The nature of the complaints from Ireland did not disquiet Strafford. He believed that he could defeat any attack on his Irish administration, and that night he wrote to his friend Radcliffe:

> To the best of my judgment we gain much rather than lose. I trust God will preserve us; and as all other passions I am free of fear, the articles that are coming I apprehend not. The Irish business is past, and better than I expected, their proofs being very scant. God's hand is with us, for what is not we might expect to have been sworn from thence?... All will be well and every hour gives more hope than other. God Almighty protect and guide us.[8]

Strafford reached London on the evening of November 10. Parliament had been sitting for a little over a week. In the House of Commons were a number of prominent members with connections in Ireland: Lord Cork's eldest son and two sons-in-law; Lord Wilmot's son; Sir William Jephson, a Munster landowner; and Sir John Clotworthy, an Ulster landowner who in the past had crossed Strafford several times. Clotworthy was an important link between the English opponents of the king and Strafford's enemies in Ireland. His election had been arranged by the Earl of Warwick.[9]

Pym's tactics were that Strafford should be thoroughly discredited before clinching the matter with a formal indictment. When the Irish complaints began, Pym stated that "all the subjects of Ireland have power to come here"—an open invitation to every notable who had been under Strafford's thumb. Mountnorris came before the Committee for Irish Affairs on the very first day that it met; Wilmot and Loftus immediately followed. As long as Strafford was at York, there was no need to hurry. But now everything was changed by the earl's sudden arrival in London.

The boldness of Strafford's move was by itself a cause for alarm. He had stuck his head into the lion's mouth simply because he had been told to do it; but from the point of view of the Commons, he had presumably come on his own initiative to snatch some unforeseen winning advantage—perhaps even to effect a military takeover. Pym's spies at Court soon informed him of the lines of attack which Strafford intended to take, and he at once realized the importance of silencing the earl.[10]

John Pym was a master of timing, a skill which he repeatedly demonstrated during the next three years. To make the correct decision was important; to act on that decision at the right moment was equally important. The decision to impeach Strafford was probably taken by Pym and his allies in both Houses as soon as they knew a Parliament was to be summoned.[11] But the attack itself had to be begun at the best possible moment. If Strafford did not come to London at all and was impeached *in absentia*, the effect of his conviction upon the government and country would be lost. Moreover, from Yorkshire he could flee to Ireland to take command of the feared Irish army and march on Ulster. Therefore, the attack would have to wait until Strafford was in London, if he came at all.

Suddenly Strafford was in their midst. His advice to the king was to accuse the Parliamentary leaders of treasonable relations with the Scots.[12] There was not time to be lost. Charles had announced his intention of withdrawing from the Tower the garrison which had been placed there by Lord Cottington. The 11th was set as the date for the king to review these troops, and it can hardly have been an unintentional coincidence that the same day was set by Strafford to charge the Parliamentary leaders with treason. The king would be ready with an armed force to guard the prisoners when they arrived.

Pym had to act quickly and for once he was unprepared: a well-briefed, well-documented indictment was not yet ready. It was a question of hours, and Strafford had the momentary advantage of surprise. Pym could not have stopped the earl from taking the offensive, if Strafford had risen in the Lords on the 11th to make accusations of treason. On the morning of November 11, Strafford took his seat in the House of Lords. The moment when his charges against his enemies should have been brought—if it was to be done at all—was allowed to slip by. The only reasonable supposition is that, when the moment for action came, Charles drew back as he had so often drawn back before. After a short time, Strafford left the House without uttering a word. He had made his first large tactical error.

The Commons, meanwhile, were in a state of violent agitation. The military arrangements at the Tower were discussed. Rumors were repeated that Strafford had boasted that the City would soon be subjected; courtiers around the king had said the same. The inevitable reference to some great popish plot was made. Next, Sir John Clotworthy revealed that Sir George Radcliffe had said in May that the Irish army would give the king his way with England. When the atmosphere was sufficiently heated, Pym saw that his time was come. He rose and moved that the doors should be locked. A select committee was named to prepare for a conference with the Lords "and the charge against the Earl of Strafford."[13]

The committee thus named had in a few hours to draw up the charges which were originally intended to be the result of an exhaustive inquiry. Consequently, they were vague and rambling. The committee itself acknowledged that they were not yet prepared to send up specific charges supported by evidence. Lord Falkland protested against charging a man before satisfying the House that there was evidence and a case against him. But Pym swept him aside, arguing that locking up Strafford would separate him from the king, after which the Commons could take their time with collecting evidence. The House agreed with Pym and directed him to carry up the impeachment without delay, demanding also Strafford's immediate arrest and sequestration from the House.[14] In Pym's position, Strafford would probably have acted just as unfairly, for the ordinary forms of judicial procedure were insufficient to cope with a minister who, armed with the authority of the Crown, was going to resort to force.

Meanwhile, Strafford was with Charles at Whitehall. One of the friendly Peers left his seat and came to the palace with news that the attack on Strafford had begun. There was a general commotion among the Court: Strafford alone "with a composed confidence," said simply, "I will go and look mine accusers in the face." He hoped to reach the House of Lords before Pym, and be in his place of honor to rebut when he was accused. But Pym beat him to the Lords by a nose.

Pym read to their lordships that the Commons of England in Parliament assembled, accused Thomas Wentworth, Earl of Strafford, Lord Lieutenant of Ireland, of High Treason. The Peers had expected no less than this and told Pym to withdraw while they examined the charge. Now Strafford with haughty mien strode through the group of waiting Commoners at the doorway up the floor to his place. There were those among the Lords who had no wish to allow him to speak, lest he accuse them of complicity with the Scots. Moreover, the Lords, as a body, felt even more personally aggrieved than the Commons by his arbitrary method of government. As he advanced to his place, a shout rose along the benches, "Withdraw! Withdraw!" Pym's message was read to the earl. The Lord Keeper told Strafford he must withdraw to await the Lords' decision. In less than an hour the powerful minister found himself become a prisoner. He found himself kneeling at the Bar to receive the directions of his Peers from the Earl of Manchester. He was to be sequestered from the House and confined until the hearing of the cause. He protested against the unprecedented severity of this measure, but Manchester silenced him with the information that he could now reach the ear of the Lords only by petition. He was deprived of his sword and taken into custody by Maxwell, the Gentleman Usher of the Black Rod. As Black Tom went through the City on his journey to Black Rod's house, the hostility of the crowd was terrible. Strafford had made his first major error of timing; giving Pym the first blow, his downfall had been swift.

The proscription was eventually extended to all the king's ministers. Archbishop Laud, old and breaking under the strain, was impeached in the Lords, silenced when he sought to reply, and removed to the Tower. Sir Francis Windebank, the Secretary of State, and some others fled to the Continent. Lord Keeper Sir John Finch, leaving the Woolsack, appeared before the Commons in his robes of office, carrying the Great Seal of England in his bag, and defended himself in such moving words that the members were silenced. Nevertheless, his eloquence served only to delay the Commons while he fled the country. These proscriptions were done by the Commons, with the support of the City and the military forces of Scotland, and accepted by the Peers.

It had now come to a duel between Strafford and Pym and his Parliamentary allies. Black Rod's house was not a fortress like the Tower, and Strafford's failure to attempt to break out and flee, along with his calm after his arrest, showed that he was confident that he could beat down the charges against him. To fail to prove the charges would be a disaster for the opposition, from which they might not easily recover.

The opposition had to bring down Strafford for the simple but compelling reason that he was the only minister of the king with dangerous abilities. As Wedgwood points out:

> His management of the Irish Parliament in 1634, his attempts to play off the House of Lords against the House of Commons in the spring of 1640, his tactics at the Council of Peers—these and many other things besides his original leadership of the Commons in 1628, bore witness to his skill in political management if he were given the least advantage. His ruthlessness and vigour had also to be reckoned with. As long as he remained alive, he was a potential danger. This could not now be said of any of the King's other councillors, not even of the Archbishop, who was old and had lost all hope and energy.[15]

During the next weeks, the committee appointed to draw up the charges against Strafford worked hard, brought witnesses out of Yorkshire and Ireland, and tried out numerous allegations. From time to time the committee reported and the articles were discussed in the House. Just in case the impeachment should fail for lack of judicial proof, Pym also investigated the possibility of using a Bill of Attainder against his foe. A Bill of Attainder did not rest upon the law: it was instead a legislative act which simply decreed a man guilty of a crime, regardless of how his case stood under the law.[16]

On November 12, the firebrand Denzil Holles resigned from the Committee. He had realized that Pym was out for Strafford's life; and, deeply as he disagreed with the earl's politics, he did not want to be a party to taking the life of his late sister's husband. Sir Walter Earle and

John Hampden were named in his place.

On November 13, Sir George Radcliffe was impeached. He would have been Strafford's chief witness for the defense, but this move stopped him from appearing. Orders were given that all records, letters, and papers connected with Strafford should be opened to the Committee. On the 18th, members of Parliament, wherein Strafford had two brothers and still some friends, were forbidden to visit him without permission or to tell him what took place in Commons. On the 19th, a request for bail was refused, and on the 20th, Pym asked leave of the Lords to question the Privy Council.[17] His purpose was to get evidence that Strafford had intended to use his Irish army against the English. Young Harry Vane had found his father's notes of the meeting of the Council of Eight for Scottish Affairs, at which the use of the Irish army was discussed, and had secretly given them to Pym. But Pym could not use the notes without revealing that they had been stolen from the Elder Vane. Therefore, he hoped to get evidence about the Irish army from the Councillors, especially Sir Harry Vane, by querying them about the Council meeting.

This unprecedented demand to violate the traditional secrecy of the King's Privy Council should have brought a howl of protest from the Lords, among whom there numbered many past, present, and future Councillors. But, unfortunately for Strafford, his high-handed dealing with many Peers during his tenure in power had made him many enemies. Lord Cork hated him. Northumberland and Newcastle were alienated. Leicester was unfriendly. Clanricarde, the English Earl of St. Albans, hated him, and so did Newport, Holland, Arundel, as well as all of the opposition Peers. Those who pleaded the privilege of the King's Councils were outvoted and Pym gained another notable advantage against Strafford.[18]

On November 21, Audley Mervyn, a member of the Irish Parliament, appeared with a remonstrance from Dublin. The Irish Commons, which in March had voted Strafford the best governor Ireland ever had, now brought charges against him for tyranny, oppression, and injustice.[19] In Strafford's absence the Irish Parliament had turned against him, and Christopher Wandesford, Lord Deputy, exerted no control at all.

On November 24, thirteen days after Strafford's arrest, Pym brought the Articles of Strafford's impeachment before the Commons. On the following morning, they were submitted to the Lords, and that afternoon Strafford was brought to hear them. Afterwards, he asked for sufficient time to prepare his answer, leave to have legal counsel and call witnesses, and to know the names of the witnesses testifying against him. He was told that such questions should be presented to the Lords by petition. When he left the Lords, he was taken through derisive crowds to the Tower of London. For thirteen days, he had remained in the lightly-guarded house of Maxwell, made no attempt to escape; apparently, he expected to win the contest.

Strafford's commitment created an extraordinary situation: He was a fallen minister, barred from his seat in the Lords, stripped from all his offices, awaiting trial for treason, but he was still the power behind the throne. Charles, brow-beaten and bullied by Parliament and the Scots, still looked for guidance to the man he could not save from the Tower. The Lord Keeper received permission to carry messages between Charles and Strafford, and messages were voluminously exchanged. Visitors from Parliament had to get permission to see the prisoner and to promise to reveal nothing. To lessen the aid given by these go-betweens, the Lords eventually forbade any visitors to Strafford after dark.[20]

The preparations went forward for Strafford's trial, but they did not occupy the House of Commons to the exclusion of all other matters. "Reformation goes on . . . as hot as toast," wrote an observer. Altar railings were pulled down all over the country, while Laud's prisoners, Prynne, Burton, and Bastwick, were received in London amid general thanksgiving. A few days later, the Londoners presented a petition for the abolition of episcopacy. On December 18, Laud himself was accused.

Hardly a voice was raised in Commons to defend the king, his ministers, or his bishops. One reason for this quiescence was the fierceness with which any dissenting member was silenced by the dominant party. Another reason was a series of measures pushed through the excited Commons by Pym to curb the king's friends; measures dealing with every sheriff and justice of the peace who had had a hand in the king's exactions of revenue. Collectors of ship money, coat and conduct money, monopolists were all deemed to have committed criminal offenses, affecting nearly half the House and all of the king's friends. Lest the laws be put into effect, no man, who had passed revenue through his hands in any manner, dared speak against the extremists. The judges, especially those who decided against Hampden, were systematically impeached or terrorized. On December 21, Lord Keeper Finch was impeached, and he fled that night. The persecution of the Catholics was resumed. It was announced that the law against priests would be put into force. The queen's friends went in terror of their lives. On January 5, Secretary Windebanke fled to France. A Franciscan was executed. There were more to follow.

The towering eminence of Strafford's personality was never more evident than these winter days when he was confined to the Tower. No one doubted that the whole issue in the struggle between the new order and the old turned upon the fate of this man. By the New Year the general excitement began to focus upon the specific issue of Strafford's trial. There were witnesses to be brought from Ireland, evidence to be gathered and tested, managers to be selected, trained, and briefed. Strafford was slightly encouraged by some of this, especially when the Lords and Commons showed any signs of falling out, as they did, for example, over the interrogation of witnesses. The Commons had insisted upon members of their House being present whenever the Lords examined witnesses; the Lords remembered their privileges and almost refused on the grounds that Lord Strafford was a Peer. But in the end they gave in.[21]

Strafford petitioned to be allowed legal counsel. The Lords did not immediately decide this point. Instead they named seven lawyers who might help him draw up his answer, if they wished.[22] It was a test of their courage. None of them refused.

Apart from these graces, the Lords had little mercy on their prisoner. Indeed, as Wedgwood states, their lordships

> except where they scented an attack on privilege, not only gave the Commons their way but even encouraged them. Early in December they ordered Sir William Balfour, the Lieutenant of the Tower, to have the Earl of Strafford confined to three rooms only, to keep two soldiers constantly in the outer of these, to lock his door at night and to allow him to take exercise only under escort. Strafford bore it with equanimity; indeed his behaviour in the Tower caused grave misgivings to the prosecution. He was steadfastly cheerful and good-humoured, attended the chapel daily, choosing to sit in Prynne's old seat where he could see the altar, took exercise under the guard of Balfour, talking amicably the while, ordered fresh liveries for his servants, and inspected the new silver-handled heading axe with detached, half-humorous interest.[23]

Petitions from Irish malcontents swelled to a steady stream, and the Irishmen who had presented the Remonstrance were added to the

Committee for drawing the charges. Cheered on by Lord Cork's friends, the Commons welcomed any complaint of injustice from Ireland, and rewards even were offered to those who would complain. The judgments against Loftus and Mountnorris were reversed, and Strafford soon learned from his friends that the heart of the charges was to be his Irish administration. This was more reassuring than threatening to Strafford, for he sincerely felt that he had done nothing illegal or dishonorable in Ireland.

Meanwhile, the Scot's Commissioners charged Strafford with being the primary incendiary who brought dissension between the two countries and turned the face of the king against Scotland.[24] Sir David Foulis, Strafford's old enemy of Yorkshire days, petitioned next for release. By Christmas there was such a backlog of unheard witnesses and accumulation of evidence that the examination continued during the recess. Sir Harry Vane's memory was interesting: it improved when he understood the specific evidence needed from him. Lord Cork was obliging throughout: "Old Richard," said Strafford, "hath sworn against me gallantly."[25]

The king's friends and the waverers in the Commons smelled the danger to themselves in the air and absented themselves in great numbers; consequently, on January 15, 1641, it was decided that forty members should constitute a quorum. A week later, Pym began to investigate the sheriffs and justices, thus securing that quarter for the duration of the trial, for most of the threatened members would buy subsequent immunity with present silence.[26]

On January 30, the Earl of Strafford was finally brought before his Peers to hear in detail the full charges against him.

William Railton, one of Strafford's most trusted advisers, was shocked the day before while on a visit to the Tower by the threatening crowds around the gates. He asked the Lords for the safety of their prisoner to bring him to Westminster by night, and lodge him there secretly until morning. Railton's request was ignored and Strafford was brought up the Thames by boat from the Tower in daylight. Under guard, he landed at Westminster stairs and made his way with the soldiers to the Parliament buildings. Along the way, there were threats and curses from the crowds, but no violence.[27]

Lord Strafford came into the House of Lords weak and pale after two winter months confinement in the unhealthy, chilling damp of the Tower.

Even among the unfriendly Lords there was a visible stir of pity. One of his friends in the House moved that he be granted the privilege of sitting, instead of standing at the Bar, which was granted.

He was then charged before his Peers with high treason. Without a flicker of emotion on his dark face, Strafford heard nine general and twenty-eight specific accusations. When the Clerk of the House had finished reading the Articles, Strafford's leading counsel, Richard Lane, asked that the earl might have a few days grace in which to prepare his answer. Very grudgingly did the Lords grant his request: Strafford was given two weeks to prepare his defense; the Commons had taken two months. With that, he was returned to his prison.[28]

Once more in the Tower, Strafford was jubilant, almost certain of acquittal. He wrote tenderly to his wife that night, and in a more businesslike manner to the Earl of Ormonde, a trusted friend in Ireland. In both letters he used the phrase: "The charge is now come in, and I am able to tell you that I conceive there is nothing capital [in them]."[29] In his opinion, the House of Commons had failed to make a case against him for treason. Faced at last with specific charges, and given two weeks in which to reply, Strafford had reached the crucial point of decision at which he must choose his prime strategies of defense. Immediately, almost instinctively, on that day before the Lords, he had silently compared the charges with English law and found "nothing capital." Under the law, the Commons could not make their case stick. Subject to later refinement, or change, Strafford had immediately decided to ground one major line of defense in English Statue Law.

The Preliminary Articles charged in general terms that Thomas Wentworth, Earl of Strafford, had traitorously:

1. Subverted the fundamental laws of England and Scotland.
2. Assumed self-regal power and exercised the same tyrannically.
3. Helped himself to the State revenue and exchequer.
4. Encouraged papists.
5. Stirred up war between England and Scotland.
6. Betrayed the army to the Scots at Newburne and Newcastle.
7. Subverted Parliament and created enmity between the king and his people.

Next followed Twenty-Eight Articles of accusation which were specific elaborations of the general charges, naming time, place, persons, and acts.

While Strafford prepared his defense, King Charles pursued a policy of moderation in an attempt to win over some of his critics and divide the opposition. He passed an opposition measure which bound the Crown to call a Parliament at least every three years. He elevated some of the opposition Peers to the Privy Council. Concurrently, the king opened negotiations for the marriage of his eldest daughter to the only son of the Prince of Orange, Stadtholder of Holland, hoping thereby to gain the financial support of one of the richest houses of Europe.

On February 17, Strafford appealed in the Lords for more time to prepare his answer to the charges. After a lengthy and heated debate, he was granted another week.[30]

John Pym knew that the general feeling of the Lords Temporal was against Strafford and that one of his large hopes of acquittal was the bishops. It was expected that the old alliance between the Crown and the Church would hold and that the Lords Spiritual would side with Strafford—twenty-six votes in the House of Lords which the prosecution might find difficult to overcome. Consequently, Pym began to whip up support in Commons for a bill against the exercise of temporal or judicial power by the clergy, this being inconsistent with their spiritual duties. Pym's cue was picked up by Laud's enemy, Bishop Williams of Lincoln, recently released from the Tower. In the Lords, William argued with a great display of learning that although the bishops could not legally be prevented from judging Strafford, nevertheless they should, as men of the church, abstain from taking part in a *causa sanguinis* which involved a death sentence. Thereupon, the bishops, anxious to preserve the church and not desiring further to anger a Puritan Commons, withdrew.

The withdrawal of the bishops from the case was serious tactical defeat for Lord Strafford. One of his first defensive moves should have been to make sure of their votes, or at least of their unfettered participation as judges. But Charles was preoccupied with his policy of moderation, aimed at dividing the opposition, and Strafford was busy preparing a forensic case. The support of the bishops would have helped both of them to attain their mutual objectives, but there is no evidence that either king or earl tried to make this maneuver. Twenty-six votes in the House of Lords had been thrown away.

On February 24, Strafford came to the Lords to deliver his answer to the charges. When King Charles arrived, he astonished everyone by having the defendant brought privately to him before the proceedings began. They spent an hour alone together, presumably reviewing the general plan of defense. Later, when Charles took his seat on the throne and Strafford came to the Bar, the king saluted his fallen minister with great warmth and affection. This pantomime was a clear sign that the king wished his Lords to acquit Strafford. By themselves, these were intelligent moves for they indicated to the Peers that the decision on Strafford's guilt was to be made by them, not the king: they were not to pass the buck along to Charles, depending upon his right of final appeal to settle the issue.

The Commons had accused Strafford of treason by nine general charges, which were supplemented and explained by twenty-eight further articles that formed the statement of the charges made. They may be grouped under five heads:

I. Statements of policy and advice given, subversive of the fundamental laws of the realm and designed to bring about arbitrary government.

II. Procured a new and illegal commission to the Council of the North, and used his powers to oppress and arbitrarily rule the people living within its district.

III. Ireland: numerous charges:
A. Interfering with the administration of justice.
B. Exercising martial law in time of peace.
C. Treating disobedience to illegal orders of the Privy Council as crimes.
D. Ejecting men from their estates without process of law, and imprisoning such as resisted.
E. Exacting taxes and enforcing decrees by the quartering of soldiers.
F. Manipulating the customs for his own profit to the detriment of traders.
G. Enforcing his illegal and arbitrary exactions by fines, imprisonment and whipping.
H. Raising an army of papists to be used in England.

IV. Scotland: accused of endeavoring to stir up strife between the English and Scots, and plotting to break the pacification between Charles and the Scots.

V. A series of charges related to recent events:
A. He had advised the king that he was released from all rules of government.
B. He was a party to the exaction of ship money and other imposts.
C. He was concerned in the illegal jurisdiction of

the Star Chamber.

D. He advised the king to seize the bullion at the
   Mint, which belonged to private owners, and to
   debase the coinage.
E. He had illegally taxed Yorkshire to maintain his
   troops.
F. He had procured the defeat of the army and the loss
   of Newcastle to stir up strife between England and
   Scotland.
G. He had threatened the City of London in order to
   enforce a loan.

In short, nothing that had happened since 1628 had occurred except by
his advice and procurement.

Strafford made a written reply to these charges which took three hours
for his counsel to read. In effect, the Commons had impeached not one
man, but a system of government. In reply, Strafford's defense was a
political creed, a personal justification, and a veiled attack upon his
accusers. Initially, he asserted that certain charges proved only that he had
effectively and efficiently minded the king's business. All charges
impugning his personal integrity, he denied on the grounds of misreport
or misrepresentation. Moreover, he denied many charges as false: the
vaunted death sentence of Mountnorris had actually amounted to a few
days' arrest. He denied any personal knowledge of the oppressive acts in
Ireland that were charged to him. Many acts he did not deny, but justified
as legal according to English and Irish precedent and law. The
contribution of the Yorkshire gentry for the upkeep of the army had not
been imposed by him but agreed upon by the Great Council of Peers. All
arbitrary measures related to the Bishops' Wars were necessary because
the country was at war.[31]

When his answer was finished, the accused asked leave to call witnesses
for the defense and to cross-examine those of the prosecution. The Lords
would not answer this request until they had discussed it with the
Commons, a sign that the alliance between the two Houses was especially
strong and, therefore, dangerous.[32]

On Friday, March 5, the Commons sent Bulstrode Whitelocke to the
House of Lords with his message:

That the House of Commons have considered of the Earl of
Strafford's answer, and do aver their charge of High Treason against

him, and that he is guilty in such manner and form as he stands accused and impeached, and that this House will be ready to prove their charge against him, at such convenient time as their Lordships shall prefix, and intend to manage the evidence by Members of their own, and desire a conference...to consider of some circumstances concerning the trial.[33]

Many conferences between the two Houses took place before the "circumstances concerning the trial" were agreed upon. C. V. Wedgwood has summarized the procedural agreements made between the Houses as follows:

The Peers wished Strafford to have the benefit of counsel, the Commons did not; they compromised by allowing him counsel for matter of law, but not for matter of fact. Next came the question of witnesses; here again a compromise was reached and Strafford was permitted to call his own witnesses and cross-examine the witnesses for the prosecution, but not on oath. He was allowed to call members of Parliament, but the Commons added a rider that no such members were under obligation to appear. Strafford himself was only informed of this permission three days before his trial, so that it was impossible for him to bring witnesses from Ireland. The Irish Commons had in any case taken the precaution of impeaching Lord Chancellor Bolton, Lord Chief Justice Lowther and the Bishop of Derry so as to make it impossible for them to be called as witnesses.

Another knotty point was the prosecution. The Commons insisted on managing it themselves through a Committee. However, they wished to be present during the hearing, consequently the trial had to be held in Westminster Hall as the House of Lords was not large enough, and a further argument ensued as to whether they should wear their hats or no; it was beneath the dignity of the House of Commons to sit bare, but the Peers would not hear of them sitting covered in their presence. In the end they agreed to come not as the House of Commons, but as a mere committee, in which case they could be hatless without foregoing their dignity.[34]

These procedural arguments were not begun by the Lords in order to give the defendant any advantage or fair play; the points of contention were merely to preserve the privileges of all the Peers.

Strafford had clearly erred when he waited to learn their lordships' pleasure on the question of calling witnesses. This was a point of privilege which they were not likely to forego, no matter what feelings they had for him. He should have quietly brought his witnesses to England and had them in London ready and waiting.

One further event in the House of Lords seriously darkened Strafford's prospects: Littleton, the new Lord Keeper and a personal friend, fell ill and could not preside over the trial. Consequently, Lord Arundel, as Earl Marshall, became the main referee of the trial's procedure and development. Arundel, a conservative, might have been favorable toward the defendant, but his pride had been hurt the year before when he lost command of the army—on Strafford's advice, or so he thought. Throughout the trial, Arundel was hostile to the prisoner. The date for the trial was set for Monday, March 22, 1641, and Sir William Balfour, commander of the Tower, was told to bring the Earl of Strafford to Westminster Hall between eight and nine o'clock in the morning.

The initiative in London was kept by John Pym, who resolved to sharpen the feelings of the mob, in case they might be needed. Popular excitement, which had cooled during February, was fueled and fired throughout March. On the first, Laud was brought through angry crowds to the Tower. On the same day, the Commons published the charge against Strafford, doing so without the Lords' consent.[35] The accused's reply was not published. The charges were speedily distributed all over England and their effect was frightful. The accusations, read and discussed everywhere, were accepted as proven facts. The Irish and Scottish Remonstrances soon followed. Strafford became a monster more terrible than anyone had first thought. "Black Tom" had betrayed king and country; encouraged a Romish coup; warred on loyal subjects; twisted the law; whipped, pilloried, tortured, and hanged defenseless thousands; starved to death thousands of small Ulster children. Here indeed was the author of the ills of three kingdoms.

The Lords took exception to this impermissible breach of privilege by the Commons against a Peer of the Realm, but no break occurred between the Houses. Strafford did not trouble himself to publish his answer to the charges. He believed that he could disprove or shake all of them. Unfortunately for him, he did not figure the mob into his calculations, and he underestimated the effect that unproven charges could have upon his Peers and the state of feeling in London. Pym was firing up the London population; and, knowing the effect of forewarning in persuasion, he used the effect of reiteration of the prisoner's alleged crimes to build up resistance to any contrary evidence. Strafford produced no effective counterstroke to ward off this tactic of Pym's.

Strafford's personal troubles daily increased:

> He was short of money, worried about his debts, and anxious about his defenseless family in Dublin. He was selling timber off his Irish estates and bringing over some of his plate from Dublin to raise money on it. In the intervals of working out his defense he was seeing his brothers-in-law, the Earl of Clare, and the Earl of Cumberland, and the dowager Lady Clare; for fear of the worst he wished to have his family affairs settled and the future of his wife and infant daughter, and his three elder children secured: no easy matter in the confused state of his public and private revenues. His creditors, all this time, were petitioning the Lords that they might not suffer if the Wentworth estates were confiscated, and the Londoners displayed their Christian charity by demanding that the arch-enemy should be more rigorously confined than he was at present.[36]

The family of his second wife, the Holles-Clares, at least, came to his aid at this time. Long estranged, they now buried any differences. The old countess assured him of her affection and care for her grandchildren. His brother-in-law, Lord Clare, intervened persistently in his favor in the House of Lords. Denzil Holles tried to form a party in the Commons which would drop the impeachment in return for concessions by the king on church policy.[37]

Meanwhile, Strafford put the finishing touches to his defense. Lane, his principal counsel, assisted him with the legal aspects. Afterwards, Lane said that the defense was not only the most brilliant he had ever heard but was primarily thought out by Strafford himself.[38] The accused built upon the foundations of his first answers. He still aimed to break up the solid front of opposition marshalled against him by Pym and his associates; to bring the two Houses of Parliament into conflict; and secure an acquittal. He hoped to vindicate his view of government by awakening political England to the doubtful legal, political, and moral position of his accusers. Above all, he still hoped to turn the tables and bring down his and the king's enemies. If he won, it would be a solid blow to the policy of the king's opponents; and, in the subsequent confusion, Charles and he would regain much lost ground, perhaps all.

Strafford was fighting for his reputation, his fortune, and his life. But, no one knew better than he that the stakes were much bigger than one man's life. He was fighting to preserve his king, and to preserve the political system in which he believed and tried to establish. It is this which raises the trial from a legal to a historic level.

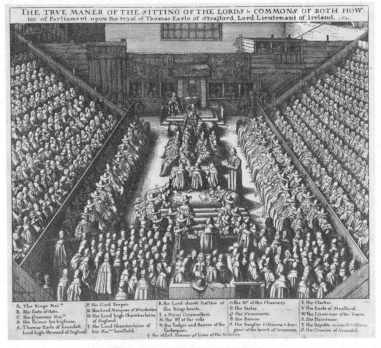

The Trial of Strafford (Hollar)

4

The Trial
Articles One to Nineteen: Tentative Strategies, Tactical Probes, First Salvoes

On Monday morning, March 22, at seven o'clock, the Earl of Strafford came from the Traitor's Gate of the Tower, took his place in one of six barges, which carried 100 soldiers of the Tower and fifty pairs of oars, and was rowed up the Thames to his place of trial. Upon his landing at Westminster, he was conducted into the Hall by two hundred of the trained bands. The formality of carrying the axe before his procession was omitted.

Within the Hall itself, a throne, for form's sake, had been erected with its back against the west wall. In front of the throne was the seat of the Earl of Arundel, Lord High Steward of the Lords and presiding. In front of Arundel, and moving from west to the east wall, were seats to be occupied by the judges if they were summoned to give opinion on points of law. There was also a table for the clerks. Running along the length of both sides of this west-east arena were the places of the Peers. Farther back from Arundel and the clerks, still moving from west to east, came the Bar, behind which was a desk for Strafford, and four secretaries were to be ready to supply him with any papers that he might need. Farther east still were the lawyers whom he might employ to argue on his behalf if any legal question should be raised, though, according to the custom of those days, they could not speak on questions of fact. On one side of Strafford's desk were seats for the managers who appeared for the Commons, while a witness-box on the other side completed the arrangements of the court. Along the entire length of the other two walls, the north and south walls, arose tiers of seats, much like bleachers, of which the best were reserved for members of the Commons and the Scots commissioners, with the balance going to spectators who were able, by favor or payment, to obtain admission. Of the twenty-six bishops, none was present among the Lords.

Accompanied by Balfour, Strafford knelt at the Bar until Lord Arundel commanded the House to proceed. The prisoner was dressed in black, wearing his George as his sole ornament.[1] Standing at the Bar, Strafford waited for about one-half hour, until at nine o'clock when the king, queen, and Prince of Wales entered. Charles did not sit upon the throne because there had been wide objection from both Houses to his official presence. The ten-year-old prince took his highest place among the Peers on the steps of the throne itself, while the king and queen took a place in a curtained alcove above the seats of the Peers, which had been arranged like a box in a theatre. The Commons had put up a lattice in front of the box to prevent the royal presence from being felt, but this was a little too much and Charles tore it down. The royal couple were constant in their attendance, in the hope that their presence might put heart into the prisoner, and impose some restraint upon the managers of the prosecution.[2] As Henrietta Maria records, they never returned to the palace without grief in their hearts and tears in their eyes.

The proceedings of the first day were purely formal. The Earl of Arundel called upon the prisoner by name, telling him that he was to answer before his Peers to a charge of high treason. John Pym, Speaker of the Managers' Committee for the Accusation, presented the articles which were read by the Clerk of the House of Lords. Strafford's answers were also read in the same manner. The reading of the articles and answers lasted until 2 p.m., when the court adjourned and Strafford was taken back to the Tower. The people of Westminster, "whose politics differed on principle from those of the Londoners, received him as he left the hall with expression of sympathy and respect, which he answered with unruffled civility."[3]

That afternoon the Commons met and ordered that:

In case the Earl of Strafford shall ask leave or shall have liberty to speak . . . in defense before the Members . . . shall enter into . . . their evidence, then they shall . . . forbear to proceed any further in the managing of their evidence, until they have reported unto the House and received further order from them.[4]

This was a very careful piece of business. If Strafford managed to make a break in the development or *dispositio* of the managers' argument, they were to retreat to their House and regroup.

Tuesday, March 23, 1641

For the Prosecution: Pym, Maynard, Glyn.
Witnesses: Lord Mountnorris, Sir Pierce Crosby, Sir
                 John Clotworthy, Lord Ranelagh, Nicholas Barnwell,
                 Mr. Egar, Sir Edward Warder, Sir Robert Pye,
                 Sir Adam Loftus—Vice Treasurer of Ireland.
For the Defense: Strafford.
Witnesses: none.

On this day, the trial began in earnest.[5] The managers of the prosecution were well-chosen. John Pym was the Speaker of the Committee and its leading spirit. He was ably supported by John Glyn, John Maynard, and Geoffrey Palmer, three of the best young lawyers in the House. George, Lord Digby, son of Lord Bristol, added considerably to the force of the attack by his sharp work in rebuttal. The managers were chaired by Bulstrode Whitelocke, a less effective speaker, but a man of great legal learning. They were assisted by John Hampden, Walter Stroude, Oliver St. John, Sir Walter Earle, and Sir John Clotworthy.

John Pym made the opening statement for the prosecution. He began with an attempt to build a bridge of common ground and of mutual concern for the kingdom between the prosecution and the Lords, which was intended to make the atmosphere favorable for his arguments to follow:

> This [trial] my Lords is a Great Cause, and we might sink under the weight of it, and be astonished with the lustre of this noble assembly, if there were not in the cause strength and vigor to support itself, and to encourage us. It is the cause of the King; it concerns His Majesty in the honor of his Government, in the safety of his person, in the stability of his Crown. It is the cause of the Kingdom; it concerns not only the peace and prosperity but even the being of the Kingdom.[6]

In his reply to the charges of the Commons, the accused initially summarized his administrations in Ireland and the North and enumerated the accomplishments which had been effected under his hand. Pym did not intend that the earl's assertions of effective and productive vice-royalties should go unchallenged: therefore, he proceeded to a direct assault upon the accomplishments claimed by Strafford. The wicked earl,

Pym said, had taken much care to set a face of honesty, truth, goodness, and justice upon his actions. Therefore, it was his duty to tear off the "vizards of truth and uprightness" and show the Lords his actual intentions and actions "in their own blackness and deformity." Pym thereupon took Strafford's so-called accomplishments and proceeded to rebut them one by one. Mainly, Pym took the same data[7] offered by Strafford and by using the topics of paradox and attributed motives as warrants, he drew his own counterclaims. His warrant types were primarily authoritative (depending upon his own credibility as a source) and motivational (which depended upon the value and emotional structure of the audience and which assumed a hostility towards Strafford).

After enumerating the accomplishments of his administrations, Lord Strafford had answered the twenty-eight articles in detail. He disputed many questions of fact, but his main defense was that, even if all twenty-eight charges were proved, none of them amounted to treason under English law.

Strafford had based his claims upon English statute law or precedent. Pym did not really try to shake this position in his opening statement. Instead, he warned the Lords against the legal correctness of the earl's acts and then shifted to a different argumentative ground, using an entirely different warrant as support for his claims:

> We shall charge him with nothing but what the Law in every man's breast condemns, the light of Nature condemns, the light of common Reason, the rules of common Society.[8]

Condemned by the laws of nature, reason, and society—everything but the law of England. The type of issue had been stated by Lord Strafford as being a *legal* issue, and he would be judged by the letter of the law and precedent. Pym also implied that the issue was legal but then he put forth a different *kind* of law as a basis for judging the case. In effect, Pym was attempting to make the issue juridical, depending upon the Lord's judgment of his acts as right or wrong, instead of legal or illegal. Was this approach to be the central point of accusation of the prosecution? Pym did not state it thus on the second day of the trial, and I must await the unfolding of further events before specifying the precise foundation underlying the whole case of the Commons.

When Pym had finished his opening statement, he called witnesses to prove points omitted from the articles: (1) intimidating members of the Irish Parliament; (2) misappropriation of revenue; (3) illegally billeting soldiers; and (4) advancing papists to positions of power in the Church of Ireland.

So far, what the Commons had presented was not very impressive and to regain lost ground John Glyn asked permission to read the Remonstrance of the Irish Parliament as proof of Strafford's injustice. Strafford protested that the matters in the Remonstrance were not in the charges and hence were irrelevant; the Commons insisted that it had bearing.

"Your Lordships may observe," exclaimed Strafford, "that the Remonstrance is fallen out since my impeachment of high treason here. . . . It is a strong conspiracy against me!" The word exploded in the Hall. Was Strafford on the point of accusing the opposition of treasonous conspiracy with the Scots while the country was at war? Pym jumped to his feet. "My Lords, these words are not to be suffered; charging the House of Commons with conspiracy. We desire your Lordships' justice in this!" But instead of thundering any counter-accusations, Strafford fell to his knees to ask the Peers' pardon for his sudden outbreak. Nothing had been further from his mind than to accuse the honorable House of Commons. The Commons had made a slip in denying an accusation before it was made. Perhaps Strafford was biding his time and intended to make some accusations of his own later. Clearly, the hint of conspiracy had unsettled the managers. The Remonstrance was finally read but the edge of it was blunted; the managers quickly dropped it and proceeded hastily to the question of misappropriating the revenue.

Since none of the accusations brought against him thus far had been included in the original articles, but had arisen from his opening statement, Strafford asked for a little time to collect his thoughts before answering in detail. At the conclusion of the request for more time, he held out the olive branch to the House of Commons, saying that he hoped:

> to recover in great measure the favor and good opinion of the honorable House of Commons...[where] I spent a great deal of my time. And...it is known to many who sit here what my carriage and behavior hath been there. And I desire no more (and I am sure it will be granted; they are so just and good) but that they will reserve toward me an opinion of charity, that I give such an account, as may preserve me to be the same in their opinion that I was formerly....I

doubt not but I shall take off their hard opinion, and procure to myself their compassion and favor, and that I shall go in peace and quietness to my grave, leaving all public employments forever. I humbly beseech the Commons to incline a gracious opinion toward me for I am the same man in opinion that I was when I was one of them.[9]

At this point in the trial, Strafford's rhetorical purpose was not necessarily to gain an acquittal, but to preserve the constitutional position of the Crown. If the Commons would call off their attack, he would offer them a deal: his political life for their cooperation with the king. It was a plausible tactic and Strafford might indeed have been willing to retire permanently, if the result would have preserved the present constitution of the government. But while Strafford's head was on, Pym and his party could never feel their own heads safe. They knew that Strafford had been on the verge of charging them with treason when he had been silenced by his arrest. Could a man like Strafford be permanently relegated to obscurity? Probably not; and Pym knew that when Strafford returned there would be another treason trial.

Strafford made his offer; the Commons refused. He asked them to recall his service to their House; they called him "apostate!" His request for a little time to prepare an answer to the unforeseen charges, they denied. He appealed to the Lords, who spent half-an-hour discussing his privileges as a Peer before they finally sustained the Commons. But Strafford had not wasted his half-hour. He sent out for some papers and spent the rest of the time hurriedly writing notes.

Strafford chose to turn back the attack on his services. He once again stated one after the other the accomplishments of his administrations, with the addition this time that he added detailed backing to the warrants for each claim. In answer to the new charges, he produced the king's own warrants, the instructions from the Council to the Lord Lieutenant, and letters of recommendation from the clergy—all of which showed that his acts were officially authorized.

When Strafford had finished, Pym rose again to say:

What I have said in answer to the preamble was not by way of charge, but only for disproof of that whereby my Lord of Strafford would take away or nullify the charge. So that if the charge remains in force, the *services performed* by him are not effectual to mitigate it.[10]

Pym thus did no more than admit that Strafford had proven his services, and the thrust of the managers to discredit him had been turned aside because Strafford had been able to back his warrants with strong evidence. Pym sat down with a promise that the separate articles would prove all.

The second day had passed in a confusing flurry of assertion, denial, and counter-denial between Strafford and the managers. But the weakness of the day's work by the Commons was underscored when the Lords directed the managers to proceed on the morrow to the proofs concerning the particular charges. Thereupon, the court adjourned.

Wednesday, March 24, 1641

Maynard opened the day[11] for the prosecution with a powerful statement of the position of the Commons of England against Lord Strafford:

> My Lords, I humbly address myself to the body of the charge . . . and I desire to open what is the nature, what the height and quality of the offense of which this Lord stands accused.
>
> My Lords, it is a charge of the highest nature that can be against a man, a charge of high treason. It is a *treason not ending in one single act . . . but a habit, a trade, a mystery of treason. . .*
>
> My Lords, it was [a twofold treason]: to deprive us of . . . *the fundamental, the ancient laws of the Kingdom*; to introduce instead an *arbitrary government bounded by no laws. . . .*
>
> *Other treasons,* yea, a treason against the person of a Prince (which is the most high treason that can be) *fall short of this treason.*[12]

There it was: the central point of accusation and the primary claim of the House of Commons against the accused. Lord Strafford was impeached, not with simple but *cumulative treason*: for though in each particular article, such a crime could not be detected; yet when all was viewed in the mass from one point of view, he should undoubtedly be found the most wicked traitor who was ever arraigned at the Bar.

To make it possible for their lordships to view the accusations within a single perspective and appreciate their weight *in toto*, Maynard next went over each of the twenty-eight specific articles, briefly summarizing the gist of each and indicating the kind of evidence which would be offered in support of each one. He then proceeded to the first article.

THE FIRST ARTICLE

The Charge

That the said Earl of Strafford the 21st day of March, in the Eighth year of His Majesties Reign, was President of the Kings Council in the Northern parts of England.

That the said Earl being President of the said Council, on the 21st of March, a Commission under the Great Seal of England, with certain Schedules of Instructions thereunto annexed, was directed to the said Earl, or others the Commissioners therein named; whereby among other things, Power and Authority is limited to the said Earl, and others the Commissioners therein named, to hear and determine all Offences and Misdemeanours, Suits, Debates, Controversies and Demands, Causes, Things, and Matters whatsoever, therein contained, and within certain Precincts in the said Northern parts therein specified, and in such manner as by the said Schedule is limited and appointed.

That amongst other things in the said Instructions, it is directed, That the said President, and others therein appointed, shall hear and determine, according to the Course of Proceedings in the Court of Star Chamber, divers Offences, Deceits, and Falsities therein mentioned, whether the same be provided against by Acts of Parliament, or not, so that the Fines imposed, be not less than by the Act or Acts of Parliament provided against those Offences, is appointed.

That also, amongst other things in the said Instructions, it is directed, That the said President, and others therein appointed, have Power to Examine, Hear and Determine, according to the Course of Proceedings in the Court of Chancery, all manner of Complaints for any matter within the said Precincts, as well concerning Lands, Tenements and Hereditaments, either Free-hold Customary, or Copy-hold, as Leases, and other things therein mentioned; and to stay proceedings in the Court of Common Law, by Injunction, or by all ways and means, as is used in the Court of Chancery.

And although the former Presidents of the said Council had never put in Practice such Instructions, nor had they any such Instructions, yet the said Earl in the Month of May, in the said Eighth year, and divers years following, did put in Practice, Exercise and Use the said Commission and Instructions; and did direct and exercise an exorbitant and unlawful Power and Jurisdiction on over the Persons and Estates of His Majesties Subjects in those parts and did Disinherit divers of His Majesties Subjects in those parts of their Inheritances, Sequestered their Possessions, and did Fine, Ransom, Punish, and Imprison them to their Ruin and Destruction; and namely Sir Coniers Darcy, Sir John Bourcher, and divers others against the Laws, and in Subversion of the same. And the said Commission and Instructions were procured and issued by advice of the said Earl.

And he the said Earl, to the intent that such illegal and unjust Power might be exercised with the greater License and Will, did Advise and Procure further directions, in and by the said Instructions to be given, that no Prohibition be granted at all, but in cases where the said Council shall exceed the limits of the Instructions. And that if any Writ of *Habeas Corpus* be granted, the party be not discharged till the party perform the Decree and Order of the said Council.

And the said Earl in the 13th year of His Majesties Reign, did procure a new Commission to himself, and others, with the said Instructions and other unlawful Additions.

That the said Commissions and Instructions were procured by the Solicitation and Advice of the Earl of Strafford.[13]

For the Prosecution: Maynard.
Witnesses: John Gower, Evers Gower, John Mulgrave,
                      F. Thorpe.
For the Defense: Strafford.
Witnesses: Guildford Slingsby, William Railton, Thomas
                      Little.

Maynard argued the article by (1) reading the Commissions for government in the North which allowed the Lord President to assume strong powers, and (2) calling witnesses who testified that they had been arbitrarily dealt with by the Northern government.

Clever as Maynard was, he could not make headway with an attack on Strafford's northern policy. The entire charge was a makeshift of contradictions. For example, Strafford had never been acting President of the North after the time he had convinced the Council to grant increased powers to that Court. Consequently, the managers tried to support their claim of personal ambition by redating some of Strafford's actions and the king's commission.

By this time in the proceedings, it had become clear to Strafford that prosecution and defense were basing their cases upon rival interpretations of law and justice. Therefore Strafford in his defense did not immediately answer the charges of the first article but rose to deride the theory of "cumulative treason":

> My Lords, there is a great deal of difference betwixt the case of a man answering for a . . . known treason by the Statutes of the Realm, . . and him that answers a mixed charge, . . . There is nothing in this that can be treason, and when a thousand misdemeanors will not make one felony, shall twenty-eight misdemeanors heighten it to a treason? . . .[14]

How could a number of alleged misdeameanors, if proven, be made to add up to treason? Here Strafford put forth his initial line of defense and drove home the massive doctrine of English liberty: "No law, no crime!" What law had he broken? Show him a law he had broken!

He also reflected upon the fair play of the proceedings. If he had been charged with a petty misdemeanor, he would have been allowed counsel and examination of witnesses. As it was, he was given neither privilege and had had no leave to summon witnesses before the previous Friday, and was debarred from witnesses from Ireland, whence came the greatest part of the charges. With that, he turned to demolish the managers on the point of the first article by calling witnesses to correct the falsified chronology of events.

The managers did little in reply but remind their lordships that even though article one as a particular charge was not treason, all twenty-eight articles did amount to subversion of the fundamental laws of the kingdom, and this was what they pressed as treason.

THE SECOND ARTICLE

The Charge

That shortly after the obtaining of the said Commission, dated the 21st of March, in the Eighth year of His Majesties Reign, (to wit) the last day of August then next following, he the said Earl (to bring His Majesties Liege People into a dislike of His Majesty, and of His Government, and to terrify the Justices of the Peace from executing of the Laws: He the said Earl being then President, as aforesaid, and a Justice of Peace) did publicly, at the Assizes held for the County of York, in the City of York, in and upon the said last day of August, declare and publish before the People there attending for the Administration of Justice according to Law, and in the presence of the Justices sitting, That some of the Justices were all for Law, and nothing would please them but law; but they should find that the Kings little Finger should be heavier than the Loins of the Law.[15]

For the Prosecution: Maynard, Glyn.

Witnesses: William Long, Sir Thomas Leyton, Marmaduke
               Potter (by deposition), Sir William Ingram,
               Sir David Foulis.

For the Defense: Strafford.

Witnesses: Dr. Duncombe, Sir William Pennyman.

The second article charged Strafford with saying that "the little finger of the King is heavier than the loins of the law." Again, Maynard was hard put to hold things together; the trouble this time: his witness was deaf. Strafford had a field day with Sir Thomas Leyton because he had testified to words spoken by the accused. Yes, he was at York in the company of Leyton, but he had spoken the words in reverse order: "The little finger of the law was heavier than the king's loins." Besides, Leyton is deaf and even now "must be whooped to at the Bar before he can hear."

A little later, Sir William Pennyman testified that the circumstances were as Strafford had related them. Pennyman was a Member of the House of Commons. He had hardly finished his testimony for the defense when Maynard said unpleasantly that Sir William should have communicated his knowledge to the House of Commons before coming out like this in court. Strafford saw the opening and quickly drove a wedge into it. If the witnesses for the defense

> were to be punished, I should think myself a very unhappy man
> indeed. Rather than prejudice any man [to threats]....I would put
> myself on God's mercy and not make use of any Member of either
> House as witnesses...for I account it as an unjust thing to overthrow
> another to save myself.[16]

Maynard unwisely kept after Pennyman, and Strafford appealed to the Lords:

> This gentleman is my noble friend and I would give him my life on
> any occasion. No man should suffer for me; I protest I had rather
> suffer ten thousand times myself.[17]

The situation was becoming embarrassing and John Glyn rose to bring

Maynard off the hook. When Lord Arundel intervened, the Commons withdrew their threats.

The second article was by this time almost as much weakened as the first, and Maynard asked leave to produce another witness, Sir David Foulis. Strafford objected to Foulis being haled out of Fleet Street Prison to testify against him. The witness was in jail because he had lost a suit against the earl and could not be other than prejudiced. Strafford was overruled by Arundel on the ground that only the weight of testimony was arguable. Foulis confirmed the Commons' evidence word for word.

The managers closed this article with the rather weak statement the the Lords should decide the argument of fact in their favor because their witnesses to the point outnumbered the accused's by five to two.

Thereupon the Court adjourned for the day.

The first two days of the trial set the pattern for what followed. The Commons made their anxious wish for Strafford's death too clear, and created thereby an increasing sympathy for him. "They have so banged and worried him as it begets pity in many of the auditors," wrote one observer.[18] The thirst of the Commons for his blood also caused Strafford to give up his bootless effort to conciliate them either by his manner and remarks of respect or his projection of the fondly-recalled days when he was one of them. The managers of the prosecution, especially Maynard and Glyn, kept up a continuous attack upon him and his witnesses. They proceeded beyond legal prosecution to threats and intimidation. They, of course, tried to discredit his witnesses, who naturally enough were his friends, dependents, and servants since he had not been allowed time enough to send to Ireland for independent witnesses. The managers became irritable when he excepted against their witnesses. After Crosby, the prosecution blandly produced Cork, Mountnorris, Lord Esmond, and others with evident personal scores to settle. Even a petty official who had been dismissed for extortion was called. The Lords permitted all witnesses to testify (legally correct), but some observers began to suspect that behind the lofty accusations about subversion of fundamental laws, there lay much "private practice for private men to work out their own ends and preferments thereupon."[19]

Immediately upon his rebuttal of the first and second articles, the managers tried to close the accused's mouth and hurry him along. The Commons assembled as a committee and proclaimed that all Strafford's objections were simply to gain time, for what dark end they feared but knew not. They objected that he had friends among the Peers who assisted his delaying action by constantly asking for adjournments to discuss the points raised. They objected also to the length of his answers and his general style of precise argument; he should be required to answer briefly without enlarging on every issue.

The first two articles were fought out primarily upon a tactical level. The Commons attempted to get their assembled data accepted as true facts, so that subsequent-warrants and claims could be set upon a secure base. Strafford hoped to defend against these data, weakening the base before the managers could move to connect a bit of information to any claim. Thus the tactical argumentative struggle over the first pair of articles was waged on the line of whether the facts would be accepted by the Lords.

But what of higher strategy? By what paths should the prosecution or the defense seek to win the Lords to their sides? The broad and massive doctrine of English law was at once marked by both sides as the primary objective to be captured. Law divided the issues clearly and could possibly prevent any attack from the rear where speed of argument could win, or attack of attrition where sheer mass of argument might win. The law and its great tributary, English precedent, offered sure means of carrying the war into the heart of the opposing side and rending it asunder. Thus English law stood like a king on a chessboard, apparently able to give victory to whomsoever captured it.

Once English law had been chosen as the primary objective, neither prosecution nor defense could move along its line of strategic advance until the law had been gained. This is the case because the warrant of a case *appears* to be incidental to the explicit claim made in an argument; but without the general assumption which is expressed by the warrant, the facts of a case cannot be connected to any claim, nor can the relationship between data and claim be validated.

To capture the "chessboard king" of English law, each side needed to employ a tactic powerful enough for this task. In other words, the warrant needed to be sustained with strong backing: the backing for a warrant is employed to certify the acceptability of the assumption which is expressed by the warrant; that is, the purpose of any support for a warrant is to "psychologically underwrite" the acceptability of the warrant, from which the ultimate claim will be drawn. Hence, Strafford immediately stated that he had acted within the law, and made ready to cite statutes and precedents to justify his conduct. By the end of the second day, his plan was to point out persistently that, even if he had committed every action cited in the charges, they were not treason. On the other hand, Pym and Maynard had immediately asked the Peers to take no notice of the single articles *seriatim*, but to look upon the charges as one whole of "constructive treason." Thus did things stand at the end of the third day and the second article. How long each side would see the law as their true strategic objective along the best line of advance or defense remains to be seen.

Thursday, March 25, 1641

THE THIRD ARTICLE

The Charge

That the Realm of Ireland having been, time out of mind, annexed to the Imperial Crown of this His Majesties Realm of England, and governed by the same laws; The said Earl being Lord Deputy of that Realm, to bring His Majesties Liege Subjects of that Kingdom likewise into dislike of His Majesties Government, and intending the Subversion of the Fundamental Laws, and Government of that Realm, and the destruction of His Majesties Liege-People there; did upon the 30th day of September, in the Ninth Year of His Majesties Reign, in the City of Dublin (the chief city of that Realm, where His Majesties Privy-Council, and Courts of Justice do ordinarily reside, and whither the Nobility and Gentry of that Realm do usually resort for Justice) in a public speech, before divers of the Nobility and Gentry of that Kingdom, and before the Mayor, Aldermen, and Recorder, and many citizens of Dublin, and other His Majesties Liege-People, declare and publish, that Ireland was a *conquered nation*, and that the King might do with them what he pleased: And speaking of the Charters of former Kings of England made to that City; He further then said, That their Charters were nothing worth, and did bind the King no farther than he pleased.[20]

For the Prosecution: Maynard, Glyn, Digby, Clotworthy, Pym.
Witnesses: Robert Kennedy, Earl of Cork, Lord Gorminstone,
                Lord Killmallock, Sir Pierce Crosby, Mr. Fitzgarrett.
For the Defense: Strafford.

Witnesses: Guildford Slingsby, Lord Dillon, Sir Adam
Loftus, Sir Robert King, Lord Ranelagh, Sir
George Wentworth.

Before the managers could begin the third article, Strafford rose and asked permission to go back to the first and second, so that he might give further satisfaction to their lordships. Maynard and Glyn objected and reminded the Lords of the rule they had agreed upon with the lower House: Commons submits the evidence; Strafford answers; the Commons reply and then move on to the next charge. They asked that the order be upheld and that the prisoner be not permitted to invert the course on pretense of new matter; otherwise, it would be impossible for them to make good the charge. The Commons were upheld and Strafford received another harmful procedural setback: his rivals now controlled the *dispositio* of the case.

The Commons advanced this article as a prime verification of the accused's tyrannical will which had given no law to the subject but what he himself had arbitrarily decided. If this were permitted, the whole power and liberty of the subject would be lost. The managers' witnesses all upheld the charges of the article.

To the charge of article three, the prisoner called witnesses whose testimony indicated that his words were taken out of context and distorted; and that whatever had been said that day, it had not been taken by the Irish Parliament as threatening or indeed made much of an impression, so harmless had been the words, "Ireland is a conquered nation."

The defense tried to score a point by calling Sir George Radcliffe to the stand. Maynard, of course, objected that Radcliffe was charged with treason and therefore it was unfit to hear one so charged in order to clear another so charged. As expected, Lord Arundel declared that Radcliffe could not be examined, whereupon Strafford observed that, "If it were only matter of misdemeanor, or nearly any other crime, he might be examined, though charged."[21] Strafford concluded with the assertion that what he had spoken was so far from being treason, a thousand such expressions would not make up one felony.

In reply, Maynard reminded the Peers:

The Commons do not press these words singly and dividedly to be treason; but take all together, they discover that disposition, that counsel, that resolution that my Lord of Strafford had taken on him: the ruin and subversion of the Common Law in both Kingdoms.[22]

And so concluded the reply and the third article.

THE FOURTH ARTICLE

The Charge

That Richard Earl of Cork, having sued out Process in Due Course of Law, for recovery of his Possessions, from which he was put, by colour of an Order made by the said Earl of Strafford, and the Council-Table of the Realm of Ireland, upon a Paper Petition, without Legal proceeding, did the 20th day of February, in the 11th year of His Majesties Reign, threaten the said Earl (being then a Peer of the Realm) to Imprison him, unless he would cease his Suit, and said, That he would have neither Law nor Lawyers, dispute or question his Orders. And the 20th day of March, in the said 11th year, the Earl of Strafford, speaking of an Order of the said Council-Table of that Realm, made in the time of King James, which concerned a Lease which the said Earl of Cork claimed in certain Rectories or Tythes, which the Earl of Cork alledged to be of no force, said, that he would make the Earl, and all Ireland know, that so long as he had the government there, any Act of State made there, or to be made, should be as binding to the Subjects of that Kingdom, as an Act of Parliament; and did question the said Earl of Cork in the Castle Chamber there, upon pretence of breach of the said Order of Council-Table; and did sundry other times, and upon sundry other occasions, by his Words and Speeches, Arrogate to himself a Power above the Fundamental Laws, and Established Government of the Kingdom, and scorned the said Laws and Established Government.[23]

For the Prosecution: Glyn, Maynard.

Witnesses: Lord Ranelagh, Earl of Cork, John Waldron,
               John Kay, John Hoy, Lord Killmallock, Sir
               Pierce Crosby, Earl of Castlehaven, Roger Lotts.

For the Defense: Strafford.

Witnesses: Lord Dillon, Sir Adam Loftus, Mr. Leake.

John Glyn had scarcely called Lord Ranelagh, his first witness; he had barely stated his theme—that Strafford had illegally tried common law cases on paper petitions in Castle Chamber—when the accused jumped to his feet: Might Lord Ranelagh be asked if he did not follow exactly the same procedure himself as President of Connaught? Instantly the managers objected to the question and asked for the court to be adjourned. The Lords complied. And next day Ranelagh was excused from answering, the point tending to an accusation of himself. Glyn never got back on the right track again with article four.

Friday, March 26, 1641

The first item of business on Friday was to excuse Lord Ranelagh from further testimony on article four.[24] Then, in an effort to build up momentum again. Glyn called the everready Lord Cork. By his testimony, Cork substantiated all that had been charged regarding the use of paper petitions. The other witnesses all deposed that Strafford had said that he would make an Act of State equal to an Act of Parliament.

In his reply, Strafford argued that the Council Board in Ireland was itself a Court of Record, and therefore had full jurisdiction over Cork's case.

For his words—that an Act of State should be as binding as an Act of Parliament—Strafford congratulated the Earl of Cork's quick memory "that could swear them roundly, without missing a letter or syllable as they are laid in the charge." But this was only a passing cut at Cork, an attempt to amuse the crowd. Strafford turned back to the charge, anxious that the words should be fairly interpreted, for they lay at the very root of his theory of mixed government:

If an Act of State be not made against an Act of Parliament...and if made by way of provision for remedying some present mischief in the Commonwealth, till the Parliament may provide redress for it, they are as binding during the time they are in force as an Act of Parliament. I confess, though, the comparison is not good, because they may be made according to law and justice...wherein the prerogative of the Crown hath a part, as well as the property of the Subject. The propriety of the Subject [and] the Prerogative of the Crown are the...tables of the law....And, they go hand in hand, and long may they do so...not rising one above another in any kind, but kept in their own channels. For if they rise above these heights—the one or the other—they tear the banks and overflow the fair meads equally on one side and the other. And, therefore, I do...desire they may be kept at that agreement and perfect harmony one with another, that they may each watch for...the other. And, therefore, this being a care of the Prerogative, as long as it goes not against the Common Law of the land, it is the law of the land, and binds.[25]

And so, stating his theory of government, his lordship concluded his defense. Strafford's deft use of testimony and law had cut the support away from Glyn's assertion of fact and he was forced to give way, reduced to concluding:

The justice of the order in Lord Cork's cause is not material; or whether within the jurisdiction of the Council Table: the charge being that . . . my Lord of Strafford threatened the Earl of Cork.[26]

So, justice and jurisdiction were admitted and Strafford was, at last, charged only with threatening Cork. This was pretty thin, compared with the high-sounding phrases of the original charges of article four. Glyn weakly concluded with a promise that the future articles would prove all. The Lords adjourned.

Saturday, March 27, 1641

THE FIFTH ARTICLE

The Charge

That according to such his Declarations and Speeches the said Earl of Strafford did use and exercise a Power above, and against, and to the Subversion of the said Fundamental Laws, and Established Government of the Realm of Ireland, extending such his Power, to the Goods, Free-holds, Inheritances, Liberties, and Lives of His Majesties Subjects of the said Realm; and namely the said Earl of Strafford, the 12th day of December, A.D. 1635, in the time of full Peace, did in the Realm of Ireland, give, and procure to be given, against the Lord Mountnorris (then, and yet a Peer of the said Realm of Ireland, and then Vice-Treasurer, and Receiver-General of the Realm of Ireland, and Treasurer at War, and one of the Principal Secretaries of State, and Keeper of the Privy Signet of the said Kingdom) a Sentence of Death by a Council of War, called together by the said Earl of Strafford, without any Warrant, or Authority of Law, or Offense deserving any such Punishment. And he the said Earl, did also at Dublin, within the Realm of Ireland, in the month of March, in the 14th year of His Majesties Reign, without any Legal or due Proceedings, or Trial, give, and cause to be given, a Sentence of Death against one other of His Majesties

Subjects, whose name is yet unknown; and caused him to be put to Death in Execution of the same Sentence.[27]

For the Prosecution: Maynard, Glyn.

Witnesses: Lord Mountnorris, Lord Dillon, Lord Ranelagh,
                Earl of Cork, William Castigatt, Patrick Gough,
                Lord Conway, Earl of Ely.

For the Defense: Strafford.

Witnesses: Lord Wilmot, Sir Adam Loftus, Lord Dillon,
                Sir Robert Farrer, Sir George Wentworth.

Article five was a very heavy charge against Strafford, and John Glyn moved swiftly to the attack. Upon assuming the Deputyship in Dublin, Wentworth came almost immediately into collision with Lord Mountnorris, Vice-Treasurer and active member of the Council. During 1634 and 1635, the Deputy had occasion to complain constantly of Mountnorris' irregular practices in office, and he began to look for a way to rid himself of this unscrupulous and undependable official. When he found a plausible excuse, the Deputy struck, and it was the methods used against Mountnorris with which he was now charged.

John Glyn first read the death sentence against Mountnorris, averring it to be against the fundamental rules of law because pronounced without trial, hearing, or answer. Next, Mountnorris was called to give his version of the story. From the testimony, it appeared that a servant of Strafford's, attending the Deputy during a severe attack of gout, dropped a stool upon his painful foot. Strafford, enraged with pain, had struck the servant with his cane. The event being merrily discussed at a dinner, Mountnorris said that he "had a brother who would not have taken such a blow" from Strafford. When the Deputy learned of Mountnorris' words, he saw his chance and called a Council of War. Mountnorris was an officer in the army commanded by Strafford; therefore, upon an article of "moving sedition, and stirring up the soldiers against the general," he was charged with words spoken at the Lord Chancellor's table. Mountnorris was so surprised that he made no defense. His words being proved, he was committed to prison and sentenced to death for inciting mutiny against Strafford.

Lord Dillon substantiated Mountnorris' testimony. But before Glyn could stand him down, Dillon added that the Council gave their votes upon the understanding that mercy would be shown by the Crown. To their request, Strafford had stretched out his right arm and said that he would rather lose his arm than Mountnorris should a lose a hair of his head. The Deputy only wanted to frighten Mountnorris into resigning his office.

Lord Ranelagh told the story as Mountnorris had given it. But Glyn slipped when he let Ranelagh go on to say that the Deputy had shown the Council a letter from the king giving direction to proceed in a Martial Court for reparation and honor of the Lord Deputy. In his cross-examination the accused successfully drew mitigating admissions from each witness as to the army being on the march, whether he had sat as judge or party, and whether he tried to influence the vote. When Glyn had finished, the Earl of Strafford began his defense.

Strafford admitted nearly all the facts brought out by the prosecution and based his defense against article five upon an interpretation of law. He arranged the parts of the charge into separate heads and made his reply:

1. He had exercised martial law in time of peace.

To this he answered: (a) That all armies, in peace or war, have always been, and must be governed by martial law. (b) That the Irish army is a standing army and therefore it makes no difference whether military justice proceeds in wartime or peace; and that the army would fall apart if the officers tried to suppress mutiny or enforce discipline through civil law instead of martial law. (c) That regulating the army by martial law had always been practiced by the Lords Deputy, particularly Falkland, Wilmot, Grandison, Chichester, and even Lord Cork himself when he had served in a temporary capacity. (d) That he had a particular warrant in his own Commission for just such power. (e) That in Lord Mountnorris' case, he was commanded to proceed martially against him by none other than the king, whose letter he produced.

2. The second head was: That he was both accusing party and judge in Mountnorris' case.

To this, he replied that he had sat at the Council Board because the Lord Deputy was the one *sine quo non* and the Council could not sit otherwise. But that he sat as party, not judge is proved because: (a) He sat uncovered (unofficially) at the hearing. (b) He refused to give his opinion. (c) He requested the Council to proceed as if he were not there. (d) He did not vote. (e) He forbade his brother, George Wentworth, to vote.

3. The last head was: That he had not fairly heard the exceptions made by Mountnorris against his witnesses.

To this, Strafford repeated that he had not been a judge in the case, and no exceptions were made against any witnesses. To which he added, that just as he had been moderate in his proceedings, so had he been moderate in the execution of the sentence: for the vaunted death sentence had really amounted to a few days' imprisonment and the Deputy had obtained Mountnorris the king's pardon. He restated that the proceedings had been instituted to repair the honor of the king's Lord Deputy and to make Mountnorris submissive to legal authority, for the lord was known to be of an exorbitant and licentious tongue and spirit.

Strafford concluded with a sharp contrast: If the House of Commons would prove to be as fair with him as he had been with Mountnorris, he would be content. And so, after some discussion touching the methods of proceeding with the next articles, the court was adjourned for the weekend.

Monday, March 29, 1641

THE SIXTH ARTICLE

The Charge

That the said Earl of Strafford, without any Legal Proceedings, and upon a Paper-Petition of Richard Rolstone, did cause the said Lord Mountnorris to be disseized and put out of possession of his Free-hold, and Inheritance of his Manor of Tymore in the County of Armagh, in the Kingdom of Ireland, the said Lord Mountnorris having been 18 years before in quiet Possession thereof.[28]

For the Prosecution: Glyn, Maynard, Palmer, Stroude.
Witnesses: Lord Mountnorris, Lord Cork, Mr. Anslow,
                 Lord Ranelagh, Sir Adam Loftus, Lady Mountnorris
                 (by petition), Earl of Bath, William Brettergh.
For the Defense: Strafford.
Witnesses: Lord Primate of Armagh (by deposition),
                 Henry Dillon, Guildford Slingsby, Lord Dillon,
                 Sir Adam Loftus.

The sixth article proved on examination to be so discreditable to Mountnorris that Glyn was forced to insist that "the merit of the case is immaterial," so long as Strafford's procedure was proved illegal. Strafford was charged with bringing vice-regal power to bear on Mountnorris to make him return an estate to a poor man, from whom the lord had taken it by means of sharp practice. When the managers shifted their ground from the justice of the case to the strict letter of the law, Strafford immediately produced the king's authorization to proceed against Mountnorris. Again, Glyn, outmaneuvered, had nothing left to do but argue that the Lieutenant had exceeded the authority given him by Charles.

Such embarrassing, sharp defeats taught the prosecution to examine their charges and evidence more carefully. Hence, when they had finished with article six, Stroude rose and said that, for the present, the Commons would pass by article seven and the first two parts of article eight. As a result of their second thoughts, Strafford was never charged with the "illegal eviction of Lord Dillon and hundreds more of the king's subjects," nor with the "illegal imprisonment of Viscount Loftus and the Earl of Kildare." Indeed, no further charges of illegal eviction were brought. The House was then adjourned until the next day.

Tuesday, March 30, 1641

THE EIGHTH ARTICLE

The Charge

That the said Earl of Strafford, upon a Petition of Sir John Gifford, Knight, the first day of February, in the said 13th Year of His Majesties Reign, without any legal Process, made a Decree against Adam Viscount Loftus of Ely, a Peer of the said Realm of Ireland, and Lord Chancellor of Ireland, and did cause the said Viscount to be imprisoned, and kept close Prisoner, on pretence of Disobedience to the said Decree.

And the said Earl, without any Authority, and contrary to his Commission, required the said Lord Viscount to yield up unto him the Great Seal of the Realm of Ireland, which was then in his Custody, by His Majesties Command, and imprisoned the Chancellor for not obeying such his Command.

And without any Legal Proceeding, did in the same 13th year imprison George Earl of Kildare, a Peer of Ireland, against Law, thereby to enforce him to submit his Title to the Manor and Lord-ship of Casteleigh in the Queens Country (being of great yearly value) to the said Earl of Straffords Will and Pleasure, and kept him a year Prisoner for the said Cause; two Months whereof he kept him close Prisoner, and refused to enlarge him, notwithstanding his Majesties Letters for his enlargement to the said Earl of Strafford directed.

And upon a Petition exhibited in October, A.D. 1635, by

Thomas Hibbots, against Dame Mary Hibbots Widow, the Earl of Strafford recommended the said Petition to the Council-Table of Ireland, where the most Part of the Council gave their Vote and Opinion for the said Lady; but the said Earl finding Fault herewith, caused an Order to be entered against the said Lady, and threaten her, that if she refused to submit thereunto, he would imprison her, and fine her Five hundred pounds; that if she continued obstinate, he would continue her Imprisonment, and double her Fine every month; by means whereof she was enforced to relinquish her Estate in the Lands questioned in the said Petition, which shortly after were conveyed to Sir Robert Meredith, to the Use of the said Earl of Strafford.

And the said Earl in like manner did Imprison divers others of His Majesties Subjects, upon pretence of Disobedience to his Orders, Decrees, and other illegal Command by him made for pretended Debts, Titles of Lands, and other Causes in an Arbitrary and extrajudicial Course, upon Paper-Petitions, to him preferred, and no Cause legally depending.[29]

For the Prosecution: Glyn, Maynard, Palmer.

Witnesses: John Hoy (son of Dame Mary), Mr. Fitzgarret,
                   Thomas Hibbots, Lord Mountnorris, Earl of Cork,
                   Sir Adam Loftus, Lord Renula, Lord Primate of
                   Ireland (by deposition).

For the Defense: Strafford.

Witnesses: Lord Dillon, Sir Philip Mainwaring.

On Tuesday, the managers passed over the seventh article, and the first two parts of the eighth, and charged the prisoner with a part of the eighth which concerned Lady Hibbot's land: that he had forced her from her rightful possessions, and afterwards (behind a front man named Sir Robert Meredith) took a bribe of 7,000 pounds to return her rights to the lands. To these points, the managers took the testimony of several witnesses, but the evidence was weakened because it was based upon hearsay.

In reply, Strafford showed that a majority of the Council Board had subscribed to her sentence. He also at some length described with what fraud and deceit the lady had come to her lands, and upon what reasons they were restored.

In his defense against the first eight of the articles, Strafford portrayed, probably honestly, the diligent and faithful, but wronged, public servant.

As those with personal scores against him paraded again and again to the witness stand—Cork and Mountnorris especially—Strafford smoothly answered them without the least semblance of emotion, a pose which did much to enhance the type of data which depended upon speaker opinion and asserted information. At the trial, the reactions of some of the Lords and many of the private spectators was beginning to swing in his favor. For example, the prosecution of articles five and six caused many to note that:

> The Lord Mountnorris was a great man...in the affairs of Ireland, having raised himself from a very mean condition to the degree of a viscount and a privy-counsellor. He had always...wrought himself into trust and nearness with all deputies...informing them of the defects and oversights of their predecessors; and, after the determination of their commands, and return to England, informing the state here, and those enemies they usually contracted in that time, of whatsoever they had done amiss; whereby they either suffered disgrace or damage....In this manner he began with the Lord Chichester and continued...upon the Lord Grandison, and the Lord Falkland...[so] that either the deputy of Ireland must destroy my Lord Mountnorris...or my Lord Mountnorris must destroy the deputy. [30]

THE NINTH ARTICLE

The Charge

That the said Earl of Strafford, the 16th day of February in the 12th Year of His Majesties Reign, assuming to himself a Power above, and against Law, took upon him by a General Warrant under his Hand, to give Power to the Lord Bishop of Downe and Conner, his Chancellor and several Officers thereto to be appointed, to Attach and Arrest the Bodies of all such of the Meaner and Poorer sort, who after Citation, should either refuse to appear before them, or Appearing, should omit, or deny to Perform, or undergo all Lawful Decrees, Sentences, and Orders, issued, imposed or given out against them, and them to Commit, and keep in the next Goal [sic], until they should either Perform such Sentences, or put in sufficient Bail, to show some reason before the Council-Table, of such their contempt and neglect; and the said Earl, the Day and Year last mentioned, Signed and Issued a Warrant to that Effect; and make the like Warrants to several other Bishops, and their

Chancellors, in the said Realm of Ireland, to the same effect.[31]

For the Prosecution: Glyn.
Witnesses: Sir James Montgomery.
For the Defense: Strafford.
Witnesses: Lord Primate of Ireland (by deposition),
                    Lord Dillon, Mr. Thomas Little.

In a short piece of work, Glyn stated that it was illegal to bring a man before an ecclesiastical court on a general warrant. The testimony from a single witness showed that Strafford had granted a general warrant to an Irish bishop, this charged as being against the liberty of the subject.

Strafford replied that as Lord Deputy, he thought it necessary for churchmen in Ireland to have such strong assistance; otherwise no respect or obedience would be given them by the papists and schismatics. If the power granted the bishops was illegal, then he was sorry for it. He had acted, he said, on the precedent practice of all other Lords Deputy, who in their time granted several such warrants. Himself, he had granted only one general warrant. He concluded that it was not treason to mistake the law. This concluded the trial for Tuesday.

Wednesday, March 31, 1641

THE TENTH ARTICLE

The Charge

That the said Earl of Strafford being Lord Lieutenant, or Deputy of Ireland, procured the Customs of the Merchandise Exported out, and Imported into that Realm, to be Farmed to his own Use.

And in the Ninth Year of His now Majesties Reign, he having then Interest in the said Customs (to advance his own gain and lucre) did cause and procure the Natives Commodities (according to which the Customs were usually gathered) at far greater Values and Prices than in truth they were worth (that is to say) every Hide at Twenty shillings, which in truth was worth but Five shillings; every Stone of Wool at Thirteen shillings Four pence though the same were really worth but five shillings, at the utmost Nine shillings; by which means the Custom, which before was but a Twentieth Part of the true value of the Commodity, was Enhanced sometimes a Fifth Part, and sometimes to a Fourth, and sometimes to a Third Part of the true value, to the great Oppression of the Subjects, and Decay of Merchandise.[32]

For the Prosecution: Maynard.
Witnesses: Lord Ranelagh, Sir James Hey, Robert
                Goodwin, Henry Brawd, John Welsh, Robert
                Cogan, Lord Renula, Patrick Allen.
For the Defense: Strafford.
Witnesses   Lord Cottington, Sir Arthur Ingram,
                Lord Dillon.

Maynard charged that Strafford had grafted the public revenues of Ireland from the Crown into his own pocket. He accomplished this by raising the customs duties and then leasing the management of the customs. Thus, his previous crimes were against the subject only, while this was against the king himself.

To prove the charge, Maynard submitted the rate book, showing a rise in import and export duties. Further, it was shown that Strafford paid 14,000 pounds per annum for the farm of the customs and took in a gross of 40,000 pounds. The prime witness, Lord Ranelagh, deposed that the Irish Customs were: 1636—36,000 pounds; 1637—39,000 pounds; 1638—54,000 pounds; 1639—59,000 pounds.

Glyn and Maynard concluded that Strafford had abused the great trust put in him. By diverting such great sums of money from the Crown, Strafford had been the hidden cause of the extraordinary methods of raising money which Charles had used during the Personal Rule. This act of itself, therefore, was enough to make good the charge of high treason against him.

Strafford knew his judges well on this point. Farms granted by the Crown were presently held by many of the Lords. Nor were the others without a farm presently in their hands likely to strike down a minister on this point, for they might be the farmers tomorrow, though they were empty-handed today. The defense proceeded from this type of warrant.

The Lieutenant's reply made light of the article: for though all of its parts were granted to be true, no interpretation of English law could imply the least hint of treason. Yet, to clear his honor of any stain, he would nonetheless answer the charges:

1. The chief grievance of the Commons seemed to arise from the Book of Rates. Therefore, he wished to point out that these had been established by the Lord Deputy Falkland, three years before his own assignment to Ireland.

2. He admitted that he came by his customs farm through a sublease

from the Duchess of Buckingham. But he had never before heard treason charged when an Englishman had made a good bargain for himself.

3. The king had hoped that the Irish customs might be improved for the benefit of the Crown. Hence, not of his own accord, but at the king's express command had he assumed the farm of the customs.

4. He had wished no personal profit. Indeed, his own share never rose to the heights asserted by the prosecution. From the gross income of the Royal Irish Customs, the Lords—to get the true picture—should first subtract the 14,000 pounds that he paid for the farm; next they should subtract five-eighths from the remainder, which went to the Irish Exchequer; the remainder should be divided among four holders of the farm, with whom Strafford had to share the net. The remainder, Strafford's share, came to 3,400 pounds a year.

The earl concluded, saying, "Nothing can be imputed to me unless that the Kingdom of Ireland is an increased and growing Kingdom, and that the trade enlarged to such a proportion as to make the customs of far more value." Therefore, he was confident that their lordships "would take this article [more] as an exercise in rhetoric by the gentlemen, his adversaries, than as a thing charged in earnest by them." With this flourish, he concluded his defense on the article.

Apparently, Strafford had scored heavily with regard to what was legal and illegal in the customs game, for the managers declared after a short conference that, for the present, they would lay aside article eleven, wherein he was charged with illegal restraint of Anglo-Irish trade and subsequent issuance of import-export licenses on the articles which he had thus restrained.

THE TWELVETH ARTICLE

The Charge

That the said Earl of Strafford being Lord Lieutenant, or Deputy of Ireland, presently, on the 9th Day of January, in the 13th Year of His now Majesty's Reign, did then, under the color to Regulate the Importation of Tobacco into the Realm of Ireland, Issue a Proclamation in His Majesty's Name, Prohibiting the Importation of Tobacco without Licence of him and the Council, there from and after the 1st Day of May, A.D. 1638, after which Restraint, the said Earl, notwithstanding the said Restraint, caused divers great Quantitites of Tobacco to be Imported to his own use, and freighted divers Ships with Tobacco, which he Imported to his own Use: and that if any Ship brought Tobacco into any Port there, the Earl and his Agents used to Buy the same to his own Use, at their own Price; and if that the Owners refused to let him have the same at Undervalues, then they were not permitted to Land the same there: By which undue Means the said Earl having gotten the whole Trade of Tobacco into his own hands, he sold it at great and excessive Prices, such as he list to impose for his own Profit.

And the more to assure the said Monopoly of Tobacco, he the said Earl, on the 23rd day of February, in the 13th Year afforesaid, did Issue another Proclamation, Commanding That none should put to Sale any Tobacco by Whole-sale, from and after the last day of May, then next following, but what should be made up into Rolls, and the same Sealed with two Seals, by himself appointed, one at each end of the Roll. And, such as was not sealed, to be seized, appointing Six Pence the Pound for a Reward to such Persons as should seize the same: and the Persons in whose Custody the Unsealed Tobacco should be found, to be committed to Gaol, which last Proclamation was coloured by a Pretence, for the restraining of the Sale of unwholsome Tobacco, but it was truly to advance the said Monopoly.

Which Proclamation the Earl did rigorously put in Execution by Seizing the Goods, Fining, Imprisoning, Whipping, and putting the Offenders against the same Proclamation on the Pillory, as Namely Barnaby Hubbard, Edward Cavana, John Tumen, and divers others: and made the Officers of State, and Justices of Peace, and other officers, to serve him in the Compassing and Executing these unjust and undue Courses; by which Cruelties, and unjust Monopolies the said Earl raised 100,000 pounds *per annum* Gain to Himself. And yet the said Earl, though he Enhanced the Customs, where it concerned the Merchants in general, yet drew down the Impost formerly taken on Tobacco from Six Pence the pound to Three Pence the pound, it being for his own Profit so to do.

And the said Earl, by the same, and other Rigorous and undue Means, raised several other Monopolies, and unlawful Exactions for his own Gain, *viz.* on Starch, Iron-pots, Glasses, Tobacco pipes, and several other Commodities.[33]

For the Prosecution: Maynard, Whitelock, Clotworthy, Glyn.
Witnesses: Timothy Crosby, John Welsh, Mr. Plunkett,
              Patrick Allen, Patrick Gough.
For the Defense: Strafford.

Witnesses: Guildford Slingsby, Lord Dillon.

In article twelve, the Commons charged that Strafford had created a monopoly of the Irish tobacco trade, so as to enrich himself. Maynard proved that such a monopoly had existed and that the entire trade was under the control of the Lord Lieutenant. He next read the Remonstrance of the Irish Commons, which declared that the earl had sold five hundred tons of tobacco for a price of 100,000 pounds. Maynard argued that Strafford had raised sums for himself which exceeded all the king's revenues in Ireland. Therefore, he was guilty of treason since he had troubled the peace and robbed the people of their goods.

Strafford's reply indicated that he had engineered a complex speculation in the sale of tobacco, holding it as a monopoly, and aiming at considerable profits not only for the Crown but for himself. The initial steps to set up his scheme were expensive and involved heavy borrowing by Strafford from the Exchequer, for which he had the King's Warrant. The king had been confident that his ultimate return would be worth the initial investment.

Strafford's exhibition of the king's order had shaken the charge. Glyn tried to recoup but he could not prove that Strafford had misappropriated any money. The earl had truly followed the order of Charles, and Glyn had to make the best of it. Treason as defined by Statute Law was limited to an attack upon the person of the king. With this series of articles, the Commons tried to make the manipulation of the king's money amount to an attack on the life of the king. When Glyn concluded the twelfth article, the Lords adjourned for the day.

Thursday, April 1, 1641

THE THIRTEENTH ARTICLE

The Charge

That Flax being one of the principal and Native Commodities of that Kingdom of Ireland, the said Earl having gotten great Quantities thereof into his Hands, and growing on his own Lands, did Issue out several Proclamations, *viz*. The one dated the One and Thirtieth of May, in the Twelfth of His Majesties Reign; and the other Dated the One and Thirtieth Day of January, in the same Year; Thereby prescribing and enjoining the Working of Flax into Yarn and Thread, and the Ordering of the same in such Ways, wherein the Natives of that Kingdom were unpractised and unskilful: Which

Proclamations so Issued, were, by his Commands and Warrants to His Majesty's Justices Of Peace, and other Officers, and, by other Rigorous Means put in Execution; and the Flax Wrought, or ordered in other manner then as the said Proclamation prescribed, was Seized and employed to the Use of him and his Agents: and thereby the said Earl endeavored to gain, and did gain in effect the Sole Sale of that Native Commodity.[34]

For the Prosecution: Maynard, Glyn.
Witnesses: Benjamin Croky, Sir John Clotworthy, Lord Ranelagh, Patrick Gough, Mr. Fitzgarret.
For the Defense: Strafford.
Witnesses: none.

In this article, Maynard showed that Strafford had brought the production of flax in Ireland under rigorous control. Then, he produced the Remonstrance of the Irish House of Commons, which declared that as a result of the rigorous execution of the controls on production, many thousand of people perished from want of food. Maynard concluded that although the article by itself did not imply treason, yet it did add much weight to the total accumulation of treason.

Strafford replied that, as before, he would repeat, and would ever repeat, that nothing in the charge was treasonous. To the facts asserted in the charge, he answered: (1) That the Proclamations were necessary to bring some order into the yarn trade, lest the merchants ruin it. (2) That nothing was more common and set by precedent and usage than for the Council of Ireland to conform the Irish to the customs of England. (3) That persons had died by the Proclamation, he denied the fact completely.

In the managers' reply, Glyn's argument revealed much of the weakness of both sides' tactics of unsupported assertions. For example, to the point of seizing yarn, the managers were able to prove only one cart load to have been seized by Strafford's officers. Strafford, likewise unable to offer any real proof, had asked by way of an answer how one cartload could possibly have been sufficient to starve 1000, 2000, or 3000 men. To this, Glyn said: "If a cart load be not sufficient to starve 1000 men, yet if there was more than 1000 starved, then more than one cart load was seized.[35]

So it went, in this and other articles, with both sides often behaving like novice high school debaters, arguing and wrangling over the smallest, non-essential points and details.

Such *minutia* concluded the thirteenth article. The fourteenth charged Strafford with forcing import-exporters to take unlawful oaths as to the quantity and destination of their cargoes. But this article was dropped from the charges, and the managers proceeded to the fifteenth.

THE FIFTEENTH ARTICLE

The Charge

That the said Earl of Strafford, traitorously and wickedly devised and contrived by force of Arms, and in a warlike manner to subdue the Subjects of the said Realm of Ireland; and to bring them under this Tyrannical Power and Will, and in pursuance of these wicked and Traitorous Purposes aforesaid; The Earl of Strafford in the Eighth Year of His Majesty's Reign, did by his own Authority, without any Warrant or color of Law, Tax, and Impose great sums of Money upon the Towns of Baltimore, Bandenbridge, Talo'we, and divers other Towns and Places in the said Realm of Ireland, and did cause the same to be levied upon the Inhabitants of those Towns by Troops of Soldiers, with Force and Arms, in a Warlike Manner. And on the Ninth Day of March, in the Twelfth Year of His now Majesty's Reign, Traitorously did give authority unto Robert Savill, a Serjeant at Arms, and to the Captains of the Companies of Soldiers, in several Parts of that Realm, to send such numbers of Soldiers to lie on the Lands and Houses of such as would not conform to his Orders, until they should render Obedience to his said Orders and Warrants, and after such Submission (and not before) the said Soldiers to return to their Garrisons. And did also issue the like Warrants unto divers Others, which Warrants were in Warlike manner with Force and Arms, put in Execution accordingly, and by such Warlike Means, did force divers of His Majesty's Subjects of that Realm, to submit themselves to his Unlawful Commands.

And in the Twelfth Year of His Majesty's Reign, the Earl of Strafford did traitorously cause certain Troops of Horse and Foot, Armed in Warlike Manner, and in Warlike Array, with Force and Arms, to Expell Richard Butler from the possession of the Manor of Castle-Cumber, in the Territory of Idough in the Realm of Ireland; and did likewise, and in like Warlike Manner, Expel divers of His Majesty's Subjects from their Houses, Families, and Possessions, as namely Edward O'Brenman, Owen Oberman, John Brenman,

Patrick Oberman, Sir Cyprian Horsefield, and divers others, to the number of about an Hundred Families, and took, and Imprisoned them and their Wives, and carried them Prisoners to Dublin, and there detained until they did yield up, surrender, or release their respective Estates or Rights.

And the said Earl in the like Manner, hath, during his Government of the said Kingdom of Ireland, subdued divers others of His Majesty's Subjects there to his Will, and thereby and by the means aforesaid, hath levied War within the said Realm against His Majesty, and His Liege People of that Kingdom.[36]

For the Prosecution: Palmer, Glyn, Maynard, Pym.
Witnesses: Sergeant Savil, Patrick Gough, Richard Welsh,
                          Patrick Cleare, Nicholas Ardagh, Edmund Berne, Robert
                          Kennedy, Robert Little, Lord Ranelagh.
For the Defense: Strafford.
Witnesses: Lord Dillon, John Conley, Lord Ranelagh,
                          Nicholas Ardagh, Sergeant Savil.

Article fifteen was important to the prosecution because for the first time they were able to charge Strafford with a treason which they found in Statute Law. Manager Palmer passed over the first part of the fifteenth and pressed only the second part, which charged the prisoner with giving warrants to Sergeant Savil for billeting soldiers upon the subjects in Ireland as punishment for breaking the Deputy's laws.

Palmer intended to prove the article by two steps: (1) exhibiting the warrant for billeting, and (2) citing the English statute by which such an act constituted treason. For the first, Savil was called to produce a copy of the warrant. The fifteenth was a dangerous article to Strafford; therefore, he immediately rose and entreated the Lords that no documents should be evidenced against him except those which had been authenticated. Moreover, he said, Savil was incompetent to testify to the authenticity of the document, for if he did not lay the act upon the Deputy, then Savil himself would be answerable for it. John Pym stated that the Commons could not waive any of their evidence, and therefore asked the Lords to allow the warrant.

The Lords recessed, and after a very hot contestation between themselves, they returned after an hour and declared that the copy should not be admitted, and directed the managers to proceed. This was the first procedural point decided in Strafford's favor, and it was an important one: Was a party in his behalf forming in the Lords? Was opinion swinging in his favor?

To prove Strafford's part in the warrant, the Commons called three witnesses who testified that they had heard of such a warrant and knew of three, sometimes five soldiers billeted by it.

For the Statutes which made such actions treason, Palmer cited the *6th of Edw. 3* which stated that whosoever should carry about with them enemies of England, Irish rebels, or hooded men, and should force them upon the subject, would be punished as a traitor. Palmer cited the *7th of Hen. 6* which stated that whosoever should billet soldiers in His Majesty's dominions should be thought to make war against the king and be punished as a traitor. Palmer concluded that it was evident that Lord Strafford had broken both statutes and desired the Lords to judge him as a traitor.

The Commons considered their charge of "levying war"[37] to be conclusive, for when Palmer had finished, the managers stood up and maintained article fifteen to be high treason, and called on the Lords to take an immediate vote on the guilt of the accused. But the Peers were not impressed. They refused to take a premature decision and directed the trial to continue. Article fifteen, by which the Commons apparently charged treason under a written statute law, had failed of its intended effect.[38]

It is difficult for the twentieth-century critic of this trial to understand what the Commons hoped to gain in open court from such crude tactics and easily refuted accusations. It is true that such charges were handy for inflaming the mob at the proper time, but the articles had already been accepted by the mob as proven and therefore did not need to be pressed in court for their benefit. Even the allies of the Commons in the House of Lords could not fail to have been impressed with the ease with which Strafford now proceeded to destroy this and similar articles.

In his reply, the Earl of Strafford turned to precedent and the law. As to precedent, he: (1) stated again that nobody would deny that the customs of government were different in Ireland from those of England; (2) showed that such warrants were issued by the Deputies Grandison, Falkland, Chichester, Cork, Evers, and others; (3) produced his commission which gave him power to issue such warrants, and, to prove that he had not extended the Deputy's power, showed his Commission to be *identical* to Falkland's.

Turning to the laws cited by Palmer, the prisoner elaborately averred that he was unlettered in the law, but nevertheless desired to cite two subsequent statutes which overthrew the earlier ones that had been advanced by Palmer: (1) the *10th of Hen. 7*, whereby it is expressly declared that nothing shall be taken thereafter to be treason except what is declared in the present statue; and there was not a word there of any such treason, and (2) the *11th of Queen Eliz.*, wherein power is expressly given to the Lord Deputy to billet and lay soldiers.

While he was thus demolishing the manager's legal case against him, proving such warrants to be perfectly legal, Strafford added the unnecessary, superfluous argument that no proof had connected him with the warrant for billeting soldiers. Such added flourishes were typical of both sides during the trial, and seem to be typical of seventeenth-century argument in general; that is, to prove unquestionably a warrant that cleanly undercut the prime claim of the opposition, and then unnecessarily shift to another, and then another warrant and claim, in order to attempt several more successful rebuttals. The seventeenth-century forensic speaker seems to have depended more upon mass of argument than upon velocity.

At the close of his reply, Strafford asked for the intermission of a day, so that he might recollect his strength against the next quarrel. His health had been bad since his commitment to the Tower and was growing steadily worse under the strain. With some difficulty, he obtained rest until Saturday.

Strafford, at this stage of the trial, was basing his claims upon English law. To provide backing for the warrant of English law, he did his homework and discovered that the Statute of the *10th of Hen. 7* had not only *repealed all previous laws* defining treason, but had *fixed treason* to be what was stated in the Treason Law of Edward III. The Edward III statute was *the* English law on treason, and nothing outside that statute could be made into treason except by another law. As Lord Strafford and his advisers came to understand this law of Edward III more clearly, the accused was to use it more and more effectively.

Saturday, April 3, 1641

THE SIXTEENTH ARTICLE

The Charge

That the Earl of Strafford the Two and Twentieth of February, in the 7th Year of His Majesty's Reign, intending to oppress the Subjects of Ireland, did make a Proposition, and obtained from His Majesty an Allowance thereof, That no Complaint of Injustice or Oppression done in Ireland, should be received in England against any, unless it appeared that the Party made first his Address to him the said Earl, and the said Earl having by such usurped, tyrannical, and exorbitant Power, expressed in the former Articles, destroyed, and oppressed the Peers, and other Subjects of that Kingdom of Ireland, in their Lives, Consciences, Land, Liberties, and Estates; the said Earl to the Intent, the better to maintain and strengthen his said Power, and to bring the People into a Disaffection of His Majesty, as aforesaid, did use His Majesty's Name in the Execution of the said Power.

And to prevent the Subjects of that Realm of all Means of Complaints to His Majesty, and of Redress against him and his Agents, did issue a Proclamation, bearing Date the 17th Day of September, in the 11th Year of His Majesty's Reign, thereby commanding all the Nobility, Undertakers, and others, who held Estates and Offices in the said Kingdom (except such as were employed in His Majesty's Service, or attending in England by His special Command) to make their personal Residence in the said Kingdom of Ireland: and not to depart thence, without Licence of himself.

And the said Earl hath since issued other Proclamations to the same purpose, by means whereof the Subjects of the said Realm are restrained from seeking Relief against the Oppressions of the said Earl, without his Licence; which Proclamation, the said Earl hath by several rigorous Ways, as by Fine, Imprisonment, and otherwise, put in Execution on His Majesty's Subjects, as namely one Parry, and others, who came over only to complain of the Exorbitancies and Oppressions of the said Earl.[39]

For the Prosecution: Palmer, Glyn.

Witnesses: John Loftus, Richard Wade, Henry Parry, Robert Lynch, Mr. Lorky, Mr. Fitzgerald, Lord Roch, John Meaugh, James Nash.

For the Defense: Strafford.

Witnesses: Mr. Riley, Mr. Ralton, Mr. Gibson, Lord Dillon, Sir Adam Loftus, Mr. Wethering, Guildford Slingsby, Mr. Little.

On Saturday, Geoffrey Palmer proceeded to the sixteenth article, which charged that Strafford had established independent authority for himself in Ireland by means of a decree which made sure that no complaint could be made by inhabitants of Ireland to England, unless the first appeal had been made to the Deputy. The Irish Remonstrance complained of this restraint as the greatest thraldom put upon them since the time of the Conquest. They concluded with the charge that Strafford had deprived the Irish subjects of the remedy which they might expect from a just and gracious king and had taken upon himself a royal and independent power.

In defense, Strafford replied that what he had done was usual, necessary, just, and free from all malice and treason. To the particulars of the charge and evidence, he replied: (1) The instructions were not solicited by himself, but came from the Privy Council of England to prevent parties in Ireland from going over the head of the Deputy. (2) The Irish could not have free access to Spain or Rome, lest they should return to put fire to both the Irish Church and State. (3) The king, as great master of the family, might restrain whom he pleased from departing his kingdom; and if it was not lawful to depart England without licence, how much more necessary was this from Ireland.

When they had finished with the sixteenth article, the managers dropped the seventeenth and eighteenth. The seventeenth charged that when Strafford found the Irish army to be a ready instrument of tyranny, he recommended that the armies of all three kingdoms should be reorganized on the Irish model. The eighteenth article charged that Strafford had supported papists in order to get their help with subversion of the fundamental laws of the kingdom. A close examination of these articles indicates that they were dropped by the managers for want of proof.[40]

THE NINETEENTH ARTICLE

The Charge

That the said Earl having Taxed and Levied the said Impositions, and raised the said Monopolies, and committed the said other Oppressions in His Majesty's Name, and as by his Majesties Royal Command; He the said Earl in May, the 15th year of His Majesties Reign, did of his own Authority, contrive and frame a new and unusual Oath, by the purport whereof among many other things, the Party taking the said Oath, was to swear, that he should not protest against any of His Majesties Royal Commands, but submit himself in all Obedience thereunto; which Oath he so contrived to enforce the same on the Subjects of the Scotish Nation, inhabiting in Ireland, and out of a hatred to the said Nation, and to put them to a discontent with His Majesty, and His Government there, and compelled divers of His Majesties said Subjects there, to take the said Oath, against their Wills, and of such as refused to take the said Oath, some he grievously fined, imprisoned, and others he destroyed and exiled; and namely the 10th of October, Ann. Dom. 1639. He fined Henry Steward and his wife, who refused to take the said Oath, 5000 pounds a piece; and their two Daughters, and James Gray, 3000 pounds a piece, and imprisoned them for not paying the said fines. The said Henry Steward, his Wife and Daughters, and James Gray, being the Kings Liege people of the Scotish Nation, and divers others he used in like manner; and the said Earl upon that occasion did declare, that the said Oath did not only oblige them in point of Allegiance to His Majesty, and acknowledgement of His Supremacy only, but to the Ceremonies and Government of the Church established, and to be established by His Majesties Royal Authority; and said, That the refusers to obey, he would prosecute to the Blood.[41]

For the Prosecution: Whitelocke, Maynard, Glyn, Stroude.
Witnesses: Sir James Montgomery, Mr. Maxwell, Sir Henry
              Spottewood, Sir John Clotworthy, Richard Salman,
              John Loftus.
For the Defense: Strafford.
Witnesses: Lord Dillon, Sir Adam Loftus, G. Slingsby,
              Thomas Little, Mr. Ralton, Sir Philip Mainwaring.

Bulstrode Whitelocke opened the nineteenth article with the charge that Strafford had not been content to domineer over the bodies of men but also sought to rule their consciences, to which purpose he had forced an oath upon the Scots in Ireland. He argued that this was the most hateful treason ever heard of, to lord it over the very souls of man.

Strafford answered, "Almost every article sets forth a new treason that I never heard of before." England had been at war with Scotland at the time of the oath, and the Council had feared that the 100,000 Ulster Scots might revolt in Ireland against the king. Hence, to oblige the Ulstermen to the Crown, the king—in his own hand—had ordered Strafford to tender an oath of loyalty to them.

In his conclusion, Strafford brought forth a rule of procedure in cases of treason, which he wielded with great effect to diminish the testimony of the Commons' witnesses, *viz*: No point of fact may be admitted as evidence in a treason trial unless it is testified by *two* or more witnesses; the evidence given by only one witness must be thrown out. After stating the procedural rule, Strafford went back over the nineteenth article, showing which points of fact had been supported by only one witness. The "two-witness rule" was to become even more important to his defense in subsequent articles.

When Strafford concluded his defense, the Lords adjourned. A weekend intervened and both sides paused to assess their relative strength and gains thus far in the struggle.

John Pym

5

The Trial Concludes
Articles Twenty through Twenty-Eight:
Strafford Wins the Battle

By April 3, the thirteenth day of the trial, the managers of the prosecution for the House of Commons had reached and concluded their nineteenth article of accusation. April 4 was a Sunday and gave the Commons a chance to survey their overall strategy and assess how well they were doing. The final eight articles brought the case closer to home, since they were based upon Strafford's actions in England and Scotland. Together, the final articles—which had been based upon his activities of the past year—made up the heaviest part of the charges: If he could create the slightest doubt regarding his alleged dark role in the destruction of the Short Parliament, or as to whether he had ignited the Bishop's Wars against Scotland and had aimed to use the Irish army to bring England to heel, then he might elude them altogether.

Among the remaining articles, there was one, the twenty-third, which infuriated all Englishmen and produced more hatred of Strafford than any other, and which could be counted upon—if it were proved—to do him irreparable damage: this was the accusation that he intended to bring the Irish army to England and use it against the disaffected subjects. The prosecution had evidence on the article from one of the Privy Council, Sir Harry Vane, Strafford's old enemy. Vane was prepared to testify that at the Council Table Strafford had advised the use of the Irish army.

On the success of Vane as a witness depended the main thrust of the crucial article. This article in turn could carry the other remaining seven along in its powerful wake. Therefore, the timing of the article's introduction was important: the moment of Vane's appearance needed to be well-chosen and his testimony cleverly handled. Indeed, if Strafford were allowed to start the day by dissecting in his precise and tenacious manner the articles which led up to the twenty-third, the edge of the pivotal article would be blunted. The managers decided, therefore, to change the arrangement and development of the last eight articles. Instead of their usual *seriatim* approach, they would hit Strafford with the next five articles at once, giving primary emphasis to the twenty-third. Of course, the accused would not be forewarned of this tactic.

Strafford's life work had now reached its climax. In the face of every obstacle, he had become the first minister to the king, and even from the Tower Charles sought his advice. The cost was great. England and Scotland were embittered, determined on revenge. Through no fault of Strafford's, the monarchy was fatally cracked and flawed. The powers of the country were drifting into two separate and irreconcilable camps, with Strafford as the last pillar of the throne. From this division, growing into an unbridgeable gulf, the convulsion of the Civil War arose. But, in the spring of 1641 there remained among many Englishmen a fundamental attachment to the Crown, and many of those in both Lords and Commons who now attacked Strafford and the king were later to lay down their lives for Charles. Presently, however, these future Royalists were absorbed along with the Parliamentarians in redress of a long accumulation of grievances. The days of an apparent alliance between these two parties were rapidly drawing to a close. Nevertheless, so long as John Pym led Commons, and so long as Strafford was a threat, Pym was careful to do nothing to arouse latent royalist feeling. Not until Parliament dispatched the great minister and plunged into revolutionary policies did royalist Britain fully awake to the Parliamentary menace.

We now enter the crucial phase of the trial—the final struggle between Pym and Strafford. These two great figures now towered over political England. In 1641, no one effectively disputed their leadership and, until Strafford was struck down, the governmental scene was dominated by their personal duel on a grand scale. Both men were at the height of their powers, and their skill and oratory in forensic debate gripped and focused public attention on the proceedings in Westminster Hall. Every thrust and parry was discussed throughout London. Their differences were unbridgeable, but what gave the conflict its edge was their dissimilarity in temperament during the trial. Strafford was the natural fighter, exhilarated by challenge and at his best in conflict. Pym was a subtle and ingenious backstage manager of men, who preferred to move from one secured position to the next, taking risks only when necessary and without zest. Strafford was nicknamed "Black Tom Tyrant"; Pym was called "The Ox." Thus they faced each other across Westminster Hall.

To confront the House of Commons, Lord Strafford needed all the courage and rousing fervor with which he had been so generously endowed. His plan was still to turn back the accusations, thus descrediting his accusers, and gain the acquittal which would drive a wedge between Lords and Commons and create the party with which he and his king would retrieve their position. Against him, the Commons advanced a new concept of treason. They argued that a traitor was not only he who attacked the sovereign's person or government, but also he who attacked the sovereign in his political capacity, and, by undermining the law which constituted his greatness, exposed him to disaster and ruin.

If the Commons' concept of treason was larger, more liberal, and more modern than the old English treason laws, it had for judicial purposes the defect of ambiguity and imprecision. It might be employed to put down any opposition to the legislative branch. Yet, even if it had been conceded that Pym's view of treason was the correct one, and if care had been taken to restrict it to a conspiracy to change by violence the existing form of government, it was still hard to pin the newly made label of traitor on Strafford. He had had no deliberate intention of changing or over- throwing the government. Moreover, he had been given no fair warning to cease and desist his actions because they were henceforth to be made treason. Perhaps the law of treason needed to be changed so as to include some of Strafford's high-handed acts. But it was patently unfair, and a bad precedent for the future, to sentence him to die under an interpretation of the law which was now heard for the first time.

Strafford saw all these weaknesses in the position of the Commons. The English doctrine of treason, as it had been handed down from the Middle Ages, had fixed the crime upon acts committed against the person or authority of the sovereign. No one knew better than Strafford that in this sense he had not committed treason, and upon this rock he founded his first line of defense: *No law, no crime.*

Beyond the Commons' difficulty with unseating a rigidly-defined treason law, they had trouble holding their indictment together. Many of the acts charged to Strafford turned out to be composed of malicious gossip and hearsay, which under Strafford's attack degenerated into absurdity. Other charges were so tenuous that they were dropped for want of proof.

Strafford's defense showed great subtlety and judgment. He persistently argued that he had acted within the law and cited statutes, precedents, and the express commands of the king to justify his conduct. The Commons did successfully show that Strafford was supreme and overbearing in Ireland, that he would tolerate no defiance of his strong will, but the earl obstinately pointed out that even if he had commited all of the alleged acts, they were not treasonous. "Almost every article," he had said with scorn, "sets forth a new treason that I never heard of before."

The Commons were undoubtedly thinking more of the future than of the past. What weighed with them was not Mountnorris or Cork, or the customs of the Irish; but instead the belief that, if Strafford escaped, he would soon be found at the head of an army which would drive them from Westminster and impeach them for treasonous conspiracy with the Scots. They had to finish him off.

By the end of the nineteenth article and the thirteenth day, the case for the prosecution was faltering badly. In Strafford's name, the Commons by implication had impeached not a single man but the whole system of royal government. Strafford rose to the challenge, making his answers into a political argument, a personal defense, and an oblique attack upon his accusers.

The king and queen sat daily in their special box, hoping by their presence to restrain the prosecution. Each morning Lord Strafford knelt to the Lord Steward Arundel and bowed to the Lords and to the assembly. Never losing his civility for a moment, and often with flashes of scornful humor, he dealt with the Anglo-Irish bosses who were the principal evidence on the first nineteen articles. He took their evidence apart with the meticulous precision of a watchmaker and reassembled the parts methodically, so as to cover them, not him, with the discredit. He was so slow and careful in his work that he must have maddened the managers, and sometimes bored the Lords. Each day by logic and appeal he broke up the heads of accusation. He successfully derided the theory of cumulative treason and moved slowly to the checkmate which would win him the "king" of the game: English law.

The Earl of Strafford possessed a certain strategic comprehension. He had not that rhetorical outlook which took all things in, and which is the quality of all great speakers, but he had an intense clarity of view and promptitude to act, and he was brave in action. From the beginning of the trial, through the first nineteen articles, Strafford's design was for a slow, attritious advance on English law. His facts, his rebuttal, his data would converge on that position and break the central warrant of accusation. Accordingly, the citadel of law was invested and upon this rock he built his defense. The citadel formed at once his main defensive and offensive outpost. The initial success of Strafford's legalistic strategy veiled its inherent weaknesses. He believed so strongly that the law was impregnable that he built at first neither alternative defenses nor laid plans for an orderly retreat if his first line of defense should prove after all to be untenable. He had thrown up a massive, Maginot Line type of defense, impregnable to a frontal assault, but vulnerable elsewhere. If the Commons should change their ground and try a flanking sweep or an attack from the rear, all might be lost. So far, all was well. On the thirteenth day, the prisoner's hopes stood high.

Monday, April 5, 1641

THE TWENTIETH ARTICLE

The Charge

That the said Earl hath in the Fifteenth and Sixteenth Years of His Majesty's Reign, and divers Years past, labored and endeavored to breed in His Majesty an ill Opinion of His Subjects; namely of those of the Scotch Nation: And diverse and sundry times, and especially since the Pacification made by His Majesty with His said Subjects of Scotland in Summer, in the 15th Year of His Majesty's Reign; he, the said Earl, did labor and endeavor to persuade, incite, and provoke His Majesty to an Offensive War against His said Subjects of the Scotch Nation: And the said Earl by his Counsels, Actions, and Endeavors hath been, and is, a principal and chief Incendiary of the War and Discord between His Majesty and His Subjects of England, and the Subjects of Scotland, and hath declared and advised His Majesty, that the demands made by the Scots, in their Parliament, were a sufficient cause of War against them.

The said Earl having formerly expressed the height and rancor of his Mind towards His Majesty's Subjects of the Scotch Nation, *viz.* the Tenth Day of October, in the 15th Year of His Majesty's Reign, he said That the Nation of the Scots were Rebels and Traitors; and

he being then about to come to England, he then further said, That
if it pleased his Master (meaning His Majesty) to send him back
again, he would root out of the said Kingdom (meaning the said
Kingdom of Ireland) the Scotch Nation, both root and branch.

Some Lords and others, who had taken the said Oath in the
precedent Article, only excepted: and the said Earl hath caused
diverse of the Ships and the Goods of the Scots to be stayed, seized,
and molested, to the intent to set on the said war. [1]

THE TWENTY-FIRST ARTICLE

The Charge

That the said Earl of Strafford, shortly after his speeches
mentioned in the last Precedent Articles, to wit, in the 15th Year of
His Majesty's Reign, came into this Realm of England, and was
made Lord Lieutenant of Ireland, and continued his Government of
that Kingdom by a Deputy: at his arrival here, finding that His
Majesty, with much wisdom and goodness, had composed the
Troubles in the North, and had a Pacification with His Subjects of
Scotland; he labored by all means to procure His Majesty to break
that Pacification, Incensing His Majesty against His Subjects of that
Kingdom, and the Proceeding of the Parliament there.

And having incited His Majesty to an offensive War against His
Subjects of Scotland by Sea and Land, and by pretext thereof to
raise Forces for the Maintenance of that War, he compelled His
Majesty to call a Parliament in England; yet the said Earl intended,
that if the said Proceedings of that Parliament should not be such as
would stand with the said Earl of Strafford's mischievous Designs,
he would then procure His Majesty to break the same; and, by ways
of Force and Power, to raise Monies upon the Subjects of this
Kingdom. And, for the encouragement of His Majesty to hearken to
his Advice, he did before His Majesty and Privy-Council, then sitting
in Council, make a large Declaration, That he would serve His
Majesty in any other way, in case the Parliament should not supply
him. [2]

THE TWENTY-SECOND ARTICLE

The Charge

That in the month of March, before the beginning of the last
Parliament, the said Earl of Strafford went into Ireland, and
procured the Parliament of that Kingdom, to declare their

assistance in a War against the Scots; and gave directions for the raising of Army there, consisting of 8000 by Foot, and 1000 Horse, being for the most part Papists as aforesaid. And confederating with one Sir George Radcliff, did together with him traitorously conspire to employ the Army, for the ruin and destruction of the Kingdom of England, and His Majesty's Subjects, and altering and subverting of the fundamental Laws, and established Government of this Kingdom.

And shortly after, the said Earl of Strafford returned into England, and to sundry Persons, declared his Opinion to be, That His Majesty should first try the Parliament here, and if that did not supply, according to his Occasions, he might use then His Prerogative as he pleased, to levy what he needed; and that He should be acquitted both of God and Man, if he took some other courses to supply Himself, though it were against the Wills of His Subjects.[3]

THE TWENTY-THIRD ARTICLE

The Charge

That upon the Thirteenth Day of April last, the Parliament of England met, and the Commons House (then being the representative Body of all the Commons in the Kingdom) did according to the Trust reposed in them, enter into Debate and Consideration of the great grievances of this Kingdom, both in respect of Religion, and the public Liberty of the Kingdom; and His Majesty referring chiefly to the said Earl of Strafford, and the Archbishop of Canterbury, the ordering and disposing of all matters concerning the Parliament: He the said Earl of Strafford, and with the assistance of the Archbishop, did procure His Majesty by sundry Speeches and Messages, to urge the said Commons House, to enter into some resolution for His Majesty's Supply, for maintenance of His War against His Subjects of Scotland, before any Course taken for the Relief of the great and pressing Grievances, wherewith this Kingdom was then afflicted. Whereupon a demand was then made from His Majesty of twelve Subsidies, for the release of Ship-Money only; and while the said Commons then Assembled (with exceptions and expressions of great affection to His Majesty and His Service) were in Debate and Consideration concerning some Supply, before any Resolution by them made, he the said Earl of Strafford, with the help and assistance of the said Archbishop, did procure His Majesty to Dissolve the said Parliament, upon the 5th day of May last; and upon the same day, the said Earl of Strafford did treacherously, falsly and maliciously, endeavour to incense His Majesty against His loving and faithful Subjects, who had been Members of the said House of Commons, by telling His Majesty they had denyed to supply him. And afterwards upon the same day, did traiterously and wickedly counsel and advise His Majesty to this effect, *viz*. That having tryed the affections of His People, he was loose and absolved from all rules of Government, and that he was to do everything that Power would admit; and that His Majesty had tryed all ways, and was refused, and should be acquited towards God and Man; and that he had an Army in Ireland (meaning the Army above mentioned, consisting of Papists, his Dependants, as is aforesaid) which he might employ to reduce this Kingdom.[4]

THE TWENTY-FOURTH ARTICLE

The Charge

That in the same Month of May, he the said Earl of Strafford falsly, traiterously, and maliciously, published and declared before others of His Majesties Privy Council, That the Parliament of England had forsaken the King, and that in denying to supply the King, they had given him advantage to supply himself by other ways; and several other times he did maliciously, wickedly, and falsly, Publish and Declare, That seeing the Parliament had refused to supply His Majesty in the ordinary and usual way, the King might provide for the Kingdom in such ways, as he should hold fit, and that he was not to suffer himself to be mastered by the forwardness and undutifulness of the People: And having so maliciously slandered the said late House of Commons, he did with the advice of the said Archbishop of Canterbury, and the Lord Finch, late Keeper of the Great Seal of England, cause to be printed and published in His Majesties Name, a false and scandalous Book, Entitled, *His Majesties Declaration of the Causes that moved him to Dissolve the last Parliament*, full of bitter and malicious Invectives, and false, and scandalous aspersions against the said House of Commons.[5]

For the Prosecution: Whitelocke, Maynard, Lord Digby, Glyn.

Witnesses: Earl of Traquair, Lord Morton (by deposition), Sir Henry Vane, Earl of Northumberland (by deposition), Bishop of London and Lord Treasurer, Sir Thomas Barrington, Earl of Bristol, Earl of

Holland, Nicholas Barnewell, Archbishop of Armaugh,
Lord Conway, Sir Robert King, Lord Ranelagh,
Sir Thomas Germain, Lord Newburgh.

When Lord Strafford was brought to the Bar on Monday, April 5, Bulstrode Whitelocke told him that he was to answer the next five articles not singly but as a whole. The earl protested that he had not been warned, and that "the matter is weighty, my memory treacherous, my judgment weak." His objection was overruled when John Glyn bitterly declared that he had never known before of a prisoner who presumed to dictate to the prosecution how they should proceed.

Whitelocke then moved swiftly to the offensive. In the previous nineteen articles, the managers had proceeded carefully, trying by sheer weight of testimony to build up a massive case. Now, they dropped their "over-prove" tactic and threw a light, well-constructed case at the accused. Whitelocke moved from one article to another and abstracted from them the strongest points against the accused, and arranged them according to whether they had to do with English or Scottish affairs. The matter in the five articles which concerned *Scotland,* he summarized under five heads:

1. The Deputy had said at the Council Board: "The Scots' demands contained sufficient matter for an offensive war."

2. The Deputy said later in Council: "The Scots' demands strike at the root and life of monarchical government and are only to be answered by the sword."

3. The Deputy illegally seized Scottish goods in Ireland.

4. He had engaged the Irish Parliament in the war against the Scots.

5. He had put bad thoughts and suspicions into his Majesty against the Scots and labored to make a national quarrel between them and England.

Concerning *England,* Strafford's offensive utterances had been made either before or after the Short Parliament. His expressions before the Parliament were:

1. In the presence of Sir George Radcliffe, Strafford had said to Sir Robert Barrington at the time of the dissolution of the Short Parliament: "Seeing the English would not grant supply to the king, it seems they were weary of their peace and desired to be conquered a second time."

2. To the Primate of Ireland, he said: "It is lawful for a king, having tried the affection and benevolence of his people, and then denied their help, upon an inevitable necessity and present danger of the Kingdom,

that he might use his Prerogative for his own supply and the defense of his subjects."

3. In the presence of Sir George Radcliffe, Strafford said to Sir Robert Barrington, when he was worrying how the king might raise money for the army: "The king had 400,000 pounds in his purse, 30,000 men in the field, and his sword by his side; and if he wanted money afterwards, who would pity him?"

4. He had said to Lord Conway: "If Parliament should not grant a sufficient supply, then the king was acquitted before God and man, and might use the authority put into his hands."

5. He had said to the Council: "If the Parliament should deny help to the king, he would take any other way he could for his Majesty's service."

After the Parliament, Strafford had made two treasonous statements:

1. "The Parliament had forsaken the king, and the king should not suffer himself to be overmastered by the forwardness, obstinacy, and stubbornness of his people."

2. *"That if his Majesty pleased to employ forces, he had some in Ireland that might serve to reduce this Kingdom."*

Whitelocke had built up his case well, selecting from one article then another to make the separate charges corroborate and support one another. He ended with the strongest accusation. His order for calling the witnesses was just as skillfully arranged. Lord Traquair was friendly to Strafford, but Whitelocke screwed from him words which showed that the accused had favored war with the Scots. Bishop Juxon admitted that the earl had advised war. Sir Harry Vane and Lord Conway said that they had heard him say that the king should take money as he needed it if Parliament failed him. Vane and Conway's testimony was confirmed by Lord Bristol, Lord Newburgh, and Lord Holland.

The managers for effect had saved their strongest accusation until last. They had one more powerful card to play and hoped it might prove to be a winner, since the charge was the one which was most infuriating to the English. For this accusation to be made, the Commons had to effect another near-revolutionary straining of the law. Hitherto, the opinions expressed by the king's ministers in the privacy of the Council Board, were, as they are today, secret and confidential. The evidence consisted of what occurred at the Council sitting of May 5, 1640. Young Harry Vane had found his father's notes on the meeting, and turned copies over to Pym. But Young Harry could not be called nor his copies used without implicating him a thief and informer. Therefore, the managers had to bring the evidence into play by calling the elder Vane himself. This worthy was known to be ready to go to any lengths to revenge himself on Strafford, who had taken from him his coveted title, Baron of Raby. Consequently, the Commons demanded, and got the Lords to concede, that ministers could be called to the stand to reveal the secret deliberations of the Council.

Sir Harry Vane was called to the stand. The climax of the trial had arrived. The Hall was hushed with expectation. Whitelocke asked Vane what words had he heard the Earl of Strafford speak to the king when a dissolution of the Short Parliament was imminent. Vane was garrulous with nerves. He said that "I consider very well where I am, and the presence before whom I speak," and that "in the whole course of life never loved to tell an untruth."[6] Then came the crucial testimony:

> These words were spoken at the Committee of Eight for the Scotch Affairs....My Earl of Strafford did say in a discourse: "Your Majesty having tried all ways and being refused; and in case of this extreme necessity, and for the safety of the Kingdom, you are acquitted before God and man. You have an army in [Ireland] [7] which You may employ here to reduce this Kingdom," or some words to this effect.[8]

Vane was on the spot before King, Lords, and Commons and stumbled badly: What Strafford had meant by the words, he could not say, but "that the words were spoken, and if it were the last hour [I was] to speak, it is the truth to my best remembrance."

Suddenly, the reaction which was brewing in the Lords burst forth. Lord Savile, of all people, Strafford's old Yorkshire foe, jumped to his feet and asked Vane whether the earl had said "their" or "this" or "that kingdom."[9] Savile pointedly added that, "It is very hard to condemn a man for treason upon such petit circumstances." The Earl of Clare wanted to know what had been meant by "this kingdom." For his part, he thought the words "meant of the Kingdom of Scotland, to which the word "this" might very well be relative, "that Kingdom" being mentioned only [alone] in the preceding discourse." Lord Clare was even more ready to draw such a favorable conclusion because he could not understand "by what grammatical construction it could be gathered from his words that he meant to reduce England, which then was...not upon rebellious course." Savile and Clare pressed Vane with several motions, until Lord

Arundel directed him to repeat what he had spoken. Vane answered:

> These words were spoken—as my Lord of Northumberland hath
> testified[10]—at the Committee of Eight for the Scotch Affairs. It
> was on occasion of a debate whether an offensive or a defensive war
> with the Kingdom of Scotland. That, on some debate then, some
> being of opinion for a defensive and some for an offensive war, he
> did say the words related as I conceive. That in a discourse, the Earl
> of Strafford said these words, or words to this effect: *Your Majesty,
> having tried all ways and refused, in this case of extreme necessity,
> and for the safety of your Kingdom and People, You are loose and
> absolved from all rules of government: You are acquitted before
> God and men. You have an army in Ireland. You may employ it to
> reduce this Kingdom.*[11]

The Commons handled Vane carefully, and he did not fail them. He
said that he was positive that Strafford had used the word "here," not
"there," and had said "this Kingdom," not "that Kingdom." Lord Clare
kept after Sir Harry, asking him to restate the exact sequence of the words
and to explain how and when they had arisen in debate. But Whitelocke
stopped Vane's answer, saying that there could be no question but that
England had been intended. The Earl of Southampton thereupon rose to
support Lord Clare. He asked Vane whether he would positively swear to
those words or not. Vane said, "Positively, either them or the like."
Southampton rejoined, "Under favor, 'those or the like' could not be
positive."[12] Lord Clare persisted and demanded satisfaction to his former
questions: Did Vane really think Lord Strafford had meant England?
What had anyone else said to the point? Did he "mean by 'this Kingdom'
the Kingdom of England or the Kingdom of Scotland?"[13] Lord Arundel
intervened and reminded Clare that "Sir Harry Vane testifies to the
words, not to the interpretation."[14] And, Manager Whitelocke concluded
with a twist to Clare's question: "The question is put, Whether '*this*'
Kingdom' be *the* Kingdom."

For the Defense: Strafford.

Witnesses: Guildford Slingsby, Sir William Pennyman, Earl
                of Northumberland (by deposition), Lord Cottington,
                Marquis Hamilton, Lord Goring, Lord Treasurer,
                Sir Thomas Lucas, Thomas Germain.

The initiative now passed to Strafford, who resolved to go over the
articles as they laid in order and under every article to give his answer. This

was a mistake, for of all the articles brought that day, the twenty-third stood heaviest against him and the entire Hall waited for his answer to that particular charge. Lord Strafford had not been prepared to fight decisively at this moment, but he was drawn into the climax of the trial because the managers had tried to surprise him by advancing five articles at once. At least Strafford had been committed to a ground that suited him and he raced to collect his defenses. He had been forced to improvise his reply to the accusations. After a few moment's respite to collect himself, he rose, bowed to the Lord Steward, the king, and the Lords and proceeded to deliver a meticulous reply, which is the more remarkable because it was nearly impromptu. With a mixture of calmness and passion, he proceeded to dissect the evidence that had been brought. "Look to what is proved," he entreated their lordships, "not to what is enforced on those proofs by these gentlemen; for words pass and may be easily mistaken."

Had he been an incendiary against the Scots? Perhaps he had been. Yet, he could not see what other advice he could give the king than to make ready for war, since England was then being invaded by a Scottish army. Besides, the posture of war had been recommended by the entire Council.

Sir Harry Vane and the Earl of Northumberland had testified that he had recommended an offensive war. The king and Council had already resolved to reduce the Scots to obedience. The question before the Council, then, was whether to do this by an offensive or defensive war, to which all present were duty bound to deliver their judgments.

The Commons, when they accused him of urging the king to use his prerogative, had opened a constitutional issue. Here was Strafford's chance to produce the outstanding political document of his time, developing the rights and responsibilities of both crown and subject in a manner which showed the way toward a compromise. He chose his theme, and did not deny the words, but denied the Commons' interpretation of them:

> I have a heart that loves freedom as well as any other man and...will go as far to defend it....[But] I think that a man does the King the best service who stands for the modest propriety and liberty of the subject. It hath been once my opinion, which I learnt in the House of Commons—it hath gone along with me in the whole course of my service to the Commonwealth, and by the grace of God I shall carry it to my grave: That the Prerogative of the Crown and Liberty of the

Subject should be equally looked upon, and served *together*, but
not *apart*. [15]

The foregoing plea for the prerogative was based upon an unwritten
constitutional warrant and represented thereby Strafford's first defensive
maneuver beyond the Maginot Line which he had built around statute
law. The issue was not well-developed or well thought-out by Strafford, so
the flash was probably unpremeditated. Yet, if he wished to develop a
second line of defense based on the constitution, now was the time to
begin to insinuate it by *suggestion* into his discourse. To spring it too
quickly on the Lords would vitiate its effect. [16]

Strafford was charged in both the twenty-second and twenty-third
articles with the intention of using the Irish army in England—the
twenty-second asserting his intent, the twenty-third citing his proposed
action as testified thereto by Vane. His decision to answer article by
article now brought him to the first instance where this was charged; but
his *seriatim* development lessened his impact slightly by dividing his
answers to what was really a single accusation. Called to the point, the
Marquis of Hamilton testified that King Charles had acquainted him with
the plans for the Irish army. The army was to total 8,000 men, who, when
they were ready, were to be landed in Western Scotland at a town called
Ayre. Major General Sir Thomas Lucas of the King's Irish Army testified
that in January, 1639, Strafford had opened a map of Scotland and said,
"Now I must tell you the greatest secret in all the world!" Strafford then
pointed to the Western part of Scotland around Dunbar Firth, and said,
according to Lucas: "The Irish army is to land here." The deposition of
the Earl of Northumberland was finally read and this also supported
Strafford. Slingsby produced dated military maps drawn for the landings
at Ayre and requisitions for flat-bottomed boats for clearing the harbor
bar at Ayre. Sir William Pennyman also testified in support of Strafford's
version of the army's employment.

Lord Strafford turned back now to the words charged against him, and
attacked the ways by which the Commons had drawn their claims from
his casual phrases and private conservations:

If words spoken to friends in familiar discourse, spoken in one's
chamber, spoken at one's table, spoken in one's sickbed...if these
things shall be brought against a man as treason, this, under favor,
takes away the comfort of all human society. By this means, we

shall be debarred of speaking—the principal joy and comfort of
society—with wise and good men, of becoming wiser and bettering
our lives. If these things be strained to take away life and honor, it
will be a silent world; a city will become a hermitage, and no man
shall dare to impart his solitary thoughts or opinions to his friend
and neighbor. [17]

The Commons were trying to extend the law of treason beyond its
statutory limits. For the second time that day—indeed for only the second
time in fourteen days—Lord Strafford again went beyond his defense
based strictly on the law and developed another type of warrant. He
appealed directly to the Lords and warned them:

It hath been the wisdom of your Lordships noble ancestors that
they have always endeavored to conclude [clearly define] the
danger that may fall on the subject by treason, so that it might be
limited...and understood so as to be avoided. I hope we shall never
be so improvident as to sharpen this two-edged sword against
ourselves and our posterity, to let the lion loose to tear us all in
pieces. For, if way be given to arbitrary treason and to the wits of
men to work upon it, to prejudice or question life, it would be very
dangerous. I believe that in this Hall there would be actions of
treason that would fly as familiarly up and down as actions of
trespass. [18]

At last, Strafford now turned to the testimony of Sir Harry Vane. The
most powerful article of the impeachment depended upon the testimony
of this single witness. There had been eight members of the Council of
Scottish Affairs and Strafford intended to call all of them whom he could,
to testify as to what occurred at the meeting. Archbishop Laud was in the
Tower awaiting his own trial for treason. Secretary Windebank, as
Strafford said in one of his frequent humorous jabs at the Commons, was
"a little too far off to be heard at this time," having fled in an open
rowboat across the Channel to France. Four only remained.

The Marquis Hamilton declared upon his oath that he had never heard
the Lord Lieutenant use the words given by Vane, nor had he heard him
use any words which gave the slightest hint of bringing the Irish army to
England. He did say that he had heard the prisoner often say that all
would never be well in England until the prerogative of the crown and the
privilege of the subject were balanced together; and that Parliaments were
the happiest way to keep harmony between the king and the people.

The testimony of the Earl of Northampton was read. Therein, the Lord declared expressly that he had never heard those words, nor any like them, from the Lord Strafford. Strafford had always spoken with great honor and regard to the Kingdom of England.

The Lord Treasurer testified that Strafford at the meeting of the Council of Eight had never advised using the Irish army in England.

Finally, Strafford called Lord Cottington as his last witness from the council. Cottington answered with an aristocratic slap at the managers, who apparently tried to get him to testify against Strafford:

> I have heard the question before, and am very confident that I did never hear him say it in my hearing; and I have a great deal of reason to be confident of it. [19]

Maynard decided to cross-examine Cottington in an effort to discredit his testimony. He asked the witness whether he had heard Strafford say that the king was absolved and loose from all rules of government, or words to that effect. Cottington, along with Pennyman from the Commons, was not easily intimidated. He answered smartly:

> I have been asked that question too; and I think I never heard the words, for it a very absurd proposition, and I should not have heard it with patience. [20]

He was asked in further cross-examination by Maynard whether he had heard Strafford say that the Parliament had forsaken, or denied, or deserted the king. Cottington was obviously enjoying himself, for he answered "It is very probable Lord Strafford did say it...for it is the truth." When Maynard interrupted Cottington, the witness shot back that the gentleman should hear him out. He declared that Strafford was the last man to have told the king that he was absolved from the rules of government. On the contrary, the Lord Lieutenant wished to keep the government well within the law, and only after the Scots marched south, only after the House of Commons refused the subsidies, had he advised the king to use the prerogative, "caste and candide." [21]

When Cottington stood down, Strafford loftily congratulated Vane on remembering the disputed words so perfectly that he could remember them better "than the party that spoke the words, or any man in the company besides." He thought that Vane had been sufficiently answered, but to nail down the last possible loose end, Vane himself, Strafford cited

the Treason Statutes of *1 Eliz.* and *12 Carol. 1,* which enacted that: no
person should be indicted, arraigned, convicted or condemned of any
offense of treason unless he be accused by *two* witnesses. Vane was but a
single witness to the alleged offense.

Strafford's last claim was constitutional, the second advanced that
day. If the private opinion of a minister, delivered under his privilege as a
counselor, could be made into a treason, there would be an end to all
government. He said:

> My Lords, lay it to your heart. You and your posterity are fitted by
> God and nature, birth and education, to beautify the Royal Throne,
> and to sustain the weighty affairs of the Kingdom. If to give your
> opinions in political agitations should be accounted treason, who
> shall be willing to serve the King? What a dilemma are you in? If,
> being sworn counsellors, you speak not your minds freely, you are
> convict of perjury; if you do, perhaps of treason. What detri-
> ment...shall fall to the King and Kingdom if this be permitted.
> Which of you hereafter will adventure, yea dare adventure, so much
> as to help by your advice—unless you be weary of your lives, your
> estates, your posterity, yea your very honor? Let me never live
> longer than to see this confusion—yea, I may say it, this inhumanity
> in England.[22]

In his peroration, he made his plea to the Lords, combining an
assertion of service to the state with a warning to the nobility:

> I do not see how I am culpable of treason, unless it be treason for
> not being infallible. And if it be so, my Lords, you have this rag of
> mortality before you...[and] though you pull this into shreds, yet
> there is no great loss. Yea, there may be a great gain...to give a
> testimony to the world of an innocent conscience towards God, and
> a resolute loyalty towards my Prince....And if by spilling of mine
> [blood] there is not found a way to...[spill] the blood of the
> nobility...there is no disadvantage at all suffered by the loss of
> mine.[23]

This was an excellent day's work, considering that Strafford had such
little time for preparation. His defense for the day told upon the Peers. It
told upon others as well. Even from the Commons' benches was heard a
loud hum of admiration as the prisoner stood down that day.[24]

The managers had played their highest card, and it was Strafford who
had taken the hand. Whitelocke, Maynard, Glyn and Pym—the best of the

managers—all tried to swing the balance back in favor of the prosecution. The main burden of the reply fell on Whitelocke, and Whitelocke, brilliant lawyer as he was, was hardly the man to cope with Strafford. The crucial accusation had broken down, but the manager did what he could to support Vane's evidence. He argued that Strafford's counsel had been no mere statement of opinion, but had proceeded from a premeditated design to subvert the laws and "to set a difference between the king and his people."

Maynard argued that the accused's plea for the sanctity of private conversation actually proved a general disaffection to the commonwealth. Glyn reasserted the validity of the accusations in article twenty-three. He ingeniously added that the necessary second witness to Vane's disputed testimony was *vox populi*—the "voice of the people," which bore true witness to Strafford's intent to crush England with the Irish army. Glyn went on to attack Cottington's evidence, that Strafford had advised the king to repair all property of the subject, on the ground that advice for repair proved an intent to invade. The scrappy Cottington interrupted Glyn to restate his meaning, but Glyn, heedless, swept to his close, wherein he followed Maynard's lead and accused Strafford of pleading the privilege of the Council to cover the darkest treason. Pym weakly pointed out a minute mistake in Strafford's deductive logic and the managers were done.

When all had been said that day, it was evident that Strafford's chance of escape stood infinitely higher at the end of the day than in the morning. Certainly the Peers thought so. For nine whole hours, a very sick but lionhearted man had fought unaided against the best forensic talent of the time, and had brought them to a standstill. Whitelocke, Maynard, Glyn and Pym knew that Strafford's whole effort had produced a great impression on the Lords. Theirs had not, and the general voice inclined to the side of Strafford. At the finish, Strafford wearily rose and represented to their lordships that he had come there "in a great deal of weakness and infirmity"; his "speech and voice were spent" and therefore he "most humbly besought their Lordships to give the respite of a day to restore what little strength it shall please God to send," for he was "no longer able to speak or stand." The committee for the Commons said they would not oppose this, if it stood with their lordships' pleasure. And so the House was adjourned and appointed to meet again on Wednesday next.

April 7, 1641

THE TWENTY-FIFTH ARTICLE

The Charge

That not long after the Dissolution of the said last Parliament (*viz.* in the Months of May and June), he the Earl of Strafford did advise the King to go on vigorously in levying Ship-Money, and did procure the Sheriffs of several Counties to be sent for, for not levying the Ship-Money, divers of which were threatened by him, to be sued in the Star-Chamber, and afterwards by his Advice, they were Sued in the Star-Chamber, for not levying the same, and divers of His Majesty's loving Subjects were sent for and Imprisoned by his Advice, for that and other illegal Payments.

And a great Loan of One hundred thousand pounds was demanded of the City of London, and the Lord Mayor, and Sheriffs, and Aldermen of the City, were often sent for by his Advice to the Council-Table, to give an Account of their proceedings in raising the Ship-Money, and furthering of that Loan, and were required to certify the Names of such Inhabitants of the City, as were fit to lend, which they with much humility refusing to do, he the said Earl of Strafford did use these, and the like Speeches; *viz.* "That they deserved to be put to Fine and Ransome, and that no good would be done with them, till an Example were made of them, and that they were laid by the Heels, and some of the Aldermen hanged up."[25]

For the Prosecution: Maynard, Glyn.
Witnesses: Lord Treasurer, Thomas Wiseman, Earl of Berkshire,
                 Sir Henry Garraway—Lord Mayor of London.
For the Defense: Strafford.
Witnesses: none.

On April 7, the twenty-fifth, twenty-sixth, and twenty-seventh articles were charged. The twenty-fifth had two accusations: Strafford was charged with enforcing ship money, and threatening to hang the London aldermen unless they contributed to the king's war chest.

In his reply, the Lieutenant was more concerned to damage the Commons' theory of treason than reply to the specific charges of the article. He said that, though the entire charge were verified against him, by no interpretation of law could it reach high treason. To the argument that his treason was not individual but cumulative, he replied that such talk was to say no treason at all. Indeed, treason is defined in statute law, common law, and precedent, and nowhere is cumulative treason heard of.

To the charge regarding ship money, the accused cited the judgment given in the Hampden case. The judges had supported the king and only later had ship money been declared illegal. Therefore, he had been on the right side of the law at the time of his alleged act.

As to the alleged statement that no good was to be had from London until some of the aldermen were hanged, Strafford denied the words, called no witnesses for himself, reminded the Lords that a single witness could not make faith in a treason charge, and challenged the managers to produce another witness from the large company supposedly present when he said the words.

THE TWENTY-SIXTH ARTICLE

The Charge

That the said Earl by his wicked Counsels, having brought His Majesty into excessive Charge, without any just cause, he did in the month of July last (for the support of the said great Charges) Counsel and approve two dangerous and wicked Projects, *viz.*:

To seize upon the Bullion, and the Money in the Mint.

And to imbase His Majesty's Coin with mixtures of Brass.

And accordingly he procured One hundred and thirty thousand pounds which was then in the Mint, and belonging to divers Merchants, Strangers, and others to be seized on, and stayed to His Majesties use. And when divers Merchants of London, owners of the said Bullion and Money, came to his House, to let him understand the great mischief that course would produce here, and in other parts, and what prejudice it would be to the Kingdom, by discrediting the Mint, and hindring the importation of Bullion: he the said Earl told them, that the City of London dealt undutifully and unthankfully with His Majesty: And that they were more ready to help the Rebels, than to help His Majesty: And that if any hurt came to them, they may thank themselves; and that it was the course of other Princes, to make use of such Monies to serve their occasions.

And when in the same month of July, the Officers of His Majesty's Mint came to him, and give him divers Reasons against the imbasing the said Money he told them that the French King did use to lend Commissaries of Horse, with Commission to search into Men's Estates, and to peruse their Accounts, that so they may know what to levy of them by force, which they did accordingly levy; and turning to the Lord Cottington, then present, said, That this was a point worthy of his Lordship's consideration, meaning this course of the French King, to raise Monies by force, was a point worthy of his Lordship's Consideration.[26]

For the Prosecution: Glyn, Stroude, Maynard.
Witnesses: Sir Ralph Freeman, Thomas Skinner (by deposition), George Henley, Robert Edwards, Anthony Palmer, Henry Gogan, Sir William Parkhurst.
For the Defense: Strafford.
Witnesses: Lord Cottington.

Article twenty-six was legally the strongest charge put forth by the Commons, since seizure of bullion and debasement of the coinage were specifically declared as treason in statute law. However, the managers could not make good their accusation for want of evidence. They brought only witnesses who testified to the unfriendly reception they had received from Strafford when, on behalf of the City, they had gone to him to protest against seizure of London's bullion from the Tower. No evidence whatsoever was brought forward to indicate that Strafford had even the smallest responsibility for the seizure. The debasement of the coinage never took place; hence there was no crime. Moreover, Strafford was not responsible for thinking up the scheme.

THE TWENTY-SEVENTH ARTICLE

The Charge

That in or about the Month of August last, the Earl of Strafford was made Lieutenant-General of all His Majesty's Forces in the North, prepared against the Scots; and being at York, did then in the Month of September, by his own authority, and without any lawful Warrant, impose a Tax on His Majesty's Subjects in the County of York of eight Pence *per diem,* for every Soldier of the Trained-Bands of the County; which Sums of Money he caused to be levied by force. And to the end to compel His Majesty's Subjects, out of Fear or Terror, to yield to the payment of the same; he did Declare, that he would commit them that refused the payment thereof; and the Soldiers should be satisfied out of their Estates; and they that refused it, were in very little better condition, than of High Treason.[27]

For the Prosecution: Maynard, Glyn, Palmer.

Witnesses: Sir Hugh Chomley, Lord Wharton, Sir Henry Chomley, Sir
               William Pennyman, Sir John Hotham, Sir Henry Griffin,
               Sir Philip Stapleton, Robert Strickland, Sir John
               Burroughes, William Dowsen, William Pearson.

For the Defense: Strafford.

Witnesses: Sir Paul Neale, Sir Edward Osborne, Sir William
               Pennyman, Sir William Savile, Sir Edward Rhodes, Sir
               Thomas Danby.

The circumstances of the twenty-seventh article had arisen at the time
of the Second Bishops' War when England and Scotland were under arms.
The Yorkshire soldiers were unpaid, and had petitioned Strafford for a
month's pay. Strafford had persuaded the Yorkshire gentry to support
their trained bands, for which Charles gave him the Garter. But now
Strafford was charged with having levied the money by his own authority,
which was supported by witnesses from Yorkshire.

Strafford answered that the king, upon coming to York, had thought
it necessary to keep the Yorkshire forces mobilized because the Scots
were on the Border. Therefore, the king had directed Strafford to write to
all the freeholders in Yorkshire, to see what they would do for their own
defense. The men of the county had subsequently directed Strafford to
offer the king a month's pay for the soldiers in their names, which he did
accordingly in the presence of forty of them. Strafford's Yorkshire
witnesses testified that the action had been done on grounds of necessity,
that they had given willingly, and that no man had complained thereof
until the trial.

The prisoner concluded that nothing had been done in the Yorkshire
business except upon petition of the county, the king's special command,
the tacit agreement of the Great Council of Peers, and upon necessity for
the defense and safety of the county. Moreover, he cited commissions and
statutes which gave Lord Presidents just such authority as he had
exercised.

When the managers had finished, Glyn told the Peers that the
Commons had not yet decided whether to proceed with the twenty-
eighth article, and therefore they wished to adjourn until tomorrow.
Their lordships concurred and the next day was appointed at eight
o'clock.

Thursday, April 8, 1641

On the following day, the Committee for the charge declared that they were finished with the articles and, for reasons best known to themselves, were content to waive the twenty-eighth. Then Sir Walter Earle rose and said that he wished to revert to article twenty-two once more, for he had some new evidence to bring forth to prove that the accused had intended landing the Irish army in England.[28] Earle's move was against the advice of the more cautious Whitelocke, who now felt that they could make no clear proof of the article. But Earle insisted that he had conclusive proof of Strafford's guilt.

For evidence in support of the accusation, Earle produced Strafford's commission as General of the army, which permitted him to land his troops not only in Scotland but in any part of England or Scotland. This, he concluded, showed the prisoner's intent to bring the Irish army to England.

Strafford's reply was devastating. He showed that his commission was identical in wording to that of the Commander-in-Chief, Earl of Northumberland, and, indeed, with all the other generals of the army. The phrasing of the commission was normal for staff officers and had been routinely drawn up by the Council and sent over to him in Ireland. A mistake of Earle's about the geography of bringing troops to Scotland or England enabled Strafford to add that he "hoped the gentleman knew they came not on foot out of Ireland, but had ships to waft and transport themselves."[29] Earle was hooked and George, Lord Digby, as one narrator put it, had to "handsomely bring him off" by swift intervention. Digby assured the Lords that all their proofs on the article were not yet ready, and "in such a business as the plotting of treason, they must be content sometimes with dark probabilities." Queen Henrietta was present at the time and asked the name of the knight who was saved by Digby. Being told his name, she said, "That dog did bark but not bite, but the rest do bite close."[30]

John Glyn now asked that Lord Strafford without delay should conclude his defense. After the prisoner had finished, the prosecution would make their closing statement and the Lords could be left to decide. The tactic, as foreseen, caught Strafford unprepared. He hesitated, and then argued that "the matter touches me narrowly, even to my life, estate...honor, and posterity," and, therefore, he had no desire "to hurry the business." He appealed to the Lords that he had not been warned that he was to make his final statement that day, and humbly entreated that the "rest of the day might be granted for strengthening myself and recollecting my thoughts and spirits. Tomorrow I shall be ready with my last replies."[31] His request was granted and the Peers adjourned until Friday.

On Friday morning, about eight o'clock, the Lieutenant of the Tower came to Westminster Hall and imparted to the assembly that Strafford was again taken painfully ill, and could not stir out of his bed. Malingering was suspected by the Commons and Glyn protested the "prisoner's wilfulness, not his weakness." Arundel appointed a deputation of four Peers to go to the Tower and learn the cause of his absence. These were satisfied that Strafford was really sick and he was excused.[32] Throughout the months in the Tower, his health had been failing. Meanwhile, the Lords confirmed their earlier decision that Strafford's counsel could speak to points of law, but not fact.

Saturday, April 10, 1641

On Saturday morning, Lord Strafford presented himself at the Bar to make his final plea and closing statement. Expectation hung in the London air. Wedgwood has caught the feeling of the time:

> The spectators in Westminster Hall on the next day, April 10th, were even more tightly packed than they had been on previous occasions. The sustained duel between Strafford and his accusers was by now famous. "I prithee come to the winding up, which I think will be near Easter," wrote Sir Thomas Knyvett to a friend, "tis worth a hundred mile riding to see....Bring your dear lady too for she may be placed to see and hear as much as the men, there being every day a great many." He was not himself much won over to the prisoner, whom the prosecution had "laid open to be so foul a man." But he could not but admire his courage. "I think there was never any man of so unmovable a temper, for in all this time, although his provocations sometimes have been great, yet he hath not discovered the least passion, but when he speakes he doth it with so much bravery and modest courtship of both the Houses, and in such language as begets admiration in all the beholders, especially in a business where he can make good clear work for himself."[33]

As Strafford stood to speak that morning, John Glyn interrupted him, desiring to offer fresh evidence on the fifteenth and twenty-second articles, pertinent to the intended use of the Irish army.[34] The case had been going badly for the managers and they wished to try again to make good their strongest accusation. Strafford could not be permitted to escape them now, or else shortly the tables might be turned: he would be the accuser and they the accused.

Strafford objected to new evidence, arguing that the Commons themselves had closed the case. Glyn answered that it did not become a prisoner on trial to prescribe a method of procedure to the House of Commons of England. Strafford replied that his primary concern was to preserve his life, yet he was willing to allow them to submit new evidence if he were given the same concession. On Lord Newark's motion, the Peers withdrew for two hours and hotly contested the point. They decided in favor of Strafford.[35]

The earl immediately followed up his victory. He said to the Peers that since the Commons had been allowed to pick their special article, a common rule should be enforced for both sides and he too should be allowed to pick freely his own article for reconsideration. Upon this new contestation, the Lords withdrew again. On the face of it, the managers had the strongest procedural argument: they had named their witnesses in their reservation when the article was first argued; Strafford had not; they wished to reconsider but one charge, he several. But sentiment in the Lords had been swinging in favor of the accused, and after two hours' vehement agitation of the point in the upper House, they returned: both sides were allowed to name the articles to which they wished to recur.[36] The Peers had dealt with the emergency as became judges.

The managers were now forced to make a painful choice between dropping their new evidence or else risking retrial of several weak articles, out of which Strafford might now make capital. After a moment's hesitation and a short argument which attempted to force Strafford to name his witnesses, the managers conferred. They did not believe that Strafford had any new evidence and decided to call his bluff. Glyn made his move—saying that the Commons would proceed to their new evidence on article fifteen. Immediately, Strafford replied that he had new proofs on the second, fifth, thirteenth and fifteenth articles, and desired the prosecution to name their witnesses.[37] Instantly, the managers were stopped by a mighty roar from the Commons' benches. Pym's party rose in their places and thundered, "Withdraw! Withdraw!" Their angry cries were answered by the opposition Lords: "Adjourn! Adjourn!" they shouted to the Lord Steward. The discontented enemies of Strafford did not wait for an adjournment. With each man's countenance betraying anger and disappointment, they crowded to the doors. Some drew their swords. The Hall was engulfed in chaos, every opponent of Strafford threatening and arguing. The managers blamed each other. Both Houses left the Hall in confusion, without even setting a day for resuming the trial. Strafford's hope had been realized: The two Houses were at odds with each other. The earl had won his battle. Strafford turned and looked to his king across the frenzied tumult. "They both laughed."[38]

Sir Harry Vane, Sr.

6

Attainder
Strafford Loses the War

The members of the Commons returned to their own House in an angry mood. Among the members who angrily rushed out of Westminster Hall was Sir Arthur Hazelrig, a Leicestershire squire and close supporter of John Pym, whom Clarendon, in one of his sharp vignettes, described as "brother-in-law to the Lord Brooke, and an absurd, bold man, brought up by Mr. Pym, and so employed by that party to make any attempt." On his person that day, Hazelrig carried a draft of a Bill of Attainder. If passed by King, Lords, and Commons, the paper would cut Strafford down by Act of Parliament and sentence him to death for treason.

Ever since the beginning of the impeachment proceedings, Pym and his party had been prepared to change their strategy and switch ground from a legal to a legislative attack. They had begun by working within the classic framework of forensic speaking: accusation and defense as to past action, aiming toward justice and injustice. The English treason laws were, however, written and particular, and by the morning of April 10, it was clear to the Commons that they were failing to prove Strafford guilty by ordinary rules of evidence and the usual definitions of treason.[1]

Back in the House, John Glyn called upon Pym and the younger Vane to disclose to the members the full story of the evidence on article twenty-three. Pym produced the new evidence which they had been unable to submit to the Lords that day. It was actually not new evidence at all. Pym offered his own copy of young Vane's copy of his father's notes which were taken at the Council meeting concerning the Irish army. This was the information supplied by young Vane, upon which the managers had based their questions to elicit the elder Vane's testimony of

Strafford's alleged threat to use the Irish army in England. There was, to be sure, a great deal of copying and recopying of Vane's original notes. But now, Pym had an authentic version of Vane's minutes of the Council meeting, and this version was pressed not only as new evidence, but as if young Vane's copy was the second witness needed in a treason charge. Following the abbreviation "LLT Irn," meaning Lord Lieutenant of Ireland, were the words, "You have an army in Ireland you may employ *here* to reduce *this* Kingdom," exactly as Vane had testified at the trial.

The by-play between the two Vanes and Pym is described by Wedgwood as follows:

> The revelation of this paper and its origins in the House of Commons was followed by espostulations from old Sir Harry Vane, who declared himself astonished and appalled at his son's betrayal, but allowed himself in the end to the soothed by the advice of the Speaker and the filial expressions of young Harry. It is quite possible that this was playacting on old Sir Harry's part. One of the Committee for the Prosecution, George Digby, Lord Bristol's son, evidently thought so. It was now apparent to him, if not to his more innocent colleagues, that old Sir Harry's evidence had been prompted to him word for word from the paper which his son had betrayed to Pym; it was possible even that at some point before the trial old Sir Harry had been allowed to refresh his memory by consulting the copy of his notes. The actual notes, as he admitted, had been burnt, with the King's agreement, shortly before Parliament met.[2]

Digby seems to have been nearly alone in his disillusion. The effect of the copy was to corroborate the evidence which had been given by the Secretary before the Lords. Indeed, the constant reiteration that the copy was additional evidence produced a strong effect upon the Commons, and they now paused to reconsider their position. The "inflexible party" had wearied of the long delay. They regarded the judicial impartiality, which day to day the Lords more and more assumed, to be open treason. The atmosphere was now favorable for the introduction of the long-ready Bill of Attainder.

For many reasons the Commons now shifted their strategic plan. First, under their original strategy, they were losing because the law was against them. Second, on a Bill of Attainder, Pym could submit his new evidence on article twenty-three without giving Strafford a chance to produce any additional evidence. Third, the bill could be framed so as to profess to punish the accused because he had broken a law which should have been on the books, instead of twisting an old law to make it mean something which it did not. Fourth, Strafford and his counsel would be unable to answer the bill in court, it being legislative not judicial. Fifth, the bill went along with the feelings against the Peers, which was presently strong in Commons. The Commons would no longer be Strafford's mere accusers. They would become his judges, and force the Peers either to pass a sentence pronounced by the Commons or to risk an open, extremely dangerous breach with the powerful lower House. Sixth, a bill would permit the Peers to vote for Strafford's attainder if they wished him out of the way, without accepting the case against him as legally proved. "It was an ingenious method of meeting the scruples of those who, though politically opposed to the accused, had been troubled by the weakness of the actual charges against him."[3] In short, the Commons had changed their basic strategy from legal-forensic to deliberative-political. The Bill of Attainder was to be fitted out with many legal trappings, but underneath it all, the new approach fitted precisely into the classic framework of deliberative speaking: exhortation regarding future action and based upon the ends of political expediency or inexpediency.

A Bill of Attainder was accordingly brought in. It was read once before the House adjourned. With that Saturday's work, the third week of the great trial was brought to a close.

On Monday morning, if the hotheads among the Commons could have had their way, the bill would have been rushed through a second reading. But Pym was not to be hurried out of his stride. There was a certain amount of decency to be preserved in the matter. A precipitate abandonment of the impeachment proceedings would have been a gross error in tactics, driving the wedge deeper between Commons and Lords. The Peers, already unconvinced of the merits of the legal case against Strafford, could not be driven too far, too fast. Accordingly, the managers held a conference that Monday morning with the Lords, at which Vane's notes were read. John Pym had now gained the effect which Strafford had ruined on Saturday: the alleged new evidence was laid before their lordships without allowing the prisoner to bring his new evidence or reopening any of the articles. The Commons went even further: They said that the paper implicated Laud and Cottington in Strafford's illegal designs. Such a veiled threat could only have been intended to intimidate the indomitable Cottington, as well as Strafford's and Charles' other friends.

The sight of that portion of Vane's notes which related to Strafford's case had its desired effect on many of the Lords. Others, however, were angered by the presumption of the Commons to bring in the verdict themselves by Bill of Attainder. Lord Savile argued angrily at the conference:

> It is an unnatural motion for the head to be governed by the tail. We hate rebellion as much as treason. We will never suffer ourselves to be suppressed by a popular faction.[4]

Such strong words from Strafford's oldest enemy made Pym realize that he must handle gingerly the sensibilities of the Lords. A fissure had broken between the two Houses and Pym had to prevent its becoming an unbridgeable chasm. Accordingly, he held the House of Commons in hand and slowed down the Bill of Attainder. The Peers shall have their trial. They shall hear Strafford's final pleas. Nevertheless, John Pym and his party had no intention of letting the Peers give the final verdict.

As of Tuesday, April 13, the impeachment trial of Strafford was to continue, despite the developing new strategy in the House of Commons. Strafford was brought to the Hall for his final defense, as if nothing extraordinary had occurred in the meantime. This Tuesday was the prisoner's most important day in court. Whether Strafford was, in the end, to be proceeded against by impeachment or by attainder, the Lords would be strongly affected for or against him by his final argument. Pym had tried to prevent Strafford's closing statement from being heard, and failed.

On the morning of April 13, Lord Strafford, having heard of the pending Bill

> walked from the river to Westminster Hall to make his last speech. He was a tragic figure, tall, gaunt, with bowed shoulders, his pale face lined with pain and fatigue, but in the midst of the whispering, excited crowd, alone unmoved.[5]

In this dark time, Strafford rose to his greatest height. His troubled, ill-starred administration had shown him in many wrong attitudes, but at the end he was to play the indisputable role of the champion of rule by law. London lay gripped under the tense drama of the proceedings. For three weeks, affairs had come to a halt in the City while all awaited the outcome. Now the end was finally near.

The more detail in which this Tuesday has been described, the greater is the sense of drama. The Earl of Strafford, basing himself upon the law and constitution which he had strained and exploited in his years of power, confronted his enemies with an unbreakable defense.

"My Lords," Lord Strafford began. He desired first to state clearly the exact charge against him:

> My Lords, this day I stand before you charged with high treason. The burden of the charge is heavy, yet far the more so because it hath borrowed the authority of the House of Commons. If *they* were not interested, I might expect a no less easy, than I do a safe issue. But let neither my weakness plead my innocence, nor their power my guilt. If your Lordships will conceive of my defenses as they are in themselves, without reference to either party...I hope to go hence as clearly justified by you, as I now am—in the testimony of a good conscience—by myself.[6]

Thus he stated the hidden and unspeakable issue. The House of Commons had shifted ground on both the accused and the Lords, and now presumed to judge the cause themselves by attainder. Strafford stongly denied the charge of treason. He submitted himself willingly and without fear to the judgment of his Peers. He then quietly pointed out to the Lords that their privileges were being usurped by the Commons and their bill, that they should reassert their right to judge, and maintain their dignities:

> You, and you only are my judges. Under favor, none of the Commons are my Peers, nor can they be my judges. I shall ever celebrate the providence and wisdom of your noble ancestors, who have put the keys of life and death, so far as concerns you and your posterity, into your own hands. None but your own selves, my Lords, know the rate of your noble blood; none but yourselves must hold the balance in disposing of the same.[7]

Treason, said the accused, was of two distinct kinds: statute treason and constructive treason, "this direct, that consecutive; this individual, that accumulative; this in itself, that by way of construction." Such a statement of the charge and subsequent classification of treason, as charged, into the two types put forth by the Commons in the Articles of Accusation, gave Strafford a two-fold point of departure, from which to develop his summation without confusing the development of his arguments.[8] Strafford momentarily set aside constructive treason, and defended himself against all the charges which could convict him of treason under the law. Strafford's complicated discussion of fine points can be briefed and schematized as follows.

Strafford consolidated the charges as two main types of treason: statutory and constructive.

I. Statute Treason Only the 15th, 23rd, and 27th Articles apply here.

A. 15th Article.
Charge of levying war.

Quick summary of replies.
Almost same points made as before.

B. 23rd Article.
Use of Irish army in England.
Charge warranted by Sir Harry Vane's test-imony. Important art-icle; hence Strafford carefully replied.

Offered four reasons to nullify Vane:
1. Single testimony can't convict in treason trial.
2. Vane hesitant and dubious.
3. Entire Council of Eight disclaim Vane's words.
4. Individual witnesses disprove Vane.

C. 27th Article.
Making war on subjects.

Quick summary of replies.
Almost same points made as before.
Little new offered.

II. Constructive Treason So far, Strafford had appealed directly to their lordships' reason and sense of justice. Now, as he began to defend himself against the Commons' theory of cumulative treason, he paused to defend his own theory of government and vindicate the monarchy:

> I have ever admired the wisdom of our ancestors, who have so fixed the pillars of this monarchy that each of them deeps due measure and proportion with another, and have so handsomely tied up the nerves and sinews of the State that the straining of one may bring damage and sorrow to the whole. The prerogative of the Crown and the propriety of the Subject have such mutual relations that this [one] took protection from that, that foundation and nourishment from this. And, as on the lute, if anything be too high or too low wound up, you have lost the harmony; so here the excess of a

prerogative is oppression; of a pretended liberty in the subject, disorder and anarchy. The Prerogative must be used as God doth his omnipotence, at extraordinary occasions; the laws...must have place at all other times, and yet there must be a prerogative if there must be extraordinary occasions. The propriety of the subject is ever to be maintained if it go in equal pace with this; they are fellows and companions that have been ever, must be inseparable in a well-governed Kingdom; and no way so fitting to nourish both as the frequent use of Parliaments. By this a commerce and acquaintance is kept between the King and the subject. This thought has gone along with me these fourteen years of my public employment, and shall, God willing, to my grave. God, his Majesty, and my own conscience, yea all who have been accessory to my most inward thoughts and opinions can bear witness. I ever did inculcate this: the happiness of a Kingdom consists in the just poise of the King's prerogative and the subject's liberty and that things should never be well till these went hand in hand together.

Under the theory of constructive treason, the accused was charged with *words, counsels,* and *actions* in England and Ireland, which, taken together, were alleged in the mass to total high treason. Rearranging the order of charges for clarity in this relation, the following heads of articles would make treason of words:[9]

A. *Article 3*
    Ireland a conquered nation.
    King may do what he pleases
    there.

B. *Article 4*
    Took powers above the law;
    e.g. oppression of Cork.

C. *Article 2*
    King's little finger
    heavier than loins of law.

D. *Article 22*
    Irish army to England.
    King may do what he
    pleases.

Strafford made a clever tactical arrangement here. Moved from easily refuted article to more difficult articles and back to an easy article. By starting with mere words, and collecting all "word" articles together, he seemed to be asking, "Is treason to be made of words? Is a man to die for words spoken in temper?

Under each article, he proceeded as he had done during the trial, except he was now brief and summarized his

E. *Article 23*
"You have an army in
Ireland which you may
use."

F. *Article 27*
Tax in Yorkshire.

G. *Article 26*
Seize mint. Debase
coinage.

H. *Article 25*
Hang London Aldermen.

contradiction of the Commons'
arguments of fact:
False. Single witness.
Misrepresentation. Libel.
Prejudice. Uttered in private to friends. Words uttered in anger. Was obliged to
speak at King's Council
Board. King's Counsel should
be kept secret. Taken out of
context. Those words were
true, and the Commons know it.
A thousand such expressions
would not make one misdemean-
or, let alone a felony.

The articles also charged *actions* taken by the accused either in
England or Ireland, either before or after the war with the Scots. Again
rearranging the order of charges for clarity and logical sequence, the
following heads of articles would make for treason of actions: [10]

A. *Article 5*
Oppression of Mountnorris.

B. *Article 6*
Case of Mountnorris
vs. Rollston.

C. *Article 7*
Oppressed Lady Hibbots.

D. *Article 9*
General Warrants.

E. *Article 10*
Enriched self from Customs.

F. *Article 11*
waived.

Here the accused went through
the various acts charged to
him in the order shown. Here
the order appeared not significant to him, since he
followed the numerical order
of the Managers. This was a
slight tactical error for on
some he stood stronger in the
law than upon others. He added
little that was new, but repeated—and summarized the
heads of what had been spoken
by him before.
    He spoke lucidly, without
extensive notes, running over
one by one his answers to every article of the charge. He
was quiet and restrained, not

G. *Article 12*
   Monopoly on tobacco.

H. *Article 13*
   Monopoly on flax.

I. *Article 14*
   waived.

J. *Article 16*
   No appeal from Ireland
   to England.

K. *Article 17 & 18*
   waived.

L. *Article 19*
   Tendered illegal oath
   to Scots.

M.*Article 20*
   Incendiary in Scots war.

N. *Article 21*
   Broke Parliaments.

O. *Article 24*
   King might use Prerogative
   to rule.

P. *Article 27*
   Tax in Yorkshire.

Q. *Article 28*
   waived.

vehement or emotional. He held his audience by his incisive logic and occasional stroke of irony. For more than two hours, he worked on the 28 articles. Contemporary spectators report that hardly a soul stirred, but followed him carefully. From a critical standpoint, *this part of his final statement must be judged a superior piece of forensic and discourse for its precise and thorough discussion of single points.*

Under each article, he proceeded as he had done during the trial. He defended on the basis of: Legality of his action. Commissions given to Lord Lieutenant by Privy Council. Warrants of the king. Express written commands of the king.

So far in his closing statement, Strafford had stood four-square on English law. Such was the ground he had marked out for his defense and had labored for three exhausting weeks to capture and hold. But the

Commons had suddenly changed their strategy and now maneuvered to outflank Strafford's nearly impregnable first line of defense. A Bill of Attainder needed no legal justification, except for window dressing; the decision was political.

Up to this point in the trial, the prisoner had hardly mentioned the political and constitutional implications of his trial. To him the entire procedure was a monstrous illegality. He eyed his pursuers with unaffected scorn. He had stubbornly refused to acknowledge the basis of their legal argument. Suddenly, he stared defeat in the face. His ruin was to be decreed by a simple ordinance.

The game had changed. No longer was Strafford's rhetorical purpose to discredit the Country party, to bring Lords and Commons into collision, and to retrieve the ground lost since Ripon, to vindicate his king. It was clearly his life that was to be won or lost. The attainder had been a well-kept secret. It had been sprung on Monday, giving Strafford a scant day to rethink his strategy of defense, but now he must extend breastworks beyond that Maginot Line to protect against the Commons' attempt to bypass it completely. He had to work quickly because, if they caught him without either the advantage of a secure defensive position or the impulsion of an attack, he would be thrown into disorder and defeat.

At last, he concluded his summation of the twenty-eight articles: "I hope I am clear before your lordships," he concluded, "for in good faith, I am clear in my own poor judgment." Now, with the force and passion he had so far held back, he turned to warn the Peers against creating a new and unheard of treason:

My Lords, you see what has been alleged for this constructive, or, rather, *de*structive treason. For my part, I have not the judgment to conceive, that such treason is agreeable to the fundamental grounds either of reason or of law. Not of reason, for how can that be treason in the lump or mass, which is not so in any of its parts; or how can that make a thing treasonable which is not so in *itself*? Not of law, since neither statute, common law, nor practice hath from the beginning of the government ever mentioned such a thing.

It is hard my Lords, to be questioned upon a law which can not be shown! Where hath this fire lain hid for so many hundred years, without smoke to discover it, till it thus bursts forth to consume me and my children? Mr. Lords, do we not live under laws? And must we be punished by laws before they are made? Far better were it to live by no laws at all; but to be governed by those characters of virtue and discretion, which Nature hath stamped upon us, than to put this necessity of divination upon a man, and to accuse him of a breach of law before it is a law at all.

Let the legislators make laws for all to know and to obey, rather than strike down a man after the fact:

If a waterman upon the Thames split his boat by grating upon an anchor, and the same have no buoy appended to it, the owner of the anchor is to pay the loss; but if a buoy be set there, every man passeth upon his own peril. Now where is the mark, where is the token set upon the crime, to declare it to be high treason?

Let the Peers beware, lest they catch themselves in the always hidden snare of cumulative treason. Let their lordships understand that the very realm stands now in danger:

My lords, be pleased to give that regard to the Peerage of England as never to expose yourselves to such moot points, such constructive interpretations of law. If there must be a trial of wits, let the subject matter be something else than the lives and honor of peers! It will be wisdom for yourselves and your posterity to cast into the fire these bloody and mysterious volumes of constructive and arbitrary treason, as the primitive Christians did their books of curious arts; and betake yourselves to the plain letter of the law and statute, which telleth what is and what is not treason, without being ambitious to be more learned in the art of killing than our forefathers. These gentlemen tell us that they speak in defense of the Commonwealth against my arbitrary laws. Give me leave to say it, *I speak in defense of the Commonwealth against their arbitrary treason!*

The earl marked how high above their station the Commons now dared to reach. If he fell, they would reach as high again; perhaps higher:

It is now full two hundred and forty years since any man was touched for this alleged crime to this height before myself. Let us not awaken those sleeping lions to our destruction by taking up a few musty records that have lain by the walls for so many ages, forgotten or neglected.

My Lords, what is my present misfortune may be forever yours! It is not the smallest part of my grief that not the crime of treason, but my other sins, which are exceeding many, have brought me to this bar; and, except your Lordships' wisdom provide against it, the shedding of my blood may make way for the tracing out of yours. *You, your estates, your posterity, lie at the stake.*

Now, Strafford had come to his conclusion. The peroration of this famous speech is its most famous part. The spectators leaned forward with expectation as Strafford apologized for troubling the company for so long:

> I have now troubled your Lordships a great deal longer than I should have done. For my poor self, if it were not for your Lordships' interest, and were it not for the interest of those pledges [children] that a saint in Heaven left me, I would be loth my Lords...

Strafford wept. So far he had not faltered. But now at the mention of his earlier days and of his late wife and his children, Strafford faltered and wept. The once proud earl stood amid the wreck of his fortunes. His king looked on from his box, unable to halt the proceedings. For fourteen years, Strafford had stood proud and imperious at the head of affairs. During the past eighteen days, he had stood alone against the finest legal talent in England, backed up by the combined weight of the Commons of England. Now, the proud earl broke momentarily under the immense strain. The effect upon the entire assembled company was electric, as Manager Whitelocke himself tells us:

> Certainly never any man acted such a part, in such a theatre, with more wisdom, constancy and eloquency, with greater reason, judgment, and temper and with a better grace in all his words and gestures, than this great and excellent person did; and he moved the hearts of all his auditors, some few excepted, to remorse and pity.[11]

Strafford pulled himself quickly together and went on:

> Were it not for the interest of those pledges that a saint in Heaven left me, I would be loth my Lords—I would be loth my Lords to take the pains to keep up this ruinous cottage of mine. It is loaded with such infirmities, that in truth I have no great pleasure to carry it about with me any longer. Nor could I ever leave it at a fitter time than this, when I hope that the better part of the world would perhaps think that by my misfortunes I had given a testimony of my

integrity to my God, my King, and my Country.

I thank God that I count not the afflictions of the present life to be compared to that glory which is to be revealed in the time to come.

My Lords! my Lords! my Lords! something more I had intended to say, but my voice and my spirit fail me....

Again the strong man faltered. He could not go on. "My Lords, My *Lords, My Lords,* something more I had intended to say, but my voice and spirit fail me"—even in cold print there is something inexpressibly moving about this, and we can only imagine its effect on that crowded audience whose feelings had been already worked up to a high pitch. The critic cannot but agree with Goodrich that: "There are few passages of equal tenderness and power in the whole range of English eloquence."

My Lords, my Lords, my Lords, something more I had intended to say, but my voice and my spirit fail me. Only I do in all humility and submission cast myself down at your Lordships' feet, and desire that I may be a beacon to keep you from shipwreck. Do not put such rocks in your own way, which no prudence, no circumstances, no circumspection can eschew or satisfy, but by your utter ruin.

And so, my Lords, even so, with all tranquility of mind, I submit myself to your decision. And whether your judgment in my case—I wish it were not the case of you all—be for life or for death, it shall be rightous in my eyes,

> *Te Deum Laudamus, Te Dominum Confitemur.*

John Glyn and John Pym were to make the final argument for the prosecution. After an hour's interval, during which he revised his notes, Glyn rose to reply.[12] He reminded the Lords that the earl was charged with an intent to subvert the fundamental laws of the kingdom. The prisoner, Glyn urged, was not charged with a number of separate acts, but with one settled purpose to overthrow the law. The separate acts were but cited in order so as to reveal the hidden purpose, a clearly treasonous purpose. Glyn then ran over the articles, following the order set by Strafford's final pleas. He summarized the evidence presented by the prosecution, and disparaged the evidence of the defense. Glyn's strongest point was his refutation of Strafford's claim that the royal assumption of extraordinary powers was justified upon the warrant of extraordinary emergencies and necessities. He argued that the government had been conducted for years on the plea of special necessity:

My Lords, for many years past, your Lordships know that an evil spirit hath moved among us, which in truth hath been made the author and ground of all our distractions; and that is necessity and danger. This was the bulwark and the battery that serves to defend all exorbitant actions; the ground and foundation of this great invasion of our liberties and estates, the judgment in the Ship Money; and the ground of the counsel given of late to do anything, and to persuade the King that he was absolved from all rules of government.[13]

He derisively belittled Strafford's concern for the political and constitutional positon of the Peerage:

My Lords, throughout the passages of his discourse, he insinuates...with the Peers of the Realm, magnifying them almost to idolatry. And yet, my Lords, when he was in his Kingdom in Ireland, and had power over them, what respect showed he then to the Peers of the Kingdom when he judged some to death, trampled upon others in misery, committed them to prison, and seized on their estates? Where then was the Peerage he now magnifies?[14]

In conclusion, Glyn argued that Strafford should die. He advanced, however, a political, not a legal warrant: The prisoner must be put out of the way for the safety of the state, and, by implication, for the safety of some of their lordships. This was the great fear of the Commons: what Strafford would do if he were acquitted:

My Lords, if this lion . . . now that he is chained and muzzled under the restraint of high treason, will here take...this language and express this malignity, then how would he do if he were unchained? How would he devour? How would he destroy?

The Commons with much pains and diligence, and to their great expense, have discovered the Jonas who is the occasion of this tempest.

They have...to cast him out of the ship, and allay this tempest.

They expect, and are confident your Lordships will perfect the work—and that with expedition—lest with the continuance of the storm, both ship and tackling and mariners, both Church and Commonwealth, be ruined and destroyed.[15]

Pym followed Glyn. It was fitting that the final speech for the House of Commons should be delivered by John Pym. More than any other, Pym was the man who had brought Strafford to the Bar. More than any other, upon this man's shoulders was falling the mantle of leadership in the struggle with the crown. And more than most others, he had much to fear if Strafford were not convicted. In his speech, Pym assumed that the managers had sufficiently proved the accused's attempt to substitute arbitrary will for law and to subvert the fundamental laws of the country, and therefore took the burden "of showing the quality of the offense, how heinous it is in nature, how mischievous in the effect of it." Pym proposed to indicate the quality of Strafford's acts by examining them in relation to "that universal, that supreme law: *Salus Populi.*" He described the quality of the earl's actions as follows:[16]

1. His is an offence comprehending all other offences; here you shall find several treasons, murders, rapines, oppressions and perjuries. . . .

2. Arbitrary power is dangerous to the King's person, and dangerous to his Crown....

3. The subversion of the laws...is prejudicial to his Majesty in his honor, profit, and greatness. . . .

4. Such arbitrary courses exhaust the people and disable them, when there shall be occasion, to give such plentiful supplies as otherwise they would do....

5. Arbitrary and tyrannical power...is inconsistent with the peace, the wealth, the prosperity of the Kingdom. . . .

Those that live so much under the whip and the pillory and such servile engines as were frequently used by the Earl of Strafford, they may have the dregs of valor, sullenness, and stubbornness, which may make them prone to mutinies and discontents; but those noble and gallant affections, which put men to brave designs and attempts for the preservation or enlargement of a Kingdom, they are hardly capable of.

Shall it be treason to debase the King's coin, though but a piece of twelve or six pence, and must it not needs be the effect of a greater treason to embase the spirits of his subjects, and to set a stamp and character of servitude upon them, whereby they shall be disabled to do anything for the service of the King and Commonwealth?...

6. The exercise of this arbitrary government in times of sudden danger, by the invasion of an enemy, will disable his Majesty to preserve himself and his subjects from that danger....

7. This crime of subverting the laws, and introducing an arbitrary and tyrannical government is contrary to the pact and covenant

betwixt the King and his people....

8. It is an offence that is contrary to the end of government. The end of government was to prevent oppressions, to limit and restrain the excessive power and violence of great men, to open the passages of justice, with indifferency towards all....

9. A last consideration is the vanity and absurdity of those excuses which the Earl made for himself....

With a firm hand, Pym painted his own theory of government and the constitution, and a picture of the misery which would follow when arbitrary rule is substituted for the liberty of the subject. The king could not act outside the nation as if he were separate from it:

> The King and his people are obliged to one another in the nearest relations. He is a father, and a child is called in law *pars patris*. He is the husband of the Commonwealth; they have the same interests; they are inseparable in their condition, be it good or evil. There is such an incorporation as cannot be dissolved without the destruction of both.[17]

To have done his best to break up this harmonious unity was Strafford's crime, and for this he should be punished. Pym concluded:

> Nothing can be more equal than that he should perish by the justice of the law which he would have subverted; neither will this be a new way of blood. There are marks enough to trace this law to the very original of this Kingdom; and if it hath not been put in execution, as he allegeth, this 240 years, it was not for want of law, but all that time hath not bred a man bold enough to commit such crimes as these, which is a circumstance much aggravating his offence, and making him no whit less liable to punishment, because he is the only man that, in so long a time, had ventured upon such a treason as this.[18]

The House of Commons, in fact, had impeached and tried a system of government. Through Strafford, they were attacking the Tudor constitution as practiced by James I and Charles I. Pym's exposition on government was directed as much to the king, who was present, as to the Peers. "I believe," wrote the Covenanter Baillie, "the King never heard a lecture of so free language against his idolized Prerogative."[19]

Neither did Pym forget immediate business. He was a strong, persuasive speaker, in a sharp, businesslike style. He followed his political theorizing with a sharp, cutting denial of all of Strafford's defense. His total speech was brief. Even so, just before the end, his memory failed him. He lost the thread, wavered into silence, and had to pull out his notes; from which, after a long pause, he started to read, giving away that his effort had been memorized, carefully thought out and prepared for delivery no matter what answer was given by Strafford. Again, the difference between the natural fighter and the ingenious manager of men. The contrast between Pym speaking from notes, and Strafford who spoke from a brief outline as the moment carried his thought, is striking.[20] When John Pym had finished, the Peers adjourned for the day.

On April 14, the Bill of Attainder was read in the Commons for the second time. Apparently, Strafford's final speech had been very effective, while the managers had fared badly, and the aim now was to bring pressure upon the Lords. Yet, the debate on the bill revealed that even the Commons were not unanimous against Strafford.[21] There was a strong minority which urged again and again every point which had been made by the earl himself. One member asked how Strafford's acts could amount to treason. Another wanted to know what real proof there was that the accused intended to land the Irish army in England. The poet Waller thrust to the heart of the question when he asked for an enumeration of the fundamental laws of the kingdom, a question which brought from Maynard the retort that if he did not know them, then he had no business to sit in the House. Despite the unsatisfied minority, the House resolved that Strafford had endeavored to subvert the fundamental laws of the kingdom. This measure was nothing less than a declaration that they set no value upon the independent, judicial judgment of the House of Lords upon Strafford's cause.

It was close fighting now between Strafford and Pym, and the Commons were now seriously to offend the Peers. The day had been appointed to hear the arguments of counsel on both sides on the legal questions arising from the evidence and charges. However, the Commons sent a message to the upper House, asking the Lords to postpone the hearing of counsel and informing them that the Commons were resolved to proceed by Bill of Attainder.[22] The Lords at once took fire and threw back this insult in the faces of the Commoners. Their lordships would proceed with the trial, hear counsel, and deliver their judgment upon the Earl of Strafford. The Commons, for their part, stubbornly declared their inflexible resolve to go on with their bill.[23]

On the morning of April 15th, the House of Lords were inflexibly
resolved to:

> ...Go down to West. Hall to the trial of E. of S. to hear the E's
> counsel speake in matters of law, admitting the fact to be proved,
> yet by the law [how far] it is not treason.[24]

The hotheads among the Commons were just as determined to go by
their bill and insisted that, since it was legislative matter, they could now
reopen the articles to offer new evidence and arguments without the earl
being allowed to reply or reopen his articles.

It was on crucial occasions that the weight of John Hampden, his
character and prestige, was felt. This man, mysterious and legendary to
our own time, seldom rose to speak and he never spoke at length. Now he
came to the support of the Lords and proposed a compromise to prevent,
temporarily at least, the breach between the Houses which was Strafford's
greatest hope. Let the managers, he said, be in their places to argue only
the question of law. Pym seconded him vehemently. The House was
convinced to attend, but only unofficially as a committee-of-the-whole
and without replying to the arguments of Strafford's counsel. The details
of this arrangement were worked out by Lords Bristol and Bath on the
15th and 16th during several conferences with representatives of the
Commons.[25]

The legal argument on behalf of Strafford was duly heard on April 17.
Richard Lane was as cool a head as Strafford and when they appeared in
Westminister Hall, both of them seemed confident. Strafford, contrary to
his habitual expression, looked "well and cheerful." Lane spoke briefly
and to the point with extreme clarity.[26] He first stated that the Treason
Law of England was fixed under a single statute, the *25th of Edward III*.
The statute read:

> That if any man shall intend the death of the King, his Queen, their
> children; kill the Chancellor or judge upon the bench; imbase the
> King's coin or counterfeit the broad seal, . . . he shall be convicted
> and punished as a traitor.[27]

This was a declarative law, Lane said, and it allowed no arguments of
equity or extension, but had to be taken by the letter. It was a penal law,
and such law can admit of no extension or inference. All legal practice,
time out of mind, restricts declarative and penal laws to their precise

letter. According to the law, the Earl of Strafford was not guilty of treason.

Next, Lane turned to a later amendment to the law of Edward III, upon which the Commons had rested most of their case. In a later proviso to the treason law, it had been further provided that, in regard to the acts of a specific person, the King and Parliament should have power to determine whether these acts were treasonable or not.[28] To this important point, Lane simply stated that the proviso proved to be a sword hanging over every man's head; hence it had been *repealed* by the *1st of Henry IV,*[29] and just to make sure, the *1st of Queen Mary* had declared that:

> No man shall be punished in life or estate as a traitor but for the crime contained in the Statute *25 Edw. 3.*

And, as Lane said, "The proviso was omitted since it had been repealed by the 1st of Hen IV."[30]

Lane's legal argument was decisive. From this moment on, the greatest lawyers in the House of Commons itself—Selden, Holborne, and Bridgeman—were against Strafford's conviction.

When Lane was finished, the Recorder of London, Thomas Gardiner rose and declared that to speak now would be prejudicial to Strafford, because a legal argument at this time would have to assume that the acts were done, which was not proved. Therefore, he said, the Lords should declare which of Strafford's alleged acts were done and which were not. Then he could tell their lordships whether these acts were treason or not.[31] Upon the conclusion of the arguments of Strafford's counsel, the court was adjourned while the Lords considered the case.

A Sunday again intervened. Strafford's mood at this stage seemed assured and calm. He wrote to reassure his eldest daughter, "Your father as you desired hath been heard to speak for himself now these three weeks together." It was a letter full of paternal reassurance which promised her and the family a happy reunion and a quiet life, albeit with reduced fortunes for the future. Wedgwood believes that Strafford was genuinely hopeful of his chances; she wrote, "Nan was in her fourteenth year and her father was unlikely to write anything that would needlessly alarm her, but it seems probable that his letter reflected genuine optimism. He was never good at hiding his feelings."[32] The letter survived the centuries with Anne Wentworth's words written upon it: "This was the last letter I had from my Lord."

On the nineteenth, the bill was read for a third time in the Commons. The members argued over the guilt of the accused. Had Strafford committed treason? Assuming that the key articles were proved, did these acts make him a traitor? If he were guilty of the acts, was he guilty of definite treason, or else of subverting the laws? Was subverting the laws a kind of treason?

The most famous of the lawyers in the House, especially Selden and Holborne, battled hard against the bill. They protested that according to no law had Strafford committed treason. He must, therefore, be acquitted. A strong ally to Pym was Lord Falkland:

> Falkland was son and heir of that Deputy of Ireland whom Strafford had succeeded and whom he had never treated even with tact, let alone with generosity. Young Falkland was so well known for the nobility of his nature that no one could or would credit him with any but the purest motives. He was genuinely concerned about the justice of the matter, and more especially the meaning of the term "cumulative treason". His argument was simple and persuasive: "how many hairs' breadths make a tall man and how many make a little man, no man can well say; yet we know a tall man when we see him from a low man. So 'tis in this: how many illegal acts makes a treason is not certainly well known, but we well know it when we see it."[33]

Falkland's honest patriotism and desire for justice provided potent support for Pym. In a second speech, he argued that "in equity, Strafford deserved to die." At this, the lawyer with the highest reputation in the House of Commons on questions of jurisprudence came out for Strafford. John Selden was a life-long opponent of the Court and had supported Parliament on nearly every issue through the years. But on this point, he refused to concede that Strafford had committed treason, and argued that decisions of equity never involved a death sentence. Despite Selden's argument and reputation, the Commons resolved that to subvert the fundamental laws was to commit treason.[34]

On April 20, the Commons debated their bill further. Strafford's opponents insisted that all twenty-eight articles had been fully proved. On the 21st, the House again debated the bill. Only 263 members out of 500 were present that day, and many of those attending desired to withdraw before the final vote. There had been dangerous looking crowds in the streets all over the city, and large numbers of doubtful members or supporters of the king and Strafford had stayed away. The kitchen was getting hot, but it was the waverers and Strafford's supporters who were getting out to avoid the heat, not Pym's party. John Pym had the door locked and the key brought to Mr. Speaker; no one could leave. The additions and amendments were read twice and the House moved to a vote.

Suddenly, as the bill was being read for the last time, when excitement was at its height, opposition to it arose from a completely unexpected quarter. One of the very managers of the prosecution now turned against the bill. George, Lord Digby rose to speak of his disgust and disillusion with the methods of the House. He said that all along he had faithfully worked as a member of the committee for the prosecution. He still believed that Strafford "was the grand apostate to the Commonwealth who must not expect to be pardoned in the world." But the case against Strafford was not proved. Mr. Pym, he said, had promised more and conclusive proof of Vane's testimony. But when the vaunted evidence was produced, it was simply Vane's testimony in another form and the witness remained the only man present at the Council who had heard the alleged offer to bring the Irish army to England.[35]

George Digby was a brave man for he went further. He dared to reveal the circumstances under which the managers had thrice examined Vane before the trial. The first time, when examined about the words, Vane had said: "I cannot charge him with that."[36] Some days later, Vane was examined a second time and pressed to the part concerning the Irish army, to which he replied that he "could say nothing to that."[37] Having examined Vane twice on the article, Lord Digby thought:

> We had done with him until weeks after—my Lord of Northumberland and all others of the Junto denying to have heard anything concerning those words of reducing England by the Irish army—it was thought fit to examine the secretary once more. And then he deposed these words to have been spoken by the Earl of Strafford to his majesty: "You have an army in Ireland, which you may employ here to reduce (or some word to that sense) this Kingdom." Mr. Speaker, these are the circumstances which I confess with my conscience thrust quite out of doors that grand article of our charge concerning his desperate advice to the King of employing the Irish army here.[38]

Lord Digby now implored the House to consider whether their proceedings with a bill were justice or murder:

> I do not say but the things charged may justly direct us to enact that they shall be treason for the *future*. But God keep me from giving judgment of death on any man...*a posteriori*. Let the mark be set on the door where the plague is, and then let him that will enter, die.
>
> I know, Mr. Speaker, there is in Parliament a double power of life and death by Bill: a judicial power, and a legislative. The measure of the one is what is legally just; of the other what is...politically fit for the good and preservation of the whole. But these two...are not to be confounded in judgment. We must not piece out want of legality with matter of convenience, nor the defailance of prudential fitness with a pretence of legal justice.[39]

Digby concluded with an appeal for a decision based on impartial justice under the law:

> Let every man lay his hand upon his own heart, and seriously consider what we are going to do with a breath: *either justice or murder*—justice on the one side, or murder, heightened and aggravated to its supremest extent, on the other! For, as the casuists say, He who lies with his sister commits incest; but he that marries his sister, sins higher, by applying God's ordinance to his crime; so, doubtless, he that commits murder with the sword of justice, heightens the crime to the utmost....
>
> Let every man purge his heart of all passions. I know this great and wise body politic can have none; but I speak to individuals from the weakness which I find in myself. Away with personal animosities! Away with all flatteries to the people, in being the sharper against him because he is odious to them! Away with all fears, lest by sparing his blood they may be incensed! Away with all such considerations, as that it is not fit for a Parliament that one accused by it of treason, should escape with life! Let not former vehemence of any against him, nor fear from thence that he can not be safe while that man lives, be an ingredient in the sentence of any one of us.
>
> Of all these corruptives of judgment, Mr. Speaker, I do, before God, discharge myself to the utmost of my power; and do now, with a clear conscience, wash my hands of this man's blood by this solemn protestation, *that my vote goes not to the taking of the Earl of Strafford's life.*[40]

When Digby was finished, the member for Windsor supported him with a vigorous assertion that the Commons were about to "commit murder with the sword of justice." These were brave sentiments but the Commons were not to be put off any longer. The waverers had stayed away and the king's friends had Pym's threatened investigation of ship money levies hanging over them. The majority of those present were for the bill. The member for Windsor was later rewarded with expulsion from the House, while Digby saw the House order a copy of his speech to be burned in public by the common executioner.

The bill was put to a vote. Two hundred and forty voted for the bill, fifty-nine against. Amid the cheers of a thin House, Pym carried the bill to the House of Lords. He declared that the lower house would justify their action whenever their lordships appointed.[41]

Were the Commons against Strafford by a majority of over 3 to 1? The evidence is scanty, but there are indications that they were not. From many examples, Wedgwood cites one that is particularly striking:

> As the Commons dispersed, an agitated gentleman clutched at the arm of one of Strafford's friends. The Bill would be thrown out in the Lords, he explained breathlessly; would he please tell my Lord of Strafford, that a great many gentlemen could not help themselves for fear of Mr. Pym, but the Bill would get no further. They would not have voted for it, but they knew it would do no harm.[42]

It was significant that nearly half of the members had absented themselves from the most critical division yet of that Parliament. It was the first sign of a reverse swing of the pendulum, as the acute eye of Pym surely noticed. The opposition chiefs must drive home their advantage now, before any reaction against them had time to mature. Yet, they must beware of further alienating the upper House. The battle had entered upon its final and decisive stage.

It must not be supposed that the king and court stood idly by and let Strafford fight alone against the Commons. Several schemes were hatched at Whitehall and Westminster to save him—some intelligent, some wildly improbable. The wisest course was plotted by the king, who wished to divide the Peers and build a party for himself. Under his guidance, an influential group was beginning to form and work for a compromise that would be satisfied with Strafford's political incapacity, without his death. Lord Bristol, loyal as ever, was the statesman of this movement. He wanted to bring the House of Lords into play as the disinterested mediator of the quarrel between king and Parliament. Bristol was joined by the important and powerful Lord Bedford, head of the Russells, who began to perceive that a revolution might get out of aristocratic control.

Bedford was to be the head of the opposition ministry which the king would form at the price of Strafford's life, while incapacitating him from office. The Chancellorship of the Exchequer was to go to none other than John Pym. Holles would be Secretary of State, and the post of Master of the Court of Wards to Lord Saye. Lord Holland had been won over by an offer of command of the northern army. Other great offices were spoken of for Essex, Mandeville, and Hampden. The Marquis of Hertford joined as a prominent member.[43]

It was now the openly expressed condition that whatever changes might be contemplated, royalty must not be further attacked. The constitutional position of the king could not allow either the Lord Lieutenant of Ireland to be condemned to death or episcopacy to be abolished. The ministers, to whom he was now prepared to entrust power, must shield him from the lowering of dignity and loss of authority with which he saw himself threatened. In fact, ever since the first overtures of the court to the Peers of the opposition, it was thought that these lords were inclined in favor of Strafford.[44] If the Lords had had such great influence in precipitating the present quarrels, then it seemed reasonable to hope that they would be equally capable of quieting them. But the growing popular tendencies had already become too strong to be mastered by the influence of the Lords. Political movements may be originated and guided by personal interest; but an individual, when he has attained his own ends, cannot always succeed in confining them within definite limits. The lower House was in control. When they became more friendly to the king, the Lords saw their popularity immediately diminish. The Scots became bitterly disillusioned and they had an army which they could loose. Alliances were to be attempted by king and Lords. But nearly every attempted combination of personages was to be burst asunder by the force of events.[45]

The king was prepared to come more than half way to meet the Parliamentary party. Bedford was ready to take over. Within the space of a few days, Pym was twice admitted to interviews with Charles. What passed between Charles and Pym we have no means of knowing. It is very probable that Pym refused to be content with anything short of Strafford's life. Lord Essex, too, would not hear of a lesser penalty. Edward Hyde, later Lord Clarendon, was employed by Bedford to argue down Essex's objections. At Hyde's suggestion that fines, imprisonment, and political incapacity would be sufficient punishment for Strafford, Essex shook his head. "Stone-dead," he answered, "hath no fellow."[46] He argued that even if Strafford were disabled, the king would restore his estate and give him his liberty, as soon as he needed to use him, which would be as soon as the Parliament ended. Essex expressed a widely held opinion, which actuated the Parliamentary party: It was not so much a question of whether Strafford had been a traitor, but whether the king could be trusted.

Charles' wisest course would have been to reply upon the Peers, but he could not make up his mind to risk everything on the steady pursuance of this line of conduct. Instead, his thoughts and especially those of the queen constantly were drawn to the English and Irish armies.

There existed a strong Royalist feeling in the army, which was still under arms and in quarters in the North. It was jealous of the superior care bestowed by Parliament on the Scottish soldiers, and it was unwilling for the royal power to be further debased or pass under control of the Commons. The first to come forward were officers who had seats in Parliament, such as Captain Ashburnham who sat for Ludgershall, Henry Wilmot who sat for Tamworth, and, as no conspiracy would have been complete without a Percy, Henry Percy, member for Northumberland and brother of the earl. They were joined by two archetypical laughing Cavaliers, the poets Suckling and D'Avenant. All these considered that the army had just complaints against the House of Commons, but not against the king, who even in these troubled times found means to support the needs of his soldiers, and they resolved to offer him their services. They calculated that they could take and hold the Tower. The army was to march on London to impose conditions on Parliament. George Goring, a regimental commander and now Governor of Portsmouth, was suggested by some to lead the army, with the Earl of Newcastle as figurehead commander. When the idea was put to him, Goring received it very favorably. The queen stated that most of the officers in the army were behind the thrust. Her personal friends were among the leaders. All bound themselves with secret and formal oaths.[47]

In Scotland, a similar movement occurred among some of those who had signed the Covenant. In Castle Merchiston, a party of friends assembled around Lord Napier, at variance with the anti-monarchical tendencies which the movement had developed. Nor would they accept domination from any group which might gain ascendance in the Committee of the Estates. The Earl of Montrose, Lord Napier, and others, including the chief notables Home, Athol, Mar, united to oppose Argyle, the most powerful of the Committee. Montrose and Napier entered into direct communication with Charles. They urged him to recognize the abolition of the episcopacy and to come to Scotland in person to hold a parliament. Here was possible strong support for Charles from Scotland. Both parties looked to him for support, and he allowed his presence to be expected soon in Scotland.[48]

In Ireland, much remained of what Strafford had built. Most important, there was the army which he had raised. In the Irish army the same spirit prevailed as in the English: it would not abandon the interest of the Crown and it would not allow itself to be disbanded.

King Charles also expected extensive help from Holland. The Prince of Orange was one of the wealthiest men in Europe, and negotiations had just been completed whereby the prince's son would marry Charles' eldest daughter, Princess Mary.

It was deemed possible by the court party that a powerful reaction against Parliament could be catalyzed out of the spirit of military devotion to the throne. So far as can be ascertained, a project was mapped out for liberating Strafford from the Tower and setting him at the head of a loyalist army. To put trustworthy troops in the city and in the Tower, it was spread abroad that enlistment was under way to raise a military force for service in Portugal. Great offers were made to Balfour, Governor of the Tower, for his cooperation. Colonel Goring was told the purpose of the Portugese enlistments. Once a significant force had declared for the king, it was expected that support would come forth from even the remotest districts.[49]

It was hoped that support for such a movement would come from France. Parliament was certainly afraid of hostile interference from that quarter. Richelieu, however, perceived that Parliament was his best hope in England; after his first refusal, the queen never approached him again.

The army plot never advanced very far. Everyone was still occupied in hopes and preparations, when suddenly everything was disclosed. Goring soon saw that the daring and desperate scheme was unworkable because the Scots Army would fall on the English army if it moved South. Moreover, Goring was not to be given the supreme command for which he bargained. Goring, therefore, wished to have a retreat: these men of the plot were all haunted by the thought that failure would ruin them, and merely to have known of a plot and concealed it might be deadly. Colonel Goring, on whose cooperation the whole wild scheme was based, imparted everything to the opposition chiefs. Thus, John Pym received intelligence.[50] A military plot! This was a powerful weapon indeed, put into his hands just when circumstances would make it very useful.

The Bill of Attainder passed the House of Commons on Wednesday, April 21, and was carried to the House of Lords on the same day. John Pym had not carried the bill through the Commons to see it voted down by the Peers or rejected by the king. Accordingly, a subtle and well-planned campaign of pressure and intimidation was set in motion. Rumors of plots and foreign invasion filled the city. The Londoners were encouraged to show their feelings by petition and noisy demonstrations.[51] On April 22, Lord Digby and the member for Windsor were attacked in the House of Commons, with the later being expelled.[52] To teach a lesson to the Lords, the names of fifty-nine members of the Commons who had voted for Strafford were posted all over London. Above their names was inscribed the words: "These are the Straffordians, enemies of justice, betrayers of their country." This was an unheard of breach of parliamentary privilege, but the Commons remained silent on the matter.[53]

As the king worked with the formidable combination of Bedford and Bristol, he was still confident that Strafford would be saved by his intervention, but that the earl could not serve him thereafter. Ready to bow to Bristol and Bedford's guidance, the king wrote to Strafford on April 23 as follows:

> The misfortune that is fallen upon you by the strange mistaking and conjuncture of these times being such that I must lay by the thought of employing you hereafter in my affairs. Yet I cannot satisfy myself in honor or conscience without assuring you now, in the midst of your troubles, that, upon the word of a King, you shall not suffer in life, honor, or fortune.[54]

Strafford was kept informed of the king's plan to compromise with the opposition Peers. The Bill of Attainder had undermined his main line of defense, and he was no longer fighting to acquit the king's government; he was now fighting for his very life. Consequently, the proposed combination with Bristol and Bedford commended itself to Strafford as an effective plan, and he therefore wrote to Hamilton on April 24th, to ask for his help in the House of Lords, where Hamilton sat under his English title as Earl of Cambridge:

> It is told me that the lords are inclinable to preserve my life and family, for which their generous compassions the great God of mercy will reward them; and surely should I die upon this evidence, I had much rather be the sufferer than the judge.
>
> All that I shall desire from your lordship, is that divested of all public employment, I may be admitted to go home to my own private fortune, there to attend my own domestic affairs, and education of my children, with as little asperity of words or marks of infamy as possible the nobleness and justice of my friends can procure for me.[55]

Meanwhile, the clamor of the House of Commons was backed by growing excitement in the city. On the 24th, 20,000 Londoners sent a petition to Parliament, calling for the execution of Strafford.[56]

On Monday, April 26, the Bill of Attainder was read for the first time in the House of Lords. The Peers had been ready to hears the Commons' legal arguments that previous Saturday but the hearing had to be called off when the lower House insisted that their words were intended to the bill and not the impeachment.[57] The Lords were incensed that the Commons insisted on their bill. They were actuated by a sense of their dignity as well as justice. Lord Savile spoke their thoughts when he cried out "that the Lower House did encroach upon the Higher House's liberties and did not know their duties."[58] Just before adjournment, the Peers warned the Commoners that they were going too far:

> It was signified to the House of C. that the orders of this House hath been much disobeyed and comtempted.[59]

That evening, Edward Hyde sought to further Lord Bristol's good offices. Wedgwood describes his discussion of Strafford's case with Bedford and Essex:

Nerve-racked with the increasing anxiety of each day, Edward Hyde, one of Pym's most ardent supporters, walked that evening up to the bowling-green in Picadilly to clear his brain and breathe the fresh spring air. The gardens were crowded with people, here and there some of the peers and Parliament men passed to and fro deep in discussion; Strafford's case was the only talk, "the great business" on which all the affairs of the Kingdom waited. Bedford came up to Hyde and asked him his opinion. Bedford himself felt that the opportunity was not to be lost—Strafford's life would buy any concessions from the King, and he would prevent Strafford's death if it cost him his crown. They must therefore use the chance that fate had sent them. A little further on they met Essex and Hertford both arguing the same point. Essex was immovable in his opinions; Strafford disgraced and retired from public service would still contrive to be a power in the state. The King's unwillingness to yield him showed how the King's affections lay. "Stone dead hath no fellow," repeated Essex, shaking his wise head.[60]

About this time, Lord Cottington suddenly resigned as Chancellor of the Exchequer, and the king offered the lucrative and powerful office to Pym. The move was part of Bedford's plan for a new ministry with himself as head and based on the exile of Strafford. But Pym had already received intelligence of the army plots and no longer trusted the king. Strafford's death had become Pym's irreducible minimum. He refused the offer.

During the first stages of the Bristol-Bedford negotiations with the king, a compromise on the Attainder was reached between the Houses.[61] The Commons agreed to answer Lane's legal arguments, if their replies were understood to be directed to the point of whether the Bill of Attainder should be passed, and not to the question of what judgment should be given on the impeachment. The Lords were still irritated by the procedure by bill, but since the Commons agreed to justify its legality, this seemed to their lordships to be a sufficient retreat of the lower House from their imperious advancement of the bill. The proposed compromise was accepted by the Lords. A collision of the Houses had been imminent; it had been postponed by this simple expedient. The Lords expressed their displeasure with the disobedience and contempt of the Commons but, finally, set Thursday, April 29, for hearing the legal arguments of the Commons.[62]

Despite the decision of the Lords to read the bill and to hear the legal arguments of the Commons, the evidence indicates that although the

Lords were unwilling to enter into an open quarrel with the lower House on a point of form, they had made up their minds to spare Strafford's life. The wisest course of the king was to rely on the Lords and let matters take the course of the constitution. Unfortunately, the king could not make up his mind which path to take. The Court was full of projects; the air was full of plots; and during these agitated days, with one then another plan commended to his mind, the behavior of Charles became completely inconsistent.

On the 27th, things suddenly began to happen very quickly. Rumors of a military coup and foreign invasions swept through the city, keeping the populace near the boiling point.

The Court of Henrietta Maria had few secrets. Speculations were wild as to the price paid by the Prince of Orange for the royal marriage. Court gossips set the sum at 1,200,000 ducats and when Prince William arrived on the 19th to claim his bride, the Parliamentarians trembled in fear of what Charles could do with such a sum.[63] The king sent money to the army at York, to make sure of their aid in the event that a final break with Parliament came. He talked of going down in person to take command, while the populace speculated whether he would turn the army against the Scots or his enemies in England.

Meanwhile, plans were made for the king and queen to flee to Hampton Court, whence they would go to Portsmouth and Goring, whom they still trusted. An armed force would be sent to seize Balfour and the Tower. The Northern army would take London. The Irish army, together with any troops which Frederick Henry could send, would land at Portsmouth. During the fight, Parliament would be dissolved, and Charles would have retrieved everything.

On the 28th, it became known that for some weeks a ship, chartered by Strafford's secretary Guildford Slingsby, had been lying in the Thames at Tilbury.[64] The Commons became more suspicious; the City became mean.

On April 29, in a great conference with the upper House, Oliver St. John argued the legal case for the Bill of Attainder.[65] Both King Charles and Lord Strafford were present. St. John presented a very long argument, replete with many precedents for the course he advocated. Primarily, he argued the doctrine of the absolute legislative power of Parliament. By virtue of this power, Parliament was unlike inferior tribunals and was not bound by existing laws. Therefore, Parliament was justified in making new laws to fit new circumstances, even though the law applied to the circumstances *ex post facto*. The only guide for Parliament was care for the common, public welfare. It was the political body which embraced all, from the king to the meanest subject, and could deal with individuals for the good of the whole, could open a vein to let out corrupted blood. It had been argued that the written law must precede the offense, that where no law was written, there could be no offense; but that defense could not protect a man who had intended to overthrow all laws. St. John broke away from his long chain of statute and precedent, and in a striking paragraph, he summed up his argument for the bill:

> We give law to hares and deer, because they be beasts of chase. It was never accounted either cruelty or foul play to knock foxes and wolves on the head as they can be found, because they be beasts of prey.[66]

It is no wonder that Strafford, listening in enforced silence, should have raised his hands and eyes to Heaven in horrified appeal. On the same day, the London mob started rioting in the streets, a result of the fear of popish plots of invasion.

Charles himself was beginning to have some inkling of the growing danger. For the first time, it would seem, he had become seriously alarmed for Strafford's life. Pym's bill, to be sure, hung by a thread, but the vehemence of the mob and Pym's refusal to bargain threw the entire, rapidly-deteriorating situation into focus. The case of Lord Strafford had arrived at a supremely crucial phase, where there existed absolutely no margin for error and a single false move would tilt the balance.

At this time, Strafford seems to have favored a masterly inaction. One good chance of the Lords defeating the bill lay in their unwillingness to be driven by the Commons. And the lower House was pushing the Lords hard. They might be driven even harder during the next few days, until they would put up with it no further. For this reason, it was highly important for the Crown to refrain from any appearance of trying to influence the Peers overbearingly.

Meanwhile, young Harry Vane's famous paper, which had mysteriously vanished, was found again with the key words altered. In the crucial phrase, "there" had been substituted for "here". More of the Peers began to doubt the evidence. On Friday, April 30, the king discussed Strafford with Bristol and Bedford and they agreed that Charles should intervene in Parliament on his behalf. Unfortunately, the king did not make the right speech. By a stroke of bad luck, the Earl of Bedford was taken seriously ill during the night and Charles was deprived of his guidance. The next day, May 1, the king, who apparently had been advised by Lord Saye, went to Parliament to plead for the prisoner's life. In the early morning, the Usher of the Black Rod knocked at the door of the Commons. A whisper swept around the benches that a dissolution was imminent—an act which most men believed would be followed by violence. Maxwell reassured the members. "Fear not, I'll warrant you," he said as he summoned them to the upper House. When they arrived, the king spoke to both Houses from the throne. He had come, he said, to give three assurances. Strafford had never advised him to bring the Irish army to England. No discussion had ever taken place in his presence which assumed the disloyalty of England. He had never been advised to change any of the laws of England. He declared, therefore, that in his conscience he could not agree to the condemnation of Strafford:

> My Lords, I hope you know what a tender thing Conscience is: Yet I must declare unto you, that to satisfy my People, I would do great matters; But in this of Conscience, no Fear, no Respect whatsoever, Shall ever make me go against it. Certainly, I have not so ill deserved of the Parliament at this time, that they should press me in this tender point, and therefore I cannot expect that you will go about it.[67]

The tone of the entire address was undoubtedly a mistake. It contained one huge contradiction: The king, in effect, told the Lords to vote against the Attainder; but then he said at the same time that he could not agree that Strafford was guilty, implying that if the Lords did pass it, he would refuse to sign. Thus he offended some of the Lords by assuming the air of a dictator, calling on them to vote to order. But at the same time, he handed the waverers a way of escape; for they could read into the speech the interpretation that their vote for the bill would do no harm because the king would refuse assent. Finally, no ground of opportunity was given to Bristol and those who would have supported in Lords a reasoned objection to the bill. Strafford certainly considered the king's clumsy intervention to be in itself impolitic.[68] The bad effect of the speech even reached old Archbishop Laud high in the Tower, who wrote: "The speech displeased mightily and I verily think hastened the Earl's death."

The next day was Sunday and a great day at Court. Prince William of Orange, a boy of fifteen, was married to Princess Mary, who was only nine and who was to stay longer in England. Charles himself presided with good humor over the wedding festivities and seemed well pleased with his new son-in-law. Yet at that very hour, the pulpits of the city were ringing with fiery addresses on the necessity of bringing Strafford to justice. Disquieting rumors were in the air and kept everyone in suspense.

On that Sunday morning, Charles had sent Captain Billingsley to the Tower with an order to the Lieutenant, Sir William Balfour, to admit the captain to the fortress with one hundred men. Balfour, a good Scot, refused to let him in and informed the parliamentary leaders of what had occurred.[69] Balfour's act was open defiance and mutiny by the commander of the first fortress in the kingdom—the first act of Civil War, and Charles was helpless to prevent it. The king's attempt to use force decided Pym to reply in kind, and the Parliament leader made ready to reveal all he knew of plots in order to stir up the city against the Crown and the Peers.

On Monday, May 3, the Peers met. Strafford's position was clearly weaker because Bedford was dying of smallpox and Bristol was having trouble drawing his supporters together. In the House of Commons, John Pym—always a master of timing—acted at last on the information he had from Goring about the plot between the Court and the army.

When they met that morning, the Commons remained silent for some time, regarding one another as men looking for counsel and finding none. At last the Clerk began to read the bill which stood first of the Order of the Day. It happened to be one for regulating the trade of wiredrawing. The inappropriateness of the subject struck the members with a sense of ludicrous incongruity, and their tension exploded in a burst of laughter. Then there was silence again. After some time the doors were closed, and John Pym rose to make a serious communication. He said that desperate plots against the Parliament and the peace of the realm were afoot for bringing the army against Parliament, seizing the Tower, and releasing Strafford; that there was an understanding with France—perhaps Holland—on the subject, and that sundry papists and Jesuits in immediate attendance on the queen were deep in the plot.[70]

From lip to lip the rumor spread. The mob assembled outside the doors, where vague reports of Pym's words reached them, detected a conspiracy worse than the Gunpowder Plot for massacring Parliament and all Strafford's opponents in the city. At times the cry "To Whitehall!" was heard, at others it seemed as if the mob would storm the Tower. The fears spread around the city: The House of Commons was in flames. The army, papists, and Strafford had blown up Parliament. "In a clap," as Baillie wrote, "all the city is in alarm; shops closed; a world of people in arms runs down to Westminster."[71] All that day and all the next a mob several thousands strong, consisting partly of "porters, carmen, and other dissolute and rude fellows" and partly of substantial citizens, stormed Westminster crying "Justice! Justice!" The entrance to the House of Lords was especially besieged. The mob flung themselves upon the carriages of the Peers, clamoring to know which way they would vote. Every lord who came in or out had to run a gauntlet of Londoners armed with swords and clubs bellowing "in a loud hideous voice" their slogan of "justice and execution!"[72]

Lord Arundel, presiding as Lord Steward, came in for special and violent attention. He tried to put them off with a promise of justice, but the mob refused to let him pass from their midst until they had forced from him a promise for execution. Even then he got away with difficulty. "We will take your word for once," growled his tormentors. Lord Bristol was known to be working for a compromise. The mob denounced him as an "apostate to the cause of Christ," and threatened vengeance upon him and his "false son, Lord Digby." One voice was even heard to cry: "If we have not the Lieutenant's life, we will have the King's!"

Once inside, the Lords moved quickly to placate the mob. They accepted petitions from the crowd and then sent a delegation of Arundel, Essex, and Cambridge to the king

> to acquaint his Majestie with the content of the petitions of the citizens of London & that the citizens are fearful of this night.[73]

Lord Newport, a hard-core opposition Peer, was put in charge of the Tower garrison. A delegation was sent to question Charles about the Billingsley Affair. Another group of lords was sent outside to "tell the citizens of London that they [the Peers] will put the Bill of [Attainder] against the Earl of Strafford into expedition."[74] Finally, it was ordered "that the Bill of Attainder of the Earl of Strafford shall be considered tomorrow morning at nine o'clock."[75]

The force of these shocks immediately jeopardized both the royal

power and Strafford's position. The supporters of the king who were
implicated in the plots, fled the country. Pym called for the closing of the
ports, and a protestation of loyalty to Parliament was tendered to all
members.[76] Not only the Commons, but the Lords as well, were shocked
by the discovery that Charles had been working as a conspirator in the
broad light of day. On the 4th, the Lords received from the king an
admission that he had ordered Billingsley to occupy the Tower. The Lords
resolved that they would see to the fortress' safekeeping and directed that
Essex, Saye, and Brooke should provide 500 men from the Tower hamlets
as guards.[77] Clearly, Charles' futile attempt to employ force had
alienated several of the Lords from him and, of course, from Strafford's
cause.

The Lords and Commons continued to usurp the military authority of
the Crown. They ordered measures taken for the security of Portsmouth,
for the arming of the militia in several inland counties, and for the defense
of Jersey and Guernsey from France or Holland.[78] Outside the doors,
Palace Yard continued full of a rough, armed mob. Late on the 4th, the
House of Lords heard testimony that "the people were saying that
tomorrow they would have the King or the Earl of Strafford...that 50,000
men in arms tomorrow will take the King or the E. of S."[79]

Information came to Parliament from all quarters. Preparations had
been made to supply the army in the north with munitions. Troops were
on the move in France along the coast. At Whitehall, when night came, all
was hurry and confusion. Charles and the queen seriously debated the
question of whether they could safely remain in London. The tumults of
the last two days were serious. They talked of flight to the northern army
or to Hampton Court. Finally, they decided to stay and fight it out with
Strafford. Whitehall had no secrets from Pym. The news of discussion
about flight was bad. If either the king or queen decided to escape from
London, it would be impossible to tell what course they would take.
When the next morning arrived, Pym resolved to communicate to the
House every last detail of what he knew of plots, oaths, and coups.

On the 5th, therefore, he told everything he knew from Goring, of
plots to bring the army to London, of invasion from France or Holland, of
persons in high places about the queen engaged in the plots. The House
took immediate action. Each member was ordered to list the arms
possessed by his constituents and the names of the Lords Lieutenant and
Deputies who could be trusted to support Parliament. A resolution was

passed that any person helping to bring foreign soldiers into England would be punished as a public enemy.[80] The Peers were persuaded to gather evidence on the army plot, and to ask the king to detain all attendants of the Court.[81]

In the House of Commons, the tensions of fear and hatred were explosive. As the House was in full debate on the plots, a board in the floor of the gallery cracked under the weight of a member. Sir John Wray, with the thought of a second Guy Fawkes in his mind, shouted that he smelled gunpowder. With that, the House rushed outside, some of them shouting that the parliament house was falling and that the members were killed. When the news reached the city, the trained bands armed themselves and came to the aid of the Commons. They marched as far as Convent Garden before they learned that the Commons were not assassinated.[82]

The fate of the Viceroy of Ireland formed the central point of all these movements in the nation and in Parliament. Lord Strafford was convinced by the violent events of the past few days that his cause was rapidly being removed from all counsels of rational deliberation. Calmly surveying the situation from the loneliness of the Tower, Strafford came to the conclusion, sometime between the 3rd and the 5th, that nothing could now stop the Bill of Attainder from passing the House of Lords. He could see at least four reasons why the Peers would give way. *First,* the king's attempt to use force upon Parliament had destroyed Bristol's plans for compromise. The hearts of many lords were hardened by the resort to force and would now vote for his death. Only in this way could they prevent Strafford, as they saw it, from striking back at them. *Second,* fear of the mob would keep many Peers away from the House, or change their votes and, as the list of "Straffordians" proved, parliamentary privilege could no longer guarantee the secrecy of how each Peer voted. *Third,* the sentiments of the mob were especially inflamed over popish plots, invasions, and coups. It would, therefore, be surprising if a single Roman Catholic Peer even showed up for the vote on the bill. Normally, the Crown could count upon the Catholic Lords to be its strongest supporters. *Fourth,* the king had opposed his conscience to the bill. Clearly, then, he would veto it, if it passed the Lords. The position taken by the king provided an easy escape for any Peer who wished Strafford to live but feared to vote against the bill.

If the Lords gave way, as they probably would, nothing would stand between Strafford and death but the king, armed only with his veto, and exposed to the fury of a city in panic. Charles, of course, would honor his pledge to Strafford, but by so doing would endanger himself and the monarchy. Loyalty had been Strafford's creed. He would not save himself by placing his prince in danger. Therefore, Strafford turned to the task of persuading Charles to accept his servant's release from the pledge made on his kingly honor. In one of the most famous letters of all time, Strafford "turned against himself his conquering eloquence" and pronounced his own death sentence:

> May it please you Sacred Majesty...I understand the minds of men are more and more incensed against me, notwithstanding your Majesty hath declared, that in your Princely opinion I am not guilty of treason, and that you are not satisfied in your conscience to pass the Bill....This bringeth me in a very great streight; there is before the ruin of my children and family, hitherto untouched with any foul crime: here are before me the many ills, which may befall your Sacred Person and the whole Kingdom should yourself and Parliament part less satisfied one with the other than is necessary for the preservation of both King and people; they are before me the things most valued, most feared by mortal men, Life or Death.
>
> To say, Sir, that there hath not been a strife in me, were to make me less man than...my infirmities make me, and to call a destruction upon myself and my young children may be believed, will find no easy consent from flesh and blood; and therefore in few words as I put myself wholly upon the honour and justice of my Peers, so clearly as to wish your Majesty might please to have spared that declaration of yours on Saturday last and entirely to have left me to their Lordships; so now to set your Majesty's conscience at liberty, I do most humbly beseech your Majesty for prevention of evils which may happen by your refusal to pass this Bill; and by this means to remove I cannot say this accursed but I confess this unfortunate thing, forth of the way towards that blessed agreement which God I trust shall ever establish between you and your subjects.
>
> Sir, my consent shall more acquit herein to God than all the world can do besides; to a willing man there is no injury done, and as by God's grace I forgive all the world, with calmness and meekness of infinite contentment to my soul; so Sir, to you, I can give the life of this world with all the cheerfulness imaginable and only beg that in your goodness you would vouchsafe to cast your gracious regard upon my poor son and his three sisters, less or more, and no otherwise than as their (in present) unfortunate father, may

hereafter appear more or less guilty of this death.

    God long preserve your Majesty.

    Your Majesty's most faithful and humble subject and servant,

      Strafford.[83]

Many reasons have been given to account for Strafford's motives. But the letter fits in most clearly with the principles he had followed all his life. To the very end, he regarded the welfare of the king's sacred person and the Commonwealth as considerations higher than any one man's private interest. It was on these grounds that he now not only released Charles from his pledge but told the king to send him to the scaffold in the public interest.

Yet, Strafford had produced a very persuasive document, which might be used to save the day; and whether he did this deliberately or not is beside the point. In the first place, the letter showed him willing to die to bring about an agreement between King and Parliament. Such an offer might, if properly communicated, disassociate him from the plots of the court in the minds of the Peers and the populace of the city. It might stimulate the Peers into showing their independence of the Commons. In the second place, the letter not only released Charles from his private promise given on April 23 in a letter, but it could be used to release the king publicly from the declaration of conscience he had made before Parliament on May 1. Used in this manner, it would throw the responsibility for Strafford's case back to the House of Lords and prevent the waverers there from using the king as their escape from responsibility.

Strafford's remarkable letter was put to no use at all. Probably the king failed to understand its persuasive possibilities.

By May 5th, the final battle lines of both sides had been drawn and the ultimate outcome of the trial began to emerge. The House of Commons had long since abandoned their impeachment proceedings in favor of a Bill of Attainder: the bill itself had been constructed from the strongest, legally, of the original charges, and it cited as treason two[84] of the nine general articles and four[85] of the twenty-eight specific charges. The final attack of the Commons upon Strafford, therefore, moved forward upon *two* legal fronts.[86] First, they advanced articles 15 and 23 as treasonable offenses under *statute* law.[87] In this, the managers were correct: Strafford himself had admitted in his closing statement that these two charges were statutable,[88] but defended himself on the basis that Savile's testimony on article 15 and Vane's testimony on article 23 were the evidence of a single witness on each separate article, and that *1 Eliz. 1, cap. 6* provided that to the point of an offense of treason, more than a single witness was necessary to make faith on a given point of fact.[89] Second, the Commons advanced articles 20 and 24, along with their two remaining general charges, under the warrant of *constructive treason,* as argued by St. John, supplemented by a proviso that Parliament had the power to declare acts as treasonous.[90] Strafford defended himself against this with the counter-warrant of "no law, no crime." Important to note here is the fact that the final arguments of both sides indicate that Strafford and Lane on the one hand, and Pym, Glyn, and St. John on the other, all expected the question for decision to fall out in the House of Lords on the validity of the constructive treason argument.

As time grew short and the field of maneuver narrowed, Strafford's last strokes were the now-defunct Bedford-Bristol compromise and his desperate letter to the king. The last moves of Pym were to reveal Charles' resort to force, to inflame the mob, and to claim, ultimately, that Strafford had to be destroyed for the safety of the realm. And now, the House of Lords would decide.

The strong possibility of an unfavorable outcome for the earl was foreshadowed on May 3rd when the Lords tremulously sent a delegation of their number outside to appease the mob, telling them that the upper House would put the Bill of Attainder against the Earl of Strafford into expedition.[91] The next day, the attendance of the House plummeted from an average of eighty-six to seventy.[92] The decline in attendance was so bad that the House found it necessary to admonish its members thus: "Ordered that those lords that are now absent and have heard the evidence in Westminster Hall against the Earl of Strafford do give good reason of their absence from this House."[93]

Of the six charges in the bill, the lords who attended on May 4th—seventy out of 147 eligible Peers—finally selected four, two general and two specific, for deliberation.[94] On May 5th, this remnant of the House of Lords, almost evenly divided now—the merest handful of votes would make the difference—perceived the danger inherent in the creation of any new precedent for treason and the initiation of a method by which the lawful could be made illegal and laws stretched or set aside by Act of Parliament. Consequently, the lords present completely bypassed the Commons' keystone position that treason could be against the state as well as the person of the sovereign and focused their attention on two specific articles: the 15th and the 23rd. Both articles were reducible to the treason statute of Edward III, and this was what the supporters of the bill in Lords intended to stake out: a firm position in statute law.[95]

The opposition Peers moved swiftly now. A crucial motion was passed by a narrow margin:

> Resolved upon the question: that going by way of Bill in the discussing of the *matter of fact* in this whole cause, *the rule shall only be the persuasion of every man's conscience.*[96]

There it was, the perfect snare for Strafford, if it could be made to stick through the final vote. The House of Lords had found the question for decision to be no high-flown theory of treason or doctrine of sovereignty. Instead, they voted to break the rules of evidence by which they were bound under law.[97] The matter of fact would be decided by majority vote. Sir Harry Vane and Sergeant Savile were to be corroborated, not by the required second witness, but by Act of Parliament and the persuasion of every lordship's conscience.[98]

Once it had been decided to proceed by way of bill on the matter of evidence, it was resolved in a series of four more resolutions "that the Earl of Strafford gave warrant for the sessing of soldiers upon men's lands in Ireland"[99] and that "the sessing of soldiers was with armies and officers in warlike manner."[100] Thus was the charge of levying war under the fifteenth article proven.

Thereupon, the Lords adjourned to a committee conference with the House of Commons. A delegation of Peers asked representatives of the lower House whether the general charge of subverting the fundamental laws was to be taken as standing alone or as relative to article fifteen. The Commons replied that the charge was made relative to the article.[101] In a stroke the question of treason at common law had been disposed of, and the Commons' treasured general charges of subverting the fundamental laws had been connected, and thereby reduced, to a statutable offense.

Immediately the next morning, a sparsely-attended House of Lords, by a narrow margin, voted in a series of five resolutions, that Strafford "did counsel and advise his Majesty that he was absolved from rules of government,"[102] and that Strafford had advised the king, "you have an army in Ireland, which your Majesty may employ to reduce this kingdom,"[103] and that "these words were spoken of the kingdom of England."[104] Thus was Sir Harry Vane corroborated and the matter of fact on article twenty-three proven. Again, the law *1 Eliz. 1,* which stipulated two or more witnesses for evidence on an offense of treason, was overridden by vote.

On Friday, May 7th, the Bill of Attainder was read for the third and final time in the House of Lords.[105] Despite the outcome of the votes on the matter of fact on the fifteenth and twenty-third articles, which had taken place on the two days previous, the result on this final day was not certain to either side; consequently, both parties strained every resource to ensure the attendance of its dependable members.

The threats of the mob effectively intimidated the more moderate Peers, and even Strafford's friends began to offer elaborate explanations for being absent or abstaining from the vote. The Earl of Bristol, once one of Strafford's greatest hopes, withdrew from the struggle, and had himself excused from voting on the pretext that since he had been a witness, he could not vote on the bill.[106] The same excuse was offered by several others, including Lord Holland,[107] whose loyalty to the king would otherwise have caused them to vote in Strafford's behalf. Bedford was lying on his death-bed, and all the combinations tried by him had flown apart. The Roman Catholic Peers were in dread of their lives and would not come. Many of the other lords, like Lord Hertford, simply walked out before the vote was taken.[108] Some of them were timid; others were disinclined to support a government which had been ready to use force to decide a constitutional dispute. Even the Earl of Cumberland, brother of Strafford's first wife and his friend since boyhood, began to waver and suggest that such a close relationship to the accused disqualified him from voting.[109] The bishops, different from their stated position in the impeachment trial, could legally have voted on the legislative bill. But Bishop Williams argued that the bishops should not vote because they had taken no part in the trial, although most had been present as spectators. With incredible weakness, all twenty-six bishops followed this mistaken policy.[110]

"Through a large crowd that beseiged the doors, the peers pressed in to take their seats. It was a thin House."[111] The members present took into consideration the remaining matters of fact and voted that Strafford had endeavored to subvert the fundamental laws of England and Ireland,[112] and that he had exercised a tyrannous government above the laws and over the lives of the subjects of the two kingdoms.[113] Their lordships then:

Resolved by vote that this question be put to the judges; that upon all the Lords have voted to be proved, that the Earl of Strafford doth deserve to undergo the pains and forfeitures of high treason by law.[114]

The judges, headed by Lord Chief Justice Banks, considered the question and, after short deliberation, declared that:

We are of opinion upon all that your lordships have voted to be proved: that the Earl of Strafford doth deserve to undergo the pains and forfeitures of high treason by law.[115]

At last, the Peers were finished. Their final moment in Strafford's tragedy had come. A motion was put to the House of Lords: "Resolved...that the B of A against the E of S should pass as a law."[116]

The vote was taken. Out of a total membership of 147 nobles in the House of Lords, only 45 were present to vote on the final motion of that Friday morning. The Bill of Attainder against the Earl of Strafford was passed by seven votes, 26 to 19.

Now there was only the king. On Saturday afternoon, the mob stormed Whitehall. Inside the palace, courtiers were rushing about swords in hand, and setting points of defense in passageways and stairways from which they would defend their prince and his queen. The palace grounds swarmed with "a rabble" as Whitelocke put it, "of many thousand people."[117] Charles looked sadly on the multitudes and sent word that his final answers would be given Monday. The mob was incensed at the delay, and an attack appeared to be imminent when a bishop, probably Williams, stepped to a window and pacified the rioters with an assurance that Monday's answer would be all that they could desire.

All through the night panic ruled at Whitehall. At any moment, the mob might break into the palace. Catholic men and women at Court, in the expectation that they were soon do die, made their last confessions to the queen's chaplains.[118] All within looked forward to Monday, if it came, with grave fears. Outside, the movement begun in the city was spreading throughout the country and, from every county, men were coming up to join the city populace.

In the Tower, Strafford prepared for the worst. In this last extremity he released his friends from any further service, so that they would not go down with him. George Radcliffe, in the Gatehouse, desired to see his friend. It was not possible and Strafford replied, "I think it best you stay where you are and let us see the issue of tomorrow."[119] Nor did he think it safe to let his friend and servant, Guildford Slingsby, be seen with him since the incident of the chartered ship. On that tense Sunday, Strafford wrote to Slingsby, entreating him to endanger himself no further.[120]

This was the agony of Charles' life, to which none of his other sufferings compared. After a long night, Charles met his Council on Sunday morning. Its members advised him to yield. The judges had been asked by Lords and king whether they thought Strafford guilty of treason, and they answered in the affirmative.[121] Still unsatisfied, Charles appealed to the bishops, who, with two exceptions, advised him that his public and his private duty were separate things and that he must separate his feelings as a man from those of a sovereign.[122]

Charles still hesitated and the long afternoon passed with no decision. All day long, the street in front of Whitehall remained filled with an armed mob of several thousand. The mob took up the cry that the queen was at the bottom of the mischief, and parliamentary leaders now bruited her impeachment. Every minute it was expected that the rush would come.

At last Charles made the surrender that haunted him the rest of his life. He gave his assent to the Bill of Attainder. He announced his decision with tears in his eyes:

> If my own person only were in danger, I would gladly venture it to save Lord Strafford's life; but seeing my wife, children, and all my Kingdom are concerned in it, I am forced to give way unto it.[123]

The next morning, as he implemented with his royal signature the act of Strafford's attainder and death, the words which burst from him were: "My Lord of Strafford's condition is happier than mine!"

Lord Cleveland was charged to take word to the condemned man. Cleveland must not have had the taste for the task because it was one of the royal secretaries, Dudley Carleton, who, late on the evening of May 9, went to the earl in the Tower.

Strafford was surprised. He had sincerely enough written with a willingness to lay down his life, that release to Charles. But he evidently knew what he himself would have done with such a letter, and had not quite fathomed his master's capacities for surrender. Sincerely as he may have written the letter, he afterward concluded, apparently, that it was impossible for Charles to accept the sacrifice. Carlton had need to repeat his message before its meaning penetrated. Then Strafford answered, "Put not your trust in princes."

On Tuesday, May 11, the king made one more attempt to save Strafford's life. He sent the Prince of Wales to the House of Lords with a final appeal:

> I did yesterday satisfy the justice of this Kingdom by passing the Bill of Attainder against the Earl of Strafford; but mercy being as inherent and inseparable to a King as justice, I desire at this time in some measure to show that likewise, by suffering that unfortunate man to fulfil the natural course of his life in a close imprisonment; this if it may be done without the discontentment of my people will be an unspeakable contentment to me. . . . But if no less than his life can satisfy my people, I must say "Fiat Justitia." Thus I rest...your unalterable and affectionate friend, Charles R.
>
> If he must die, it were charity to reprieve him until Saturday.[124]

The next day, the last of his life, Strafford turned to his old friend, now his fellow prisoner, Archbishop Laud. He asked Balfour if he might see Laud, but was told that he must first get permission from Parliament. "No," said Strafford, "I have gotten my despatch from them, and will trouble them no more."

A message was, however, sent to the Archbishop reporting his friend's wish to bid him farewell. As Strafford was led away on the morning of May 12, the aged prelate stood at the window of his cell. Strafford saw him and knelt: "My Lord, your prayers and blessing." Laud could not answer; overcome with emotion, he extended his hands but fainted. "Farewell, my Lord. God protect your innocency," said Strafford as he passed on.[125]

An immense concourse of persons, estimated at 200,000, crowded to the place of execution. Strafford went to his death with fortitude and dignity. His friends said that his look was more like that of a general marching to victory, than that of a prisoner led to execution. He mounted the scaffold with calm, and there, among a few kinsmen and friends, he made his last public declaration. He told the crowd that he had always held that "parliaments in England are the happy constitution of the kingdom and nation, and the best means under God to make the king and his people happy." He wished that all who were present would consider "whether the beginning of the people's happiness should be written in letters of blood."[126] After professing his faith in the Church of England, he knelt for a while in prayer. When he was done, he took leave of his friends and sent messages to his wife and children. He then prepared himself for death. "I do as cheerfully put off my doublet at this time as ever I did when I went to bed," he said. He was blessed by his chaplain and knelt before the block. The blow fell and it was finished.

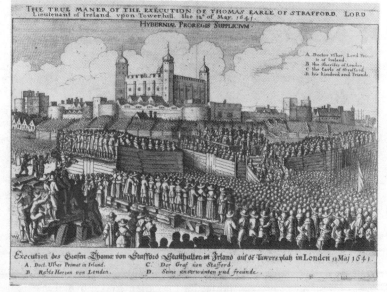

The Execution of Strafford (Hollar)

7
Conclusions

He had been Earl of Strafford, Lord Lieutenant of Ireland, Lord President of the North, Lieutenant General of the King's Army, and Knight of the Garter; then by Act of Parliament, he was merely Thomas Wentworth; now he was dead.

Why was Strafford deserted by his Peers, his king, and his friends? After all was finished, was the trial a significant happening? Was it necessary? Did the earl fight the best possible fight? What, in the end, did it all mean? Such questions are rightly asked; hence, the final chapter of this study will try to put the trial and fall of Strafford into perspective. The first part of the chapter will discuss the political reasons for his death. The second part will examine the rhetorical and legal history of the trial. The concluding pages will discuss the historical importance of the Earl of Strafford.

The Crisis of Confidence

Lord Strafford had depended upon his Peers for acquittal. He had every reason to expect justice or at least mercy from these men. But, in the end, they abandoned him to the mercies of the Commons and the king. His failure to win the upper House must be examined.

It was unfortunate for Strafford that he came before the Lords just at the time that monarchical and aristocratic government in England was entering the climax of its breakdown which finally occurred in 1640-1641, to be reestablished on terms in 1660 and 1688.

Lawrence Stone, a most profound historian of the Tudor and Stuart aristocracy, believes that the Peerage of England underwent between

1558 and 1641 a "crisis of confidence." Stone contrasts the maintenance of a fairly stout barrier between Peers and Gentry in the reign of Elizabeth with the striking, if temporary, erosion of the barrier under the early Stuarts.

During the reign of Elizabeth, the Peers were treated with utmost deference. Up to the late sixteenth century, they still lived in a semi-regal state, surrounded by swarms of attendants and served by sons of gentlemen.

By the early seventeenth century, this attitude of respectful subservience was breaking down. As early as 1578, it was remarked that Lords were far more respected in remote areas like Lancashire, Cheshire, and Stropshire where they were rare birds, than in the home counties where they were a familiar sight. During the 1620s and 1630s, significant little events kept occurring which indicated that the prestige of the peerage was declining and that the lower orders were ceasing more and more to treat noblemen with wonted deference. By the time of the Civil War, the stock of the aristocracy was lower than it had ever been before, or was to be again for centuries.

Stone, in his excellent work, spells out at length the many causes of the slump in prestige:

> They include the decline in the wealth of the peers relative to that of the gentry; the shrinkage of their territorial possessions, in both absolute and relative terms; the decay of their military power in men, arms, castles, and will to resist; the granting of titles of honour for cash not merit, in too great numbers, and to too unworthy persons; the change in their attitude towards the tenantry from suppliers of manpower to suppliers of rent; the undermining of their electoral influence due to the rise of deeply felt political and religious issues; the increasing preference for extravagant living in the city instead of hospitable living in the countryside; the spread throughout the propertied classes of a bookish education, acquired at school and university, and the demand by the State for an administrative *elite* of proved competence, irrespective of the claims of rank; the pervasive influence of the rise of individualism, the Calvinist belief in a spiritual hierarchy of the Elect, and the Puritan exaltation of the private conscience, which affected attitudes towards hierarchy and obedience in secular society; and finally the growing psychological breach between Court and Country in attitudes, real or supposed, towards constitutional

theory, methods and scale of taxation, forms of worship, aesthetic teates, financial probity and sexual morality.[1]

Many of the same forces were at work to bring about a general weakening of the hierarchical framework of upper class society in the early seventeenth century:

Respect for the episcopacy had been reduced by a century of robbery, neglect, and Calvinism; respect for the clergy had been undermined by attacks on their morals and educational short-comings, and by wider reading of the New Testament; respect for the King had been reduced by his association with a sexually depraved court, a pro-Spanish foreign policy, and a popish queen; respect for the baronetage had been sapped by the admission of men who were not even regarded as gentlemen, respect for the knighthood by the indiscriminate mass creations of James and Buckingham.[2]

The early seventeenth century thus saw a hardening of status divisions according to the law, accompanied by a decline of respect for superiors in church, state, society, and family. Therefore:

It is hardly surprising that the sharp decline in the prestige of peers eventually gave birth to a new constitutional theory. The M.P.'s had convinced themselves that the House of Commons was by its very nature an infinitely more important body than the House of Lords. John Pym described the latter as merely "a Third Estate by inheritance and birth-right," compared with "the whole body of the Commons of the Kingdom." Others took up the same theme, "this House being the representative body of the whole Kingdom, and their Lordships being but particular persons and coming to Parliament in a particular capacity." Although these ideas were undoubtedly stimulated by the policy clashes on vital issues between Lords and Commons, they struck an immediately respon-sive chord among the public, and it was this popular reaction which forced the Lords into reluctant retreat in 1641-2. This was the atmosphere which prepared the way for, and does much to explain, the popularity of the Leveller ideas in the late 1640's. William Overton argued historically that William the Conqueror and his successors "made dukes, earles, barrons, and lords of their fellow robbers, rogues, and thieves." His conclusion, "away with the pretended power of the Lords," was acceptable in circles far removed from that of his fellow Levellers.[3]

In the face of the mounting criticism of their privileges, the growing contempt for their persons, the erosion of the territorial foundations of their authority, the nobility were not prepared to mount a counterattack or attempt a reaction over the cause of the Earl of Strafford. A brief look at the statistics on attendance and voting of the Peers on Strafford's Attainder will indicate how far removed from their own fate they considered the fate of the earl to be.

There were 147 Lords. Of this number, only 45 were present and voting.

Nineteen voted for Strafford. Who were they? The question is highly conjectural,[4] but it seems probably that the following thirteen Lords were among the nineteen who were against his Attainder:

William Cavendish, Earl of Newcastle (7).[5]

Henry Clifford, 5th Earl of Cumberland (8).

Thomas Coventry, 2nd Lord Coventry (10).

Spencer Compton, 2nd Earl of Northampton (6).

James Hay, 2nd Earl of Carlisle (10).

John Hamilton, 2nd Earl of Cambridge (11).

John Holles, 2nd Earl of Clare (11).

Edward Noel, 2nd Viscount Cambden (10).

Thomas Savile, 2nd Lord Savile (9).

Edward Sackville, 4th Earl of Dorset (9).

Thomas Wentworth, 1st Earl of Cleveland (8).

Jerome Weston, 2nd Earl of Portland (8).

Francis Cottington, 1st Lord Cottington (7).

Why is it probable that these men voted for Strafford? Most of them were long-time colleagues of the earl, connected with him by kinship, or else were courtiers and creatures of the king or hardline Royalists. As a case in point, Lord Coventry had served on the Council with Strafford and taught the young earl many of the day-to-day methods of administration. Coventry became so fond of Strafford that he married his daughter to Strafford's nephew, Sir William Savile. Lord Cottington, of course, had served on the Council with Strafford, and had stuck by him throughout the trial. The Earl of Carlisle was the son of an old Scot whose loyal service dated back to when he came south with James I, and the son of Lucy Carlisle, Strafford's enamorata. The Earl of Clare was Strafford's father-in-law through his second wife. The Earl of Portland was a long-time courtier and friend of the king. Newcastle was more royalist than the king. The Earl of Cumberland was the brother of Strafford's first wife. Coventry, Northampton, Cambden, Dorset, and Portland had sons in Commons who voted against Strafford's attainder. So it went: the only lords who voted for Strafford were his friends, connections, relations, or else the most loyal and steadfast adherents of the Crown. He was unable to appeal to the other lords who required stronger reasons than justice to come out for him amidst so much danger.

Twenty-six Peers voted for the Bill of Attainder. It seems highly probable that most of the following fifteen were among the twenty-six:[6]

Mountjoy Blount, Earl of Newport (8).
Robert Devereux, 3rd Earl of Essex (8).
William Fielding, 1st Earl of Denbigh (10).
Henry Grey, 1st Earl of Stamford (10).
William Grey, Lord Grey of Warke (10).
P. Herbert, Lord Herbert of Cherbury (8).
Thomas Howard, 14th Earl of Arundel (11).
Edward Howard, 1st Lord Howard of Escrick (9).
James Howard, 3rd Earl of Suffolk (6).
Charles Howard, 2nd Earl of Nottingham (9).
Dudley North, 3rd Lord North (7).
Robert Rich, 2nd Earl of Warwick (10).
Oliver St. John, 1st Earl of Bolingbroke (11).
Francis Willoughby, 5th Lord Willoughby of Parnham (9).
Philip Wharton, 4th Lord Wharton (11).

The above were the hard-core Parliamentarians, who later formed the House of Lords during the Civil War (except Arundel, who became a Royalist) and from whom came many generals and officers of the parliamentary army.

It seems possible that most of the following four future Parliamentarians and Royalists were among the twenty-six who voted for the bill:

William Fiennes, 2nd Lord Saye and Sele (8).
Theophilus Fiennes (Lennard), 4th Earl of Lincoln (P-10).
Francis Fiennes (Lennard), 14th Lord Dacre of the South (P-3).
Edward Montague, 1st Lord Montague of Boughton (R-7).

Lord Saye was a strong Parliamentarian; but, tempted by the sweets of office, he worked with Bedford and Bristol on a compromise over Strafford's life. When their coalition fell apart, he probably voted for the bill to square himself with the Parliamentarians. The others of the Fiennes clan, Lincoln and Dacre, ran in the same pack. Montague of Boughton was with the Parliamentary party until war began. On the issue of fighting the king, he went over to the Royalists.

There were one-hundred and two abstentions or absentees among the Lords Temporal (the twenty-six bishops, the Lords Spiritual, all failed to vote):[7]

Seventeen Roman Catholic Peers, Royalist to a man, feared to come:

Abergavenny	Morley	Stafford
Arundell	Powys	Stourton
Brudenell	Rivers	Teynham
Castlehaven	Shrewsbury	Winchester
Eure	Somerset	Vaux
Montague	St. Albans	

Bristol, Holland, and Hertford abstained. Of the remainder of fifty-six, the *Daybook* shows an absentee record which indicates that forty other eligible Peers were probably not present and voting, among them names like Cavendish, Cecil, Danvers, Herbert, Howard, Ley, Manners, Sidney, Spencer, Stanley, Stanhope, Stuart.

Berkeley	Devonshire	Middlesex
Berkshire	Exeter	Mohun
Boteler	Falconberg	Mulgrave
Bridgewater	Gloucester	Northumberland
Bruce of Kinloss	Hervey	Pembroke
Capel	Kent	Purbeck
Charleton	Kingston	Richmond
Chesterfield	Leicester	Rutland
Conyers	Lindsey	Salisbury
Craven	Littleton	Spencer
Cromwell	Manchester	Stanhope of Harrington
Danby	Marlborough	Sussex
Deigncourt	Maynard	Winchelsea
Derby		

Most of these men were later to declare for the king. Some were to die in the Civil War; many were to be ruined. But they would not stand against Parliament on the issue of the Earl of Strafford. They drew the line only when Commons clearly endangered their privileges and the monarchy.

A most graphic illustration of the weakness of Strafford's appeal to the basic motives of the Lords is taken from a count of the ultra-Royalists whose sons were members of the Commons and did not vote for Strafford. There were ten of these Lords with sons so seated:

Belayse (Falconberg), Capel (Capel), Conway (Conway), Fane (Westmoreland), Goring (Goring), Poulett (Poulett), Seymour (Seymour of Trowbridge), Herbert (Herbert of Cherbury), Howard (Berkshire), Stanhope (Chesterfield).

The most striking illustration of how small was Strafford's importance to the Peers, is taken from a count of their ultimate declaration either for Charles or for the Parliament:

A report to the House of Lords in May 1642 showed that although more than half the peers ordinarily coming to parliament had remained in London, thirty-two were with the king at York. By June, sixteen more had joined him, although a few had left York or at least failed to sign the declaration of the peers in behalf of the king, testifying that they were convinced that he did not intend making war. With the subsequent additions, of the 135 male peers of England living on 22 August 1642, the day on which Charles raised his standard, about half actively backed the king with military service or contributions. Of the other half, *only about thirty may be considered Parliamentarians*—the balance being under age, abroad, or otherwise disqualified from participation.[8]

Only thirty lords joined with the Parliamentary party. Yet, of the others, Strafford could muster only nineteen to vote against the bill.

Divided and uncertain, the Lords were unwilling to make an issue with the Parliamentarians over Strafford. Moreover, in England, "unlike France or Brandenberg, a firm alliance of mutual self-interest between a highly-privileged nobility and an authoritarian Crown was not given time to mature."[9] Strafford was right: when it came to the crunch, "the English nobles would be ground to pieces between the millstones of the king and Commons."[10]

The fate of the Royalists Peers cannot be better summed-up than in the watchword of the sentries who, during the siege of Oxford, shouted down from the walls to their besiegers: "Roundhead, throw me up a mutton and I'll fling thee down a Peer!" Nor, as Stone points out, were things any better for the lords in London:

There a miserable rump huddled, neglected and despised, in an empty House of Lords. In 1645, Lord Willoughby remarked bitterly, "I thought it a crime to be a nobleman"; by the winter of 1648 there were only a handful of peers left to "sit and tell tales by the fireside in their House in hope of more Lords to drive away the time." A few months later the House of Lords was abolished, and with it the privileges which had hitherto helped to distinguish peers from gentry.[11]

These degrading situations were not a mere byproduct of the war. They were the culmination of a series of events begun when the Peers let Strafford go to his death. It is certainly arguable that if the leaders of the Commons had not been able to enlist the support of a number of prominent Peers, and to rely on the neutrality of an even larger group, they might have hesitated to take up their position against the king.

Of all this, Strafford had warned their lordships in his final statement. But he was unable to enlist the support of more than 19 out of 147 Peers.

Strafford's Failure

Any reasoned criticism of his defense must ask first of all: Was Strafford guilty of treason? The answer according to strict law must be firmly in the negative. Treason under English law, then and now, is an offense against the allegiance due the Sovereign in aid and counsel. The basic warrant of the Commons, that there were in England fundamental laws and that to subvert them was treason, was and still is erroneous. Legally, there are in Great Britain absolutely no laws, not even the Act of Settlement or the Act of Union, which Parliament may not alter as easily as a statute which provides penalties for littering a street. To break the laws is a crime. But to call treason that which falls unequivocally outside the written terms of the Statute of Treason does not justify a conviction. Lord Strafford was charged with treason; however, the evidence proved, at best, a series of high-handed and arbitrary acts, none of them treasonable. Strafford may have menaced the Constitution, but under the law he was not guilty of treason.

No one knew better than the leaders of the Commons that Strafford had committed no treasonable act. They were, however, genuinely convinced that King Charles, Strafford, Laud, and company were working to substitute arbitrary government for the rule of law. The Commons also knew Strafford better than Charles. They realized that in him the king had a minister who was capable of bringing to reality the dreams of a sovereign who longed for the full powers of the Tudor constitution. Despite the law, therefore, they resolved to destroy him.

Strafford died indeed "'twixt treason and convenience." There is absolutely no legal, and scant moral justification for the members of the House of Commons who engineered his death as a political necessity. Likewise, there is no legal or moral justification for the king: nor can a political justification be claimed for Charles because, when he yielded Strafford, the Parliamentarians realized from the surrender that victory in the constitutional struggle would be theirs. Both king and Commons alike could plead only that the act was convenient—convenient for the Commons to demand his life, convenient for the king to yield it. The law was on the side of the accused.

The undoubted rectitude, under the law, of the entire cause formed at once Strafford's greatest strength and his greatest weakness. Initially, his rhetorical purpose was not so much to save his life—since he was unaware of the full danger—but rather to drive a wedge between the House of Commons and the House of Lords and bring the two into collision. From the first, he was confident that his actions were not illegal, that he could justify himself, that he could completely discredit the lower House, and, therefore, that he would be found not guilty by the Lords. This was his first major error in judgment.

Such errors in judgment, which stemmed from an obstinate, stiff-necked belief in his own uprightness, formed the primary basis of Strafford's fall. Throughout his career, the earl's ambition, ability, and self-confidence qualified him for a high position in the royal administration. Unfortunately, he lacked the ability to earn more than the fear or hatred of the majority of his colleagues. His insight into human relations was almost always poor, and seldom could he make and keep allies. If he had learned to manage the human side of politics as skilfully as he learned to manage administrative and financial details, the outcome of his life work, including the trial, might have been different.

The Earl of Strafford's final defeat and ultimate death, then, were to a great degree brought on by himself. To be sure, the Parliamentarians saw him as the last pillar to a tottering throne, as the source of all ills, and were therefore resolved to remove him; but his own behavior did much to drive them on. There was nothing light and easy about the inflexible and arrogant earl. He met opposition with threats or force, and criticism with unreasonable perserverance in his own opinions. In her final estimate of Strafford's life, C. V. Wedgwood sums up Strafford's human shortcomings as follows:

> From the upheavals of his career, from the reports of his friends and
> his enemies, from the massive tomes of his correspondence, there
> emerges the image of a strong and resolute man, of great practical
> ability, of powerful intellect, of tireless energy; over-confident in
> his own opinions, over-certain of his own rectitude; not always
> scrupulous in the pursuit of public power and personal advantage;
> but a man of generous vision and unswerving loyalty, faithful to his
> King, just to his servants, true to his friends. [12]

These traits of Strafford's—especially persistent adherence to his own
opinions, purposes, and courses of action—did him ill-service when carried
over to the management of the trial. From the very beginning of the
proceedings, he was overly impressed by the undoubted strength of his
case under English law. This confidence led him to look upon the law as
the pivot upon which the outcome of the trial would turn. He came
quickly to believe that, if he could capture the law for the defense and
then hold the ground against the prosecution, he would be able to erect
thereupon an impregnable defense.

Thus, during the inventive-creative stages of working up his plan,
Strafford came to diagnose his entire case as a legal issue. If the
twenty-eight charges were to be answered from a strictly legal point of
view, then Strafford's justifying motive, of necessity, would be the
legality of his actions with reference to the law as it appeared in the
statute books, or was administered by the courts. His burden of proof
would be to convince the Lords that the point to adjudicate was the
legality or illegality of his actions with reference to the statute law of
treason.

Now, once Strafford chose a legal angle-of-attack upon the charges,
this selfsame choice would have caused a unique psychological integration, or perception, of the case and its facts to take place in at least four
"dimensions": (1) selection of data; (2) organization of data; (3)
association and discrimination among various data; and (4) the criteria of
judgment applied to various data and argumentative alternatives. Accordingly, once Strafford had selected the law as his major line of defense, his
subsequent field of inventive-creative maneuver was restricted. Such a
narrowing of the rhetorical alternatives occurs because once a specific
defensive strategy is selected, then the specific defensive tactics follow

from logical necessity: the nature of the initial rhetorical commitment dictates the nature of the argumentative follow-through.

As delivered, Strafford's defense is most noteworthy for its precise and thorough discussion of single points. He was especially effective when dissecting the prosecution's case. He spent hours taking apart their twenty-eight articles, bringing up from his retentive memory point after point of the evidence against him, weighing it and placing it in proper perspective. He presented an intricate argument, distinguished more by sheer mass than velocity and comparable to some of the efforts of Lord Mansfield.

In addition, it was often Strafford's technique to "unhorse" his adversaries rather than try to shout them down or wear them down. When the managers tore off reams of bombast and paraded platoons of witnesses, he often made their collective pyrotechnics seem foolish by stating quietly and simply the point at issue. For example, when the financial points of article ten were in danger of becoming a bookkeeper's nightmare because of a complex manipulation of figures by both sides, Strafford finally asked for a comparison of the king's revenue before and after his coming to Ireland. When the managers wandered far afield, he poked sharp fun at their meanderings. When they took shelter in abstruse technicalities, he appealed to the common sense of the Lords. In short, Strafford had a fund of what might be called a legal "sense of tactics": not deeply trained in the law, he grasped legal situations quickly, thought them through logically in terms of the prerogative and statute law, rhetorically in terms of argumentative force; talked the simplest English, and seldom tried to hide a weakness behind a barrage of words or legal phraseology.

Taken as a whole, Strafford's defense is marked with harmony of language, thought, and purpose. The broad principle which underpinned and unified the rhetorical resources of his arguments was the rule of law. Consistently, he focused the attention of the Lords upon a guide for legal interpretation of his actions. These features are even more striking because Strafford, like Lord Erskine and Lord Mansfield after him, spoke at a time when much English oratory was influenced by Ramian rhetoric, separated from invention and arrangement and burdened with Latin ornament and excruciating detail.

On the negative side, Strafford's defense was weakened by a large number of significant tactical errors. These were as follows:

1. Strafford had planned to forestall the impeachment by himself charging Pym and his party with treasonous correspondence with the Scots. Pym, however, charged Strafford first. Whether the earl moved too slowly or the king held him back is not known. In any case, the unfortunate result for Strafford was that he found himself in the custody of Black Rod before he could mount his own formidable attack against Pym.

2. Strafford was not in his place in the House of Lords when the general articles of impeachment were brought in. This was an error. He was barred at the door, unable to answer the charges immediately, which he could have done from his seat when Pym entered. Consequently, the earl's answer was never heard until the actual trial, at which time he was required to follow the case as it was developed by the managers. He was thus straited and unable to unfold his defense in the best possible order.

3. The loss of the twenty-six votes of the bishops must be reckoned as Strafford's most grievous tactical error. This error appears even larger in light of the fact that the accused apparently never tried to persuade the bishops to sit. There is evidence neither of personal appeal to them nor of intercession with Charles to protect the bishops and their position if they would sit and vote.

4. Strafford did not know whether he would be allowed to bring witnesses and papers out of Ireland. Instead of making secret arrangements for needed evidence to be sent over, he foolishly waited four weeks to receive this privilege formally from the Lords. Hence, much important evidence did not arrive until the particular article to which it was pertinent had already been tried.

5. The Commons blackened Strafford in the minds of the populace by their wide circulation of the charges against him. The earl apparently discounted the importance of public opinion and failed to mount a counter-effort to win the populace or, at least, to neutralize the effect of the publication of the charges. This was a very large miscalculation: At the climax of the struggle, the mob tipped the balance against him, frightening the Lords into abstention or submission, and the king into final surrender.

6. Strafford made no attempt to gain a change of venue. Yet if the trial could have been moved out of London on some pretext to a location such as Oxford or York, where the royal writ still ran, he might have been saved. As it happened, the London mob overawed both Lords and king.

The Earl of Strafford's crucial decision to defend himself on the basis of the law, and the subsequent skill of that defense, raise an important question for the critic: Should the critic *accept* Strafford's strategic assumptions, his own point of view, and proceed to analyze and criticize the defense as he delivered it? The answer to this question must be: No. Lord Strafford was well aware that the trial marked a turning point of grave importance in his career. He knew that he dared not fail and he believed that his best chance of success lay in a defense based solidly on the law. Now, Strafford was no beginner when it came to argumentation and debate; hence it is almost inconceivable that he would have designed a poor, stupid, or naive defense. Therefore, if the critic were to accept Strafford's *own* assumption, if he were to develop the criticism from Strafford's *own* angle-of-attack, then the critic would be inevitably led, from logical necessity, to assess nothing more or less than *what was done* by Strafford. Clearly, an acceptance of Strafford's "starting places" of argument would lead straight into an appraisal of the earl's logical argument, emotional proof, arrangement, style, and the like, *as delivered*. In short, if the critical judgments of Strafford's speaking were to proceed from his own assumptions as to the best trial strategy, then the critic would follow an unbroken circle, *judging the earl's tactics on the basis of the earl's own strategy*. Such a methodology of criticism would give any speaker high marks, unless the man was a complete fool. *The essence of rhetoric is sound strategy; tactics are only secondary.*

This much is clear: Strafford's entire defense, as conceived on the basis of English law, is brilliant and almost flawless; indeed, he lost with it by only a hair's breadth. Any criticism of his defense would find it to be legally, logically, and rhetorically near-perfect. Weaknesses can be found in it only at the level of microscopic detail, and these defects are all trivial. Moreover, the strengths of his defense are, in a sense, also trivial because they too follow logically from his overall strategic decisions. Taken as a forensic argument which disputed questions of fact and law, Strafford's work could serve as nothing less than a model for students of this genre of discourse. However, to take Strafford on his own terms would be to miss the major rhetorical lessons of his trial. He must be criticized, instead, on the basis of his *inventio*, i.e. his strategy; he must be criticized on the basis of whether he did indeed construct the strongest possible case from among the nearly infinite number of alternatives which were open to him as an advocate.

The alternative which the Earl of Strafford did select as his primary line of defense was the law. Through the entire fifty days from his indictment to his attainder, he put forward English law as the great leading principle to which all his efforts were connected and subsidiary, and which pointed like a beam of light through his entire plan. As Arnold points out, this kind of unity and emphasis is effective:

> Such centricity in composition has merit in almost any oral discourse but it contributes special force to forensic argument, where facts of human action and their relations to accepted systems of rules and policies are the bases of judgment. Harry Caplin has used the phrase "the complete economy of the entire speech" to suggest this degree of centricity required in effective pleading. [13]

Strafford undoubtedly achieved a high degree of unity and systematic emphasis. He created during the proceedings of each day of the trial a "complete economy" of argument, in which the principle of English law was advanced as his justifying motive.

No one can asperse the precept behind this conception of the case, or the ensuing methodology of execution: It utilized all the resources of the Crown lawyers and the peculiar strengths of the available documents and witnesses; it followed closely the accepted idea that, at the English Bar, the ground of argument was generally limited to precise law and statute; it struck hard at the forehead of the charges of the House of Commons. The strategy overlooked one overpowering weakness: It was a Maginot Line type of defense, extremely vulnerable to flanking movements. Strafford won battle after battle as the managers broke the thrust of their articles in frontal attacks against his main defense. But he lost the war because he failed to cover his defensive line with alternative strategies, which could have been made into emergency defenses if his legal position became threatened. The earl staked everything on one idea. Believing his position under the law to be impregnable, he stubbornly adhered to his original plan. When the Commons shifted ground on him, he was caught unprepared, unable to retreat or maneuver.

By the time the Commons reached their final articles, it was clear that Strafford was winning. The stage was thus set for the lower House's deadly change of strategy: the Bill of Attainder, which argued Strafford's death as politically necessary for the safety of the State. As soon as their move was revealed, Lord Strafford, still keeping his defense anchored upon its original ground, crossed the letter of the law and began hastily to build a political, defensive argument. However, he no longer enjoyed the concentration of all forces upon a single warrant (which yields rhetorical advantages similar to those of interior lines in military warfare). More important, he was too late and disposed too little: The Commons now struck at an open, vulnerable enemy.

First to be noticed—after the Commons had shifted their attack—are the precipitate, incautious stages by which Strafford advanced his new defenses, based upon claims that were warranted by the prerogative, the constitution, and the Peers' well-being. In all the previous weeks of the trial, he had mentioned only once his theory of the relation between the king and the subject; only twice, and briefly too, the danger which his conviction would present to the nobility. Faced with the Bill of Attainder at his very last opportunity to speak, he had no time to work gradually, cautiously, indirectly. He was forced to install the new defenses all in one day, while at the same time to maintain the old. Consequently, he worked fast and stated his political argument bluntly. Given the new attack by the Commons, Strafford's moves were rhetorically necessary, but hasty and crude. The new argument by Strafford swept about the Peers much too quickly: they were given no time to think carefully, no time to accustom themselves to the new doctrines and gradually assimilate them. On the other hand, the basic argument of the Commons remained pretty much the same: Strafford was still the source of all evils and the blackest of hearts; only the legal framework had been changed; the basic charges were intact. Far better for Strafford if he had developed his political warrants from the very beginning of the trial. Then, if he had to bring them fully into play, the Peers—long accustomed to their meaning and implications—could have received them without surprise.

Not only was Strafford's defensive strategy false, and not only was he unable to use *insinuatio* and suggestion in his last-minute defense, but the case in its entirety was tried the way that the Commons wanted it tried. A good defense lawyer controls the course of the case, so that the cause is developed the way he wants it developed. Strafford seldom tried to gain this tactical advantage. The Commons had received from the Lords the right to develop the articles and to call witnesses, and submit evidence, in any sequence or combination that they saw fit. Thus, they controlled the overall disposition of the trial. Strafford lamely submitted to this decision, and made no attempts to break out of this straitjacket until the last three days of the trial. Ironically, when he did finally begin to combine articles and evidence, the Lords let it stand.

The earl did manage to put his finger on the most perplexing aspect of the case: if the Earl of Strafford was guilty, who was innocent? But he made no great amplification or emphasis of this point, so that its impact was lost among the mass of other testimony and argument.

Another significant weakness of Strafford's method: he was always on the defensive. He would have been more effective if he could have devised a non-defensive plan and brought pressure against the Commons. Following an offensive strategy, he would not have stood on the defense; he would not go before the Lords as the wrongdoer, the guilty, pleading for justice, or, at best, mercy. Instead, he would go in and attack. He would indict certain of the Commons and the managers for criminal conspiracy, revealing to the Lords and the country their treasonous correspondence with the Scots. He would indict John Pym and his men for treason. But, most important of all, he would place before the Bar that country party which was trying to wrest control of the government unto themselves, men under whom the Crown and the Lords would be reduced to ciphers.

True, Strafford certainly could not have convicted John Pym and his party, nor would he be able to persuade the Lords to support such charges, even if he could prove Pym and company guilty of treason with the Scots and of trying to betray the army. He could not be a trial lawyer; he would have to be political theorist and a teacher. In doing so, he might have damned his accusers in the minds of the Londoners, that formless mass, which, if ever sufficiently informed and aroused, might rise up in its wrath and overawe the Commons.

Indeed, his defense could have juxtaposed Lord Strafford with John Pym and let the Lords draw their own conclusions. He might have tried to call Pym to the stand, to reveal the details of the correspondence with the Scots and his part in wrecking the king's efforts to win the war.

The shoe neatly could have been put on the other foot: the prosecutors could have been prosecuted. Pulling a master-stroke, Strafford could have announced that he was going to call to the stand every last member of Pym's conspiracy, whom he would then proceed to convict not only of treason with the Scots but, further, of a criminal plot to take over and use the royal government for their own collusive purposes. Such a move, obviously, would have had to be cleverly and subtly arranged, for

Strafford was on trial, not the Commons. Yet, the annals of trials are full of accusations which were effectively made from the dock, and Strafford might have gained at least a partial success. The great mystery is why he never effectively used the incriminating evidence that he had on Pym and his party.

The ordinary lawyer collates facts, analyzes evidence, and makes his appeal. There are few who, like Erskine, use history, psychology, politics, and philosophy in order to show the true underlying significance of the cause. In this sense, Strafford's entire defense was ordinary. For example, the larger danger of convicting Strafford was not amplified and fully developed. If the Earl of Strafford were convicted as a traitor, all of the Crown's advisors would stand on the same ground; the precedent would be set for executing any and all advisors on any and all illegal charges. Justice would be destroyed; the State and its courts and legal system would be taken over by the Commons; the Constitution and the Government would be paralyzed; and in the paralysis, the Crown and the Lords would see their power dissolve. Yet, this idea, which should have formed a consistent, underlying theme of Strafford's defense, was mentioned only sporadically from time to time during the trial and was never as fully developed as, for example, the Statute and Proviso of Edward III on Treason.

Along this same line, Strafford failed in another way. In this trial at this time, when Commons was making a determined attack upon the Crown, the accused was in a position to produce one of the outstanding political documents of his time, enunciating in logical terms the rights of the Crown alongside the rights of the Parliament and the subject, in a manner which would lead the way toward a compromise. Strafford touched greatness several times in his appeal, but not in his arguments for the political system in which he so steadfastly believed.

Men of vision do not build for today; they do not build for tomorrow. They build for the centuries, for the ages. Great and epochal phrases might have poured from Strafford's lips, phrases that would have reshaped the minds of men and the government of his country. He might have saved the monarchy and his king. He might have brought about the change in the constitution without bloodshed. At least, he might have saved his own life. Instead, history, politics, and the like were subsidiary to his defense built on the law and were, consequently, underdeveloped.

An argument which in addition was profound political philosophy might also have made sure of the king. Strafford, however, assumed that if—on some slim chance—the Lords did find him guilty, then the king would not assent to the conviction and would use his royal prerogative to veto the sentence. This was another of Strafford's major errors in judgment.

As Thomas Lord Erskine knew, one of the more important rhetorical problems for the defense is to advance strong reasons for acquittal which have deep personal importance to the judges. The paramount task is to make the judges *want* to decide the case for the defense. Points of law and argument merely give the judge a reason for doing what the advocate has already made him want to do. The English lords who sat in judgment on Strafford were, above all, human beings, motivated by the same hopes and fears as other humans. Therefore, the earl needed, above all, to include in his defense strong reasons for acquittal which had deep personal importance to the Lords and king. Instead of speaking directly and indirectly to either their personal well-being or the long-term weal of the kingdom, he based 95 percent of his case upon questions of fact and law. He gave his judges cold, dry legal arguments, all of which had scant powers of motivation when the mob began to threaten their lives.

If the Peers had been made to agree that Strafford's ruin entailed their own, they probably would have made his fate a point on which to stand, just as they drew the line when the parliamentary issues resolved into a direct attack upon the constitutional position of the Crown. When it came to the monarchy, their privileges, traditions, and loyalties, the great majority of the Lords were ready to fight. But Strafford did not manage—he hardly tried until the very last—to stimulate the Lords on the basis of such deep-seated springs of motivation. If he could have shown that he was merely the first victim, that his trial was the opening skirmish of a revolution, the Lords would have acquitted him.

I have suggested that the essence of Strafford's defense was the convergence of all his forces of discourse towards a legal basis for decision in the case. In his argument lasting fifty days, there are no digressions, no wasted thoughts. From his *stasis*, he developed a defense so effective that it nearly defeated the Commons, so well-constructed that it practically defies negative criticism, except at a trivial level. I have also suggested that there is in his defense much that is striking and beautiful as proof, especially his closing statement with its thorough and meticulous discussion of single points united with a deeply-moving pathos.

But Strafford overlooked one important dictum of the classic forensic rhetorician: "There is indeed no cause in which the point...is considered with reference to parties...and not from arguments relating to questions in general." With regard to considering his case in relation to "questions in general" of political wisdom or expediency, which was the basis on which the case was finally decided, Strafford was simply out-generaled by the Commons on both the tactical and strategic level. He set himself firmly upon the law and stubbornly clung to that position until he saw his position undermined. Too late did he develop a political argument with broad appeal. His argument on the law was tenacious and strong, but his inflexibility must be regarded as the negation of rhetorical generalship.

When the day arrived for St. John's legal argument, nearly all illusions had vanished. Strafford knew that he had lost the fight and would be defeated. It is his enduring glory that this made no difference to his resistance. His able and often eloquent defense clearly places Lord Strafford in the mainstream of British public address as an able practitioner of the art as it was in the 17th century. But Goodrich was clearly mistaken when he ranked Strafford as one of the most eminent British orators of all time. To be sure, Lord Strafford was extremely able in his own defense, but he simply made too many *basic* rhetorical errors to be granted a place alongside such speakers as Lord Erskine or Lord Mansfield. A great practitioner of the art of rhetoric does not fight a strategically inferior battle.

Strafford deserves, rather, a place in British public address at the head of that class of near-greats like Palmerston, Russell, Canning, *et al*. His defense is interesting to the rhetorician or historian for its thorough and unified argument from a single principle. He exemplifies the best methods of effective rebuttal and cross-examination. And, in his closing statement, he shows how a near-great speaker can rise for a moment to the height of eloquence. Nothing more hopeless than his position on that last day can be imagined; nothing more effective than his brief union of *logos* and *pathos* could have been accomplished in that untenable position; and it is this which raises his closing statement from an ordinary to a rhetorically noteworthy level.

The trial of Lord Strafford gives rhetoric more reason than usual to review its theory and practice. The earl's defensive strategy assumed that the point to adjudicate and the question for decision in the trial would emerge from the law; thus he assigned most of his time and effort to a legal defense, to the detriment of any other approach. The strength of the legal position would prevent the prosecution from making a case, went the theory, and the other possibilities for prosecution, or defense, would not matter. But it was another, unforeseen possibility that defeated him. A legal defense failed to deter the creative maneuvering of the Commons.

Lord Strafford should have abandoned a massive, single-point-to-adjudicate defense in favor of a *strategy of flexible response*. This concept dictates that the forensic defense must *possess* the means to respond with appropriate degrees of rhetorical force to any point of accusation. Moreover, the concept dictates that the appropriate means of response must be *partially developed* throughout the trial by means of suggestion, so that if the prosecution suddenly changes from one point of accusation to another, the defense will not have to begin cold with a new justifying motive. The concept seems equally applicable to deliberative speaking.[14]

The rhetorical problem is to translate the concept into hard decisions, to anticipate what points of accusation will be or could be forthcoming, and what defensive response is appropriate to meet them. The difficulty of this task can be pointed out by an analogy: A long-range rhetorical problem is comparable to the problems of an automotive racing team who want to win a grand prix race to be run many months hence, on a track not yet built, between cars not yet designed. To make matters more difficult, the possibility exists that when the race is finally run, the rules may have been changed, the track configuration altered, and the cars replaced by motorcycles. Strafford lost his fight when the rules were changed and the track altered. His trial points up again the importance of an effective audience analysis methodology, of an effective analysis of the options open to both sides, and of a strategy of flexible response.

The trial of Lord Strafford has come down through the centuries as one of the most important in English history. Strafford deserves to be remembered, however, not only as a competent forensic artist, but as a man who stood for a system of government and who courageously defended this system in a trial which he had little chance of winning. It is more by his choice of briefs and manner of death, than by his art as a speaker, that Strafford will continue to be remembered.

More than a great orator, he was a tragic and romantic hero. He fought for an ideal, but was betrayed by cowardice and perfidy in his peers and in his prince. His death was brave and generous, wasted and unnecessary. For everyone who studies it with care, there is a humanizing lesson in Strafford's trial and execution. The circumstances of the trial and of the attainder throw odium upon his pursuers. Thus, his oratory will live, not because of any intrinsic rhetorical merit which makes it great, but because of the romance, tragedy, and injustice which surrounded his fall as the Commons slaughtered a man they could not convict.

In conclusion, then, the lessons of the impeachment and attainder of Thomas Wentworth, First Earl of Strafford, are ethical and political, not rhetorical. The Earl of Strafford cannot be claimed as a defender of English liberties and law, but nevertheless he died for them, and by his death helped to preserve them to another day.

Charles I and Henrietta (Van Dyck)

APPENDICES

APPENDIX A

Attendance of the House of Lords at the Trial of the Earl of Strafford

The following tabulation of attendance of the Lords at Strafford's trial was taken from the *Braye Mss*. The Minute Book shows attendance at sessions from January 11 to April 10, 1641; and the Journal, no. 18, shows attendance on May 4. From twenty-two sessions—March 20 to April 10, plus May 4—eleven dates were selected at random. The following list shows which Peers attended all eleven sessions of the selected eleven, ten of the eleven, down to zero of the eleven.

A polygraph of attendance for all twenty-two sessions follows the tabulation.

11 of 11:

Arundel: 3-20, 3-22, 3-27, 3-30, 4-1, 4-5, 4-7, 4-8, 4-9, 4-10, 5-4.

Brooke: 3-20, 3-22, 3-27, 3-30, 4-1, 4-5, 4-7, 4-8, 4-9, 4-10, 5-4.

Cambridge: 3-20, 3-22, 3-27, 3-30, 4-1, 4-5, 4-7, 4-8, 4-9, 4-10, 5-4.

Clare: 3-20, 3-22, 3-27, 3-30, 4-1, 4-5, 4-7, 4-8, 4-9, 4-10, 5-4.

Holland: 3-20, 3-22, 3-27, 3-30, 4-1, 4-5, 4-7, 4-8, 4-9, 4-10, 5-4.

Huntington: 3-20, 3-22, 3-27, 3-30, 4-1, 4-5, 4-7, 4-8, 4-9, 4-10, 5-4.

Strange: 3-20, 3-22, 3-27, 3-30, 4-1, 4-5, 4-7, 4-8, 4-9, 4-10, 5-4.

Wharton: 3-20, 3-22, 3-27, 3-30, 4-1, 4-5, 4-7, 4-8, 4-9, 4-10, 5-4.

10 of 11:

Bath: 3-20, 3-22, 3-27, 3-30, 4-1, 4-5, 4-8, 4-9, 4-10, 5-4.

Camden: 3-22, 3-27, 3-30, 4-1, 4-5, 4-7, 4-8, 4-9, 4-10, 5-4.

Carlisle: 3-22, 3-27, 3-30, 4-1, 4-5, 4-7, 4-8, 4-9, 4-10, 5-4.

Carnarvan: 3-22, 3-27, 3-30, 4-1, 4-5, 4-7, 4-8, 4-9, 4-10, 5-4.

Chandois: 3-22, 3-27, 3-30, 4-1, 4-5, 4-7, 4-8, 4-9, 4-10, 5-4.

Conway: 3-22, 3-27, 3-30, 4-1, 4-5, 4-7, 4-8, 4-9, 4-10, 5-4.

Coventry: 3-22, 3-27, 3-30, 4-1, 4-5, 4-7, 4-8, 4-9, 4-10, 5-4.

Denbigh: 3-20, 3-22, 3-27, 3-30, 4-1, 4-5, 4-7, 4-8, 4-9, 4-10.

Kymbolten: 3-22, 3-27, 3-30, 4-1, 4-5, 4-7, 4-8, 4-9, 4-10, 5-4.

Lincoln: 3-20, 3-22, 3-27, 3-30, 4-1, 4-5, 4-8, 4-9, 4-10, 5-4.

Rich: 3-20, 3-22, 3-27, 3-30, 4-1,

4-5, 4-8, 4-9, 4-10, 5-4.

Robartes: 3-22, 3-27, 3-30, 4-1, 4-5, 4-7, 4-8, 4-9, 4-10, 5-4.

Sarum: 3-22, 3-27, 3-30, 4-1, 4-5, 4-7, 4-8, 4-9, 4-10, 5-4.

Seymour of Trowbridge: 3-20, 3-22, 3-27, 3-30, 4-1, 4-5, 4-8, 4-9, 4-10, 5-4.

Stamford: 3-20, 3-22, 3-27, 3-30, 4-1, 4-5, 4-7, 4-9, 4-10, 5-4.

Thanet: 3-22, 3-27, 3-30, 4-1, 4-5, 4-7, 4-8, 4-9, 4-10, 5-4.

Grey of Warke: 3-22, 3-27, 3-30, 4-1, 4-5, 4-8, 4-9, 4-10, 5-4.

Warwick: 3-20, 3-22, 3-27, 3-30, 4-1, 4-5, 4-8, 4-9, 4-10, 5-4.

9 of 11:

Dudley: 3-22, 3-27, 3-30, 4-1, 4-5, 4-7, 4-8, 4-9, 4-10.

Devonshire: 3-22, 3-27, 3-30, 4-1, 4-5, 4-8, 4-9, 4-10, 5-4.

Howard of Escrick: 3-22, 3-27, 3-30, 4-1, 4-5, 4-8, 4-9, 4-10, 5-4.

Goring: 3-20, 3-22, 3-27, 3-30, 4-1, 4-5, 4-8, 4-10, 5-4.

Grey of Ruthyn: 3-20, 3-22, 3-27, 3-30, 4-1, 4-5, 4-8, 4-10, 5-4.

Hertford: 3-22, 3-27, 3-30, 4-1, 4-5, 4-8, 4-9, 4-10, 5-4.

Lovelace: 3-22, 3-27, 3-30, 4-1, 4-5, 4-8, 4-9, 4-10, 5-4.

Manchester: 3-22, 3-27, 3-30, 4-1, 4-5, 4-7, 4-8, 4-9, 4-10.

Nottingham: 3-20, 3-22, 3-30, 4-1, 4-5, 4-8, 4-9, 4-10, 5-4.

Willoughby of Parnham: 3-20, 3-22, 3-27, 3-30, 4-1, 4-5, 4-8, 4-9, 4-10.

Peterborough: 3-22, 3-27, 3-30, 4-1, 4-5, 4-8, 4-9, 4-10, 5-4.

Poulett: 3-22, 3-27, 3-30, 4-1, 4-5, 4-8, 4-9, 4-10, 5-4.

Rivers: 3-20, 3-27, 3-30, 4-1, 4-5, 4-7, 4-8, 4-9, 4-10.

Savile: 3-22, 3-27, 3-30, 4-1, 4-5, 4-8, 4-9, 4-10, 5-4.

St. Albans: 3-22, 3-27, 3-30, 4-1, 4-5, 4-7, 4-8, 4-9, 4-10.

Stafford: 3-22, 3-27, 3-30, 4-1, 4-5, 4-7, 4-8, 4-9, 4-10.

8 of 11:

Bristol: 3-22, 3-27, 3-30, 4-1, 4-5, 4-8, 4-10, 5-4.

Howard of Escrick: 3-22, 3-30, 4-1, 4-5, 4-8, 4-10, 5-4.

Cleveland: 3-22, 3-30, 4-1, 4-5, 4-7, 4-8, 4-9, 4-10.

Cumberland: 3-27, 3-30, 4-1, 4-5, 4-8, 4-9, 4-10, 5-4.

Dover: 3-27, 3-30, 4-1, 4-5, 4-8, 4-9, 4-10, 5-4.

Leigh of Dunamore: 3-22, 3-27, 3-30, 4-1, 4-5, 4-8, 4-10, 5-4.

Essex: 3-22, 3-27, 3-30, 4-1, 4-5, 4-8, 4-10, 5-4.

Herbert of Cherbury: 3-22, 3-27, 3-30, 4-1, 4-5, 4-8, 4-9, 4-10.

Newport: 3-22, 3-27, 3-30, 4-1, 4-5, 4-8, 4-9, 4-10.

Portland: 3-22, 3-27, 3-30, 4-1, 4-5, 4-8, 4-10, 5-4.

Powys: 3-22, 3-27, 3-30, 4-1, 4-5, 4-8, 4-9, 4-10.

Saye and Sele: 3-22, 3-27, 3-30, 4-1, 4-5, 4-8, 4-10, 5-4.

Southampton: 3-22, 3-27, 3-30, 4-1, 4-5, 4-8, 4-9, 4-10.

Westmoreland: 3-22, 3-27, 3-30, 4-1, 4-5, 4-8, 4-10, 5-4.

Wentworth: 3-22, 3-27, 3-30, 4-1, 4-5, 4-8, 4-10, 5-4.

7 of 11:

Arundell: 3-22, 4-1, 4-5, 4-8, 4-9,
4-10, 5-4.

Brudenell: 3-22, 3-27, 3-30, 4-1,
4-5, 4-8, 4-10.

Cottington: 3-20, 3-22, 3-27, 4-5,
4-8, 4-9, 4-10.

Fauconbridge: 3-27, 3-30, 4-1, 4-5,
4-8, 4-9, 4-10.

Hastings: 3-27, 3-30, 4-1, 4-5, 4-8,
4-10, 5-4.

Monmouth: 3-22, 3-27, 3-30, 4-1,
4-8, 4-10, 5-4.

Montague of Boughton: 3-22, 3-27,
3-30, 4-1, 4-5, 4-8, 4-10.

Mowbray: 3-22, 3-27, 3-30, 4-1,
4-5, 4-8, 5-4.

Newcastle: 3-22, 3-27, 3-30, 4-1,
4-5, 4-8, 4-10.

North: 3-22, 3-27, 3-30, 4-5, 4-8,
4-10, 5-4.

Paget: 3-22, 3-27, 3-30, 4-1, 4-5,
4-8, 5-4.

Stourton: 3-22, 3-27, 3-30, 4-1,
4-5, 4-8, 4-10.

6 of 11:

Craven: 3-30, 4-1, 4-5, 4-8, 4-10,
5-4.

Northampton: 3-22, 3-27, 3-30,
4-1, 4-5, 5-4.

Suffolk: 3-27, 4-1, 4-5, 4-8, 4-9,
5-4.

5 of 11:

Derby: 3-22, 4-1, 4-5, 4-8, 4-10.

4 of 11:

Bedford: 3-20, 4-1, 4-8, 4-10.

Deigncourt: 3-27, 3-30, 4-1, 4-5.

Morley: 3-27, 3-30, 4-1, 4-5.

3 of 11:

Sussex: 3-22, 3-30, 4-10.

2 of 11:

Dacre of the South: 3-30, 4-1.

Oxford: 4-1, 4-10.

1 of 11:

Berkshire: 5-4.

Chesterfield: 3-20.

Charlton: 5-4.

Danby: 3-20.

Falconburg: 3-22.

Gloucester: 5-4.

Hertford: 5-4.

Lindsey: 5-4.

Marlborough: 5-4.

Pembroke: 5-4.

0 of 11:

Abergavenny.

Berkely.

Boteler.

Bridgewater.

Capel.

Castlehaven.

Conyers.

Cromwell.

Eure.

Exeter.

Stanhope.

Hervey.

Kent.

Kingston.

Kinloss.

Leicester.

Littleton.

Maynard.

Middlesex.

Mohun.

Montague

Mulgrave.

Northumberland.

Purbeck.

Richmond.

Rutland.

Shrewsbury.

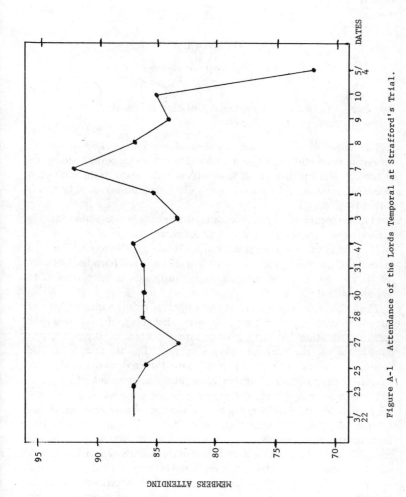

Figure A-1   Attendance of the Lords Temporal at Strafford's Trial.

Somerset.   Vaux.
Salisbury.   Winchelsea.
Spencer.   Winchester.
Teynham.

APPENDIX B

A Critical Methodology for
Rhetorical Analysis of the Trial

Part One: Audience Analysis and Adaptation as Primary Foci of
a Rhetorical Criticism

The nature of any criticism of public address is shaped by the critic's ideas concerning the nature of audience. The critic's ideas about audience, in turn, reflect his theoretical assumptions with regard to the character- istics of communicative situations. The assumptions directing this particular inquiry are:

(1) The speaking situation consists of all possible interactions among speakers, listeners, subject matter, and occasion.

(2) Within the speaking situation, audience is an *emergent*; that is, a function of listener's predispositions toward topic and purpose; listeners' reaction to the occasion; and, most importantly, how listeners respond to what the speaker does.

Thus, the critic, when confronting a work of public address which he intends to criticize, must try to discover what *mediating* factors in the speaking situation led the audience into a posture of support of, or opposition to, the purposes of the speaker. In this case, what did Strafford's judges "bring with them" into the trial which could have affected their responses to speaker, topic, purpose, or occasion?

It is clear that Strafford's judges brought with them to the trial lifetimes of loyalties, beliefs, and understandings of themselves within the scheme of things important to them. In the parlance of modern psychology, each judge had a "behavioral history" which accompanied him into Westminster Hall. Any factor in the judge's behavioral history could conceivably have affected or mediated his response to the rhetorical situation of the unfolding trial. Consequently, Lord Strafford, in order to be effective, had the knotty problem of accurately estimating what effective variables (e.g., attitudes, knowledge) were at work within the "rhetorical field-of-force." Hence, his judges can be viewed by the critic as a network of interrelated responses affected through points in time by attitudes and knowledge.

I am led, therefore, to consider audience as a variable intervening between Strafford's opinion of the accusation and the achievement of his specific purpose(s); the achievement of a specific purpose being dependent upon how listeners respond. It therefore follows that the audience to which Strafford had to adapt, *emerged* for him at successive moments of time during this trial. As a result of this point of view, the attention of the critic is focused upon *"how well"* Strafford assessed the *contingencies* which he had to prepare to meet during the trial.

Viewed in this way, effective communication depends upon two things: (1) the kind of behavioral history that has been built into a listener's action structure (system of beliefs and knowledge, habits of acting, personality) and (2) the kind of situation arranged by the speaker for the listener, which determines the kinds of stimuli to which the latter is exposed. In short, the speaker faces the problem of deciding the *kinds* of stimuli to which the listener shall be exposed. Hence, the task of the critic is to evaluate not only the "quality" and "effectiveness" of these stimuli, but also, and probably more important, the decisions *by which* the speaker selected this or that stimulus.

A speaker, with a purpose before an audience, always faces the total possible rhetorical alternatives of the communicative situation. Therefore, the critic must evaluate both the "path taken" by the speaker and the "choice of paths" from among countless possible alternatives. It is from this kind of general concept that the study proceeds.

Part Two: Specification of the Critical Methodology

Task One: *Discovery of Strafford's Rhetorical Purposes at Points in Time*

Lord Strafford did *not* have to come to trial for his life: he could have fled the country like Finch, Windebank, and many other Ministers of the Crown who felt themselves in danger. Thus, it would be a great oversimplification for the critic merely to assume that Strafford's rhetorical purpose throughout the trial was only to gain an acquittal and save his life, an end which could have been more simply accomplished by slipping back to Ireland or across the Channel. Consequently, the first aim of Task One was to ascertain precisely why Strafford allowed himself to be put on trial, and what he hoped to accomplish by confronting in this manner the enemies of the Crown.

Furthermore, it was likely that Strafford's rhetorical purpose did not remain the same throughout the trial. More likely, his purposes changed significantly as the trial unfolded and the advantage swung for or against him. The second aim of Task One, therefore, was to discover how and why Strafford's rhetorical aims varied during the trial.

Task Two: Description of the Nature of the Audience

To provide a basis for Task Three of the study—which was to estimate the feasibility, logicality, and practicability of Strafford's rhetorical purposes—the nature of the audience had to be discovered and described. Task Two, therefore, was concerned with estimating the pertinent attitudes, convictions, knowledge, and experience of the three sets of judges to whom the Earl addressed his arguments: Commons, Lords, and the Crown.

Task Three: Estimation of the Feasibility of Strafford's Rhetorical Purposes

Rhetorical feasibility[1] refers to whether or not a speaker's purpose is both logical and practicable for the situation that he faces. Conversely, a purpose may be considered rhetorically unfeasible if it was either illogical or impracticable for the situation.

At this point in the study, I possessed an estimate of Strafford's purposes at points in time throughout the trial, and an estimate of the "status" of the audience at points in time throughout the trial: I then proceeded to criticize the feasibility—in terms of logicality and practicability—of Strafford's purpose, when compared with the audiences he faced.

Before a purpose can be called feasible, the speaker must estimate whether there is a *logical* possibility that he can achieve his purpose, and then whether his *trying* to achieve it will overcome the difficulties of the situation.

The starting point of this criticism of Strafford's audience adaptation presupposed the aforementioned specific purposes at which he aimed during the trial, thus defining what he, himself, took to be overall success; that is, the "consummate" responses at which he aimed.

Estimating the logicality of Strafford's purposes served the critic as a "red flag" procedure, intended to prevent him from indulging in unnecessary criticism. For example, if a speaker's purpose was to create a new understanding, his purpose would be illogical *if* his audience possessed that understanding prior to hearing his discourse. If this should turn out to be the case, then the criticism ought to be focused mainly upon *how and why the speaker misjudged his audience*, rather than focusing mainly upon points of style or delivery.

In such cases, a discovery of illogicality reveals the speaker's purpose to have been unfeasible (unfeasible if and only if either illogical *or* impracticable[2]) and, therefore, reveals a badly mistaken analysis of the audience. If, on the other hand, the audience does not possess the understanding or belief that the speaker desires them to have, then he knows that success in the situation is at least a *logical possibility*.

Lord Strafford's purposes were indeed logical; therefore the critic now proceeded to the next step in the criticism, which was to discover the attitude-knowledge relationships which shaped the responses of Strafford's audiences.

When the logicality of Strafford's purposes had been discovered, the *practicability* of his purposes (given the audiences that he had to persuade) had to be estimated. To make such an estimate of practicability, the critic of a speaker must ascertain the attitude-knowledge relationships which shaped and influenced the responses of the audience. This kind of estimate is a mirror image of, and corresponds logically to, the *speaker's* task when he tries to discover the "status" of his audience, and then to provide himself with explanations for this state of affairs.

An attempt to explain the rhetorical situation faced by a speaker by means of reference to patterns of audience attitudes and knowledge often enables the critic to discover what things the speaker had to accomplish as prerequisites to achieving his purposes. For example, the critic could discover what kinds of prejudices the speaker had to conciliate and disarm as instrumental goals to be accomplished as he progressed towards his goals. Discoveries of extreme hostility, and the like, might lead the critic to conclude that the speaker's purpose was impracticable.

The final step in judging the practicability of Strafford's purposes was to assess the *alternative means* to his ends, during successive stages of the trial. Thus far, I have set down purpose, audience, and logicality and practicability. Now, for Strafford there did exist alternative methods of persuasion. Thus, the prime critical question was: Did he analyze his audience validly and then choose the most viable alternatives? The critic noted how and why the speaker anticipated that the choice of a particular rhetorical option would probably evoke an unfavorable response— unfavorable meaning a response which was not instrumental to the achievement of his purpose. The critic's task, then, was to evaluate the speaker's choice of alternatives.

Critical consideration of the interrelationships between purpose, audience, and feasibility provided a basis for criticizing Strafford's selection of purpose, audience analysis, and audience adaptation. These interrelationships also provided a foundation for the criticism done in subsequent phases of this study. The procedures followed in Tasks One,

Two, and Three are summarized in Figure One.

Task Four: *Describing and Criticizing the Central Ideas and Major*
                 Methods of Argument Used by Defense and Prosecution

It is imperative with any rhetorical criticism to abstract the central
ideas and major methods of argument of both sides, so that an estimate of
their respective effectiveness can be made. Consequently, the next task of
the study was to describe and criticize the ideas and methods of argument
which were used during the trial by the prosecution and defense. The
analysis and criticism which was done grouped factors which responded
to heuristic questions into "cluster areas", including:

(1) the central ideas, which are the foundations or the starting places of
the arguments;

(2) the topoi represented by the arguments;

(3) the use of suggestion:

a. the major ideas which are suggested but not argued;

b. the premises and topoi which are represented by suggestion;

(4) the structure and flow of the argument.

Since little was known about the "rhetorical anatomy" of the trial, this
mapping of cluster areas enabled the critic to evaluate the speaker's ideas
and methods in light of their feasibility of purpose, thus relating the
rhetorical force of the ideas and the arguments to the concrete
purpose-audience situation and yielding a judgment of the skill of
Strafford on the one side and the managers on the other.

The work done in Task Four is pictorially summarized in Figure Two.

Task Five: *Abstracting and Criticizing the Stasis of the Strategies*

Stasis is a heuristic device which can serve as a tool for discovering
within one's own knowledge what can be said, and what must be said, to
support a proposition. Stasis is a "line of approach" to a cause and its
accompanying "sayables" and "evidence." Stasis provides angles of
attack upon a case, a cause, a proposition: angles which yield various
points of observation from which to view a subject from different mental
vantage points. Thus, stasis can be considered structurally as an
interrogational function.

I do not intend to imply here that Strafford or the managers
consciously used the classical idea of stasis as a rhetorical device for
invention. But the *critic* can use it as a device for discovering how the
prosecution or defense viewed its position in relation to the opposing side,
as a device for discovering the "lines of approach" which were actually
taken by Strafford on one side and the managers on the other.

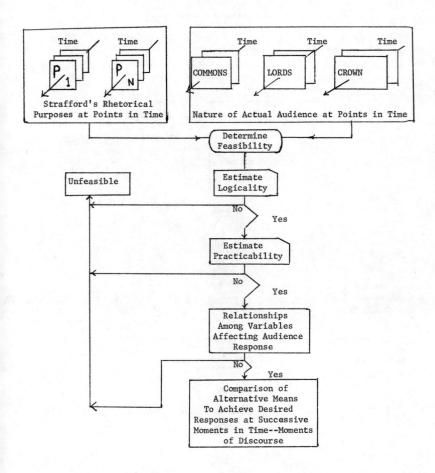

Figure B-1   Schematic Tasks One through Three.

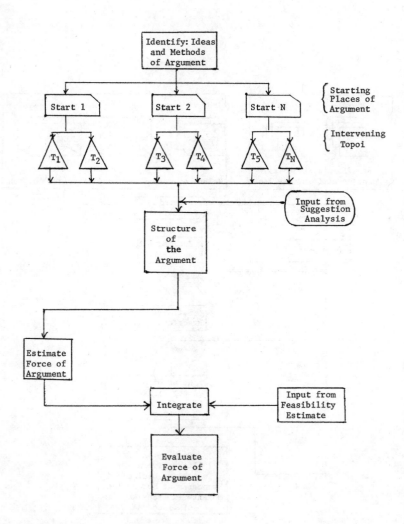

Figure B-2   Schematic of Task Four.

Consequently, the next step of the study was to group the ideas and arguments of the speakers into "stasis clusters," such as:

(1) Type of issue—conjectural, legal, juridical.

(2) Justifying motive.

(3) Central point of accusation.

(4) Question for decision; point of adjudicate.

The foregoing classification according to stasis clusters did not, by itself, give the critic much more than another *kind* of "anatomy-of-the-arguments." Yet if we remember that speakers, during the inventive stage of speech design, have their own tactics of "method finding," then the angles of attack upon a cause that had been selected by a speaker would cause this speaker to create his own unique psychological integration of the problem and its data: that is, *from* the "ground" (Gestaltist's ground) of a case and data, the angle of attack (stasis, if you will) taken by a speaker will cause a "figure" to emerge in his mind. Consequently, whether the speaker was aware of his angle of attack or not, the critic can employ stasis in at least four ways:

(1) as a heuristic device for criticizing *selection*: What influenced the speaker during his process of abstraction from the available data?

(2) as a heuristic device for criticizing *organization*: What influenced the speaker during his task of patterning the data?

(3) as a heuristic device for criticizing *association* and *discrimination*: What influenced the speaker's mental process of comparing?

(4) as a heuristic device for criticizing the speaker's *criteria of judgment*: What influenced the speaker during his process of evaluating?

The work done in Task Five of the proposed study is pictorially summarized below in Figure Three.

Task Six: *Abstracting and Criticizing the Types of Proof and Structure of Proof Advanced by Prosecution and Defense*

Proof is the process of securing belief in one statement by relating it to another statement already believed by the audience. Task Six of the study was concerned with a critical analysis of the methods of proof used by Strafford and the managers.

For the purposes of this criticism of proof, I assumed, after Toulmin, that any unit of proof may have six elements, three of which—data, warrant, and claim—are necessary to any completed proof.

a. Data

Data may be defined as a fact which is accepted as true by the audience, and which is used by an advocate as a basis from which to secure belief in another statement.

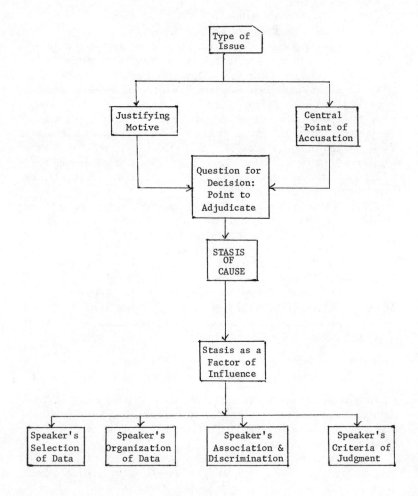

Figure B-3   Schematic of Task Five.

The data used in a unit of proof must satisfy two conditions:

(1) Some principle of reasoning must warrant the connection between a bit of information and the claim to be advanced by the advocate.

(2) The Informative statements, the facts, must be accepted by the audience before they can be input as data within the structure of a unit of proof. Thus, there is no psychological difference between evidence of fact and evidence of opinion.

b. Warrant

Evidence supplies the informative data upon which a unit of proof will be erected. The warrant provides a method by means of which the proof is derived. Because a warrant is the means by which one moves from data to claim, it states an inference and involves a so-called mental leap. Data is categorical and bound to the subject matter, warrant is hypothetical and content-free; or data are given and static, warrant is dynamic and creative.

c. Claim

The claim is the explicit appeal produced by the data and warrant; that is, the specific stand which, as a result of accepting the data and recognizing the validity of the reasoning, the audience is then prepared to take with regard to the question under consideration. A claim may be a final proposition in an argumentative discourse, or an intermediate statement that may serve as data for a subsequent proof. The relationship among the three basic elements of a proof may be mapped as shown in Figure Four.

The warrant *appears* to be incidental to the explicit appeal made by the proof, but without the general assumption that it expresses, the accepted data could not be connected to the claim, nor could the relationship between these elements be validated. This is the case because the warrant, by means of utilizing one of the "psychologically approved" relationships that may exist between data and claim, establishes a connection between these two elements. The warrant, therefore, may be said to give birth to the proof as a whole.

The following three elements may be added, when necessary, to the unit of proof:

d. Backing for the Warrant

The backing for the warrant is used to certify the acceptability of the assumption which is expressed by the warrant. The purpose of any material used to support the warrant is to "psychologically underwrite" the acceptability of the warrant which is to be employed in the proof.

e. Reservations

Specific circumstances or conditions surrounding the proof might reduce the psychological force exerted by the warrant upon the claim.

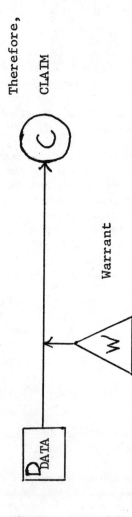

Figure B-4   Relationship Among the Three Basic Elements
of a Proof: Data, Warrant, and Claim.

The advocate will then have to include some reservations to his statement of the claim, as a kind of "escape clause."

f. Qualifier

Since claims vary considerably in the degree of strength with which they are believed by the audience, the advocate often needs a set of qualifying terms that declare how strongly he intends to affirm the claim. These terms register the degree of force which a claim is judged to possess.

The relationship among the six elements of a proof may be diagrammed as shown in Figure Five.

The elements of proof as diagrammed in Figure Five allowed an analysis of the trial's "logical proof" to be made. What is not so clear is the fact that the same structure of relationships also allows an analysis of "pathos" and "ethos" to be made. The only problem was for the critic to discover when and where the advocates *varied* their use of *types* of data, or warrants, or claims.

(1) *Data types* could be varied as follows:
  (a) audience opinion
  (b) audience information   audience-supplied evidence
  (c) speaker opinion
  (d) asserted information   "ethos"
  (e) opinions of others (testimony)
  (f) information of others (facts, statistics,
  examples, objects, etc.)   evidence

(2) *Warrant Types* could be varied as follows:
  (a) authoritative (credibility of source of data)
  (b) motivational (value and emotional structure of audience)
  (c) substantive (logical patterns accepted by audience—cause,
  sign, generalization, etc.)

(3) *Claim types* could be varied as follows:
  (a) factual
  (b) definitive (definition)
  (c) evaluative (value)
  (d) advocative (policy-action)

By analyzing and describing, in the above manner, the proofs used at the trial, I was able to arrive at an evaluation of the "quality" and "force" of the proofs used by Strafford and the managers. This was done by comparing the structure of the proofs that were used with the previously derived estimate of Strafford's feasibility of purpose—which estimate, it will be recalled, was derived from the description of rhetorical purposes, nature of audience, logical and practicability requirements, variables affecting the audience, and the comparison of the alternative means to

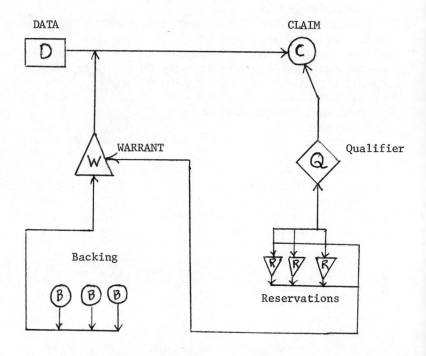

Figure B-5   Relationship   Among the Six Elements
of a Proof.

achieve the desired response.

Task Seven: *Description and Criticism of the Arrangement of the Arguments*

The aim of Task Seven was to criticize the arrangement of the arguments used throughout the trial. To accomplish this, the task was subdivided into the following subtasks:
  a. Identification of the parts of the trial and parts of the speeches.
  (1) identification of the main divisions of the trial and the speeches.
  (2) estimate of whether introductions, bodies of speeches, and conclusions accomplished their purpose.
  b. Identification of the structure of the trial and the speeches.
  (1) identification of the general structure.
  (2) identification of the order and relationships.
  (3) estimate of the intended function of order and relationships.
  c. Estimate of the "rhetorical quality" and "persuasive force" of the arrangement of the arguments.

Task Eight: *Further Analysis and Criticism of Factors Related to Speaker, Audience, Occasion, and Message.*

At this stage in the research, the critic had approached Strafford's trial from fourteen different, critical angles of attack. These fourteen critical points of view yielded a large amount of data about Lord Strafford as a public speaker. Yet there still existed several remaining critical possibilities which were related to the speaker, the audience, the occasion, and the message. Therefore, I raised some additional questions which served as further guides in this attempt to criticize the trial of Lord Strafford. These additional questions were as follows:
a. Speaker
  (1) familial history and tradition.
  (2) source and development of the speaker's ideas, values, purposes, skills, etc., including theories about speech-making.
  (3) relevant ideational-emotional-moral characteristics that speaker brought to occasion.
b. Audience
  (1) relevant predisposing factors influencing society.
  (2) relevant precipitating factors influencing society.
c. Message
  (1) speaker's specific preparation for speeches, including research, composition, and rehearsal.

(2) what was the rhetorical quality of what was said (not said; might have been said)?
(3) how does speech (trial?) relate to other ideas?
(4) how might speeches have been improved?
(5) what were the ostensible and real purposes of the participants?

d. Occasion

(1) what were the relevant antecedent factors affecting the occasion?
(2) what were the physical and psychological factors which affected the situation?

Task Nine: *Evaluation of Strafford's Style*

Here and there in their accounts of the trial, Rushworth and other reporters reach a level of specificity which they maintained long enough to give the critic a partial, though flimsy, foundation upon which to base an estimate of Strafford's style. For example, his closing speech was recorded almost word for word. Therefore, where appropriate, I evaluated such aspects of his style as clarity, correctness, appropriateness, and force. This criticism of Strafford's style followed the format below:

a. *Clarity* of Strafford's style

(1) arrangement of words
(2) coherence of ideas
(3) length and arrangement of sentences
(4) presence or absence of colloquialisms
(5) word coinage
(6) repetition
(7) examples
(8) illustrations

b. *Correctness* of Strafford's style

(1) word choice
(2) connective words
(3) specific words
(4) avoidance of ambiguous language
(5) grammatical construction

c. *Appropriateness* of Strafford's style

(1) adaptation to the audience
(2) adaptation to the subject
(3) adaptation to the speaker
(4) homely allusions
(5) avoidance of triteness
(6) familiarity of language

(7) apologetic or patronizing style
(8) use of pictorial words and sentences
(9) use of conversational language
d. *Force* of Strafford's style
  (1) concrete and specific language
  (2) position of sentences
  (3) climax
  (4) conciseness
  (5) rhythm
  (6) euphony
  (7) rhetorical questions
  (8) figures of speech
  (9) use of antithesis
  (10) emphatic words
e. Other factors of style
  (1) vivid metaphors
  (2) loaded words and phrases
  (3) imagery
  (4) questions
  (5) artistic handling of words
  (6) use of ornamentations
  (7) allusions to poetry, Scripture, and picturesque materials

Task Ten: *Erskine and Mansfield as Models With Which to Compare Strafford's Discourse*

Additional criticism of Strafford's trial was attempted by reference to two generally accepted "models" of forensic excellence: Lords Erskine and Mansfield.

I discovered something about the relative merit of Strafford's discourse by comparing it to Erskine's and Mansfield's, which, in a sense, was an attempt to get at rhetorical quality by means of examples. Now, of course, I did not expect Lord Strafford to have spoken in exactly the same manner as Erskine or Mansfield: touchstones are not models for copying. Rather, I tried to discover whether Strafford, when he was attempting, for example, to state a point to adjudicate, did so in a manner as effective as Erskine's when handling his pivotal propositions. Similarly, when I evaluated the precision and methodicity with which Strafford developed an argument, I compared him to Mansfield. By using Erskine and Mansfield as "overlays" or "points of view," I gained further insights into the quality and force of Strafford's discourse.

The entire critical effort of the research is summarized in Figure Six.

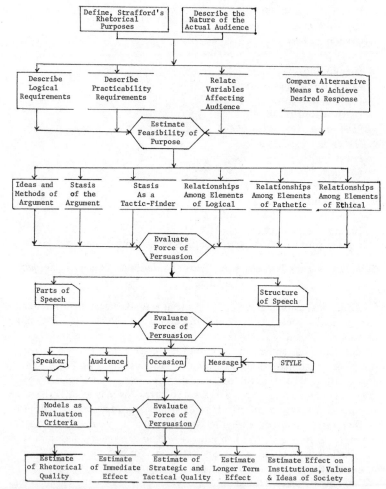

Figure B-6   Schematic of Critical Research

APPENDIX C

Charges of the Articles of Impeachment Which Were Waived by the Commons

The Seventh Article

That the said Earl of Strafford, in the Term of holy Trinity, in the Thirteenth Year of His now Majesty's Reign, did cause a case, commonly called *The Case of Tenures upon Defective Titles*, to be made and drawn up without any Jury or Trial, or other Legal Process, and without the consent of Parties, and did then procure the Judges of the said Realm of Ireland, to deliver their Opinions and Resolutions to that case, and by color of such Opinion, did without any Legal proceeding, cause Thomas Lord Dillon, a Peer of the said Realm of Ireland, to be put out of the possession of divers Lands and Tenements, being his Freehold in the County of Mayo and Roscomen, in the said Kingdom, and divers other of His Majesty's Subjects to be put out of Possession, and disseized of their Freehold by color of the same Resolution, without Legal proceedings, whereby many hundreds of His Majesty's Subjects were undone, and their Families utterly ruined.[1]

The Eleventh Article

That the said Earl, in the 9th Year of His Majesty's Reign, did by his own Will and Pleasure, and for his own Lucre, restrain the Exportation of the Commodities of that Kingdom without his License, as namely, Pipe-staves, and other Commodities, and then raised great Sums of Money for Licenses of Exportation of those Commodities, and dispensation of the said Restraints imposed on them, by which means the Pipe-staves were raised from Four pound ten shillings, or Five pound per thousand, to ten pounds, and sometimes Eleven pound per thousand, and other Commodities were enhanced in the like proportion and by the same means, by him the said earl.[2]

The Fourteenth Article

That the said Earl, by a Proclamation dated the 16th of October, in the 14th Year of His Majesty's Reign, did impose upon the Owners, Masters, Pursers, and Boat-Swains of every ship, a new and unlawful Oath, *viz.* That they (or two or more of them) immediately after the arrival of any Ship within any Port or Creek in the said Kingdom of Ireland, should give in a true In-voice of the outward bulk of Wares and Merchandises first laden aboard them, together with the several marks and number of Goods,

and their qualities and condition of the said Goods, as far as to them
should be known, the Names of the several Merchants Proprietors of the
said Goods, and the place from whence they were Fraughted, and whither
they were bound to discharge; which Proclamation was accordingly put in
execution, and sundry persons enforced to take the said unlawful Oath.[3]

The Seventeenth Article

That the said Earl having by such means as aforesaid subverted the
Government and Laws of the Kingdom of Ireland, did in March in the
16th Year of His Majesty's Reign, in scandal of His Majesty's Government,
of all His Kingdoms; and in further Execution of his wicked Purposes
aforesaid, speaking of the Army in Ireland, declare, That His Majesty was
so well pleased with the Army of Ireland, and the consequences thereof,
that His Majesty would certainly make the same a Pattern for all His Three
Kingdoms.[4]

The Eighteenth Article

That the said Earl of Strafford, for the better effecting of his traitorous
Designs, and wicked Purposes, did endeavor to draw dependency upon
himself of the Papists in both Kingdoms of England and Ireland, and to
that end, during the time of his Government in Ireland, he restored divers
Priories and Mass-Houses (which had been formerly suppressed by the
precedent Deputies of that Kingdom; two of which Houses are in the City
of Dublin, and had been assigned to the use of the University there) to the
pretended Owners thereof, who have since employed the same to the
Exercise of the Popish Religion.

And in the month of May and June last, the said Earl did raise an Army
in the said Realm, consisting of 8000 Foot, all of which except one, or
thereabouts, were Papists, and removed said One thousand Foot, and in
their places there were a thousand Papists, or thereabouts, put into the
said old Army by the said Earl.

And the more to engage and tie the said new Army of Papists to
himself, and to encourage them, and to discourage and weary out the said
old Army, the said Earl did so provide: That the said new Army of Papists
were duly paid, and had all Necessaries provided for them, and permitted
the Exercise of their Religion, but the said old Army were for the space of
one whole Year and upwards unpaid.

And the said Earl being appointed a Commissioner within eleven
several Counties of the Northern parts of England, for Compounding with
Recusants for their Forfeitures due to His Majesty; which Commission
beareth date the 8th day of July, in the 5th Year of His Majesty's Reign

that now is; and being also Receiver of the Composition-money thereby arising, and of other Debts, Duties, and Penalties, by reason of Recusancy within the said Counties, for His Majesty's Use, by Letters Patents dated the 9th day of the same July; He to engage the said Recusants to him, did Compound with them at low and under Rates, and provided, that they should be discharged of all Proceedings against them in all His Majesty's Courts, both Temporal and Ecclesiastical, in manifest breach of, and contrary to the Laws and Statutes of this Realm, in that behalf Established.[5]

The Twenty-Eighth Article

That in the months of September and October last, he the said Earl of Strafford, being certified of the Scottish Army coming into the Kingdom, and he the said Earl of Strafford being Lieutenant General of His Majesty's Army, he did not provide for the defence of the Town of Newcastle, as he ought to have done, but suffered the same to be lost, that so he might the more incense the English against the Scots.

And for the same wicked purpose, and out of a malicious desire to engage the Kingdoms of England and Scotland in a National and bloody War, he did write to the Lord Conway, the General of the Horse, and under the said Earl's Command, that he should fight with the Scottish Army at the passage over the Tyne, whatsoever should follow; notwithstanding that the said Lord Conway had formerly by Letters informed the said Earl, that His Majesty's Army, then under his Command, was not of force sufficient to encounter the Scots, by which advice of his, he did, contrary to the duty of his place, betray His Majesty's Army, then under his Command, to apparent danger and loss.

All and every which words, counsels, and actions of the said Earl of Strafford were spoken, given, and done by him the said Earl of Strafford, traitorously, and contrary to his Allegiance to our Sovereign Lord the King, and with an intention and endeavor to alienate and withdraw the hearts and affections of the King's Liege-people of all His Realms from His Majesty, and to set division between them, and to ruin and destroy His Majesty, and Majesty's said Kingdoms, for which they do further impeach him the said Thomas Earl of Strafford of High Treason against our Sovereign Lord the King, His Crown and Dignity. And he the said Earl of Strafford was Lord Deputy of Ireland, or Lord Lieutenant of Ireland, and Lieutenant General of the Army there under His most Excellent Majesty, and a sworn Privy-Counsellor to His Majesty for His Kingdoms both of England and Ireland, and Lord President of the North during the time that all and every the Crimes and Offences before set forth were done and committed, and he the said Earl was Lieutenant General of His Majesty's Army in the North parts of England during the time that the Crimes and Offences, in the 27th and 28th Articles, set forth were done and committed.[6]

APPENDIX D

Evidence and *I Eliz. I, Cap. VI*: The Basis of the Lords' Decision

"Resolved by the majority that the Bill of Attainder against the Earl of Strafford should pass as a law."[1] Thus, on May 7, 1641, the House of Lords enacted that Thomas, Earl of Strafford, should "undergo the pains and forfeitures of high treason by law."[2]

The passage of this law subsequently engendered one of the perennial controversies of English political and legal history. On one side of the issue, it is claimed that the answer of the judges[3] and the decision of the Lords were warranted by generally-accepted doctrines of law and constitutional theory.[4] The other side of the question claims that the charges against Strafford had no basis in statute or common law, that the abandonment of the impeachment proves the weakness of the case against the accused, and that in going by way of the bill, the Commons "slaughtered a man they could not convict."[5]

Resolution of the controversy over Strafford's case has been hampered by a lack of historical data because, at the restoration, Charles II ordered all proceedings of the trial to be stricken from the Journals of the House of Lords. The Journal Manuscripts were rendered almost totally unreadable and, as a result, the official record of the trial has been missing for over three-hundred years. Until recently, Rushworth has been the main source for histories of the Strafford trial. However, the usefulness of Rushworth has been marred by many lapses and errors, the most significant being that he was absent for several days from the trial at its climax. Consequently, the conclusion of the trial, the proceedings of which would help to resolve the legal controversy, has been reconstructed from fragmentary sources.

The discovery of new documents, the Braye Manuscripts,[6] now allows the historical record to be corrected and extended. On many significant points, the *Braye MSS* not only bring to light new evidence but also extend the scope of inference permitted by Rushworth, *A Brief and Perfect Relation*, *Harleian MSS 6424*, and others which were previously depended upon.

In this appendix, I am concerned to bring to bear the new data of the *Braye MSS* upon the heretofore unresolved questions of evidence and law in the Strafford case. I am concerned to show what the Lords found in the case to be (1) the points to adjudicate; (2) the questions for decision; and (3) the points of law or else of evidence which warranted each of their judgments. In my conclusion, I hope to have proved that the long-continuing controversies over Strafford's execution have been misdirected into the status of the charges under treason law; and that the crucial decision on the case by the Lords was not upon whether the charges were warranted by law, but rather upon a simple yet far-reaching point concerned with the admissibility of evidence. The *Braye MSS* of the proceedings in the House of Lords on May 5, 6, and 7, 1641, show clearly, I feel, the warrant, in both law and evidence, for the Lords' attainder of Strafford.

The indictment of Strafford contained nine general and twenty-eight articles of impeachment and upon these thirty-seven charges, the trial was convened and proceeded for nineteen days. On the nineteenth day, April 10, 1641, the impeachment proceedings broke down and were adjourned *sine die*. That same afternoon, the House of Commons brought in for a first reading a Bill of Attainder against the Earl of Strafford.

The bill had been constructed from the strongest, legally, of the original charges and it cited as treason two of the nine general articles and four of the twenty-eight specific articles. Of the six charges in the bill, the House of Lords finally selected four, two general and two specific, for deliberation.[7] What is most noteworthy about these four charges is that two of them clearly were statutory offenses under the treason law of 1641.

Before I show how the charges, which were ultimately to doom Strafford, stood under law, I must summarize the status of English treason law as of 1641.

The basis of all treason law was the statute of Edward III. By the time of Henry VIII, this law had received many extensions and additions, so that it had become both ambiguous and dangerous. For example, the taking of goods by Welshmen was treason. So also had poisoning been made treason, the penalty for which was boiling of the offenders. Likewise, to marry the king's children was treasonous, as was unchastity in the queen.

The *1st Edw. 6, cap. 12* swept away this plethora of laws by repealing all treasons between the third and sixth Edwards and declared to be statutable "only such [acts] as were made treason by . . . *25 Edw. 3.*"

As functional as this statute might have been, *1 Edw. 6* was later discovered to contain a few props to support a Protestant crown. Consequently, *1 Mary 1* abolished it and declared treason to be "only as such declared . . . in *25 Edw. 3.*"

Thus, two successive reigns abolished all intervening statutes and passed laws which fixed treason to be as stated by *25 Edw. 3.*

At this point, it is pertinent to bring up the question of the power of parliament to declare an act as treasonous. The statute *21 Rich. 2, cap. 20* declared that "to pursueth to repeal or reverse statutes of the king or parliament is treason." By way of interpretation, Lord Chief Justice William Thirning, at the request of Richard II, "layed that the declaration of treason not declared [by *25 Edw. 3* or *21 Rich. 2*] belongeth to the parliament." From this, the 1641 House of Commons inferred that parliament still had the power to declare treason upon its own authority alone.

But *21 Rich. 2, cap. 20* was specifically repealed by *1 Hen. 4.* Indeed, the first parliament of Henry IV repealed all laws passed in the twenty-first year of Richard II and pardoned all treasons made by that parliament. To this specific repeal must be connected *1 Edw. 6* and *1 Mary 1*, which fixed treason in *25 Edw. 3.* Now to apply the law to Strafford.

The *25th Edw. 3* made it treason to "compass, imagine, desire, or intend the death of the sovereign, . . . to wound the royal person, . . . [and] to make war upon the subjects." The *6th Edw. 3* stated that "whomsoever should carry about with them enemies of England, Irish rebels, or hooded men, and should force them upon the subject, shall be punished as a traitor." *1 Mary 1* made a traitor he who should "bring parties beyond the sea into this realm." *1 Eliz. 1, cap. 6* declared it treason "to make war upon the subject" and "to move or stir foreigners or strangers."

Thus, of the original indictment, articles 15 and 23 constituted treason under the clear letter of statute law. And, in the Bill of Attainder, the third and fifth charges, which had been drawn from articles 15 and 23 of the impeachment, also were statutable as treason by law.

The House of Commons, therefore, had a statutable case and there clearly was no need for the managers of the prosecution either to manufacture, as Wedgwood puts it, a new theory of treason or to amplify an attack by Strafford upon the constitution, as Russell has it, into an attack upon the person of the sovereign.[8]

Thus far, I have shown that two of the charges against the Earl of Strafford—the fifteenth and twenty-third articles of impeachment which survived to become the third and fifth charges of the Act of Attainder—

were clearly, precisely, and unequivocally grounded in statute law. Below, I intend to show proceedings in Lords from the *Braye MSS* that will demonstrate that these same two charges became the legal basis for the Lords' enactment of the bill. However, this still leaves unanswered the questions: Why, if the fifteenth and twenty-third articles made treason under law, did the House of Commons bother with a Bill of Attainder in the first place? Why not simply convict the accused straightaway with the juridical means readily at hand? Why the shift to a legislative means when the original charges were statutable?

To answer these questions, we must examine the trial of the two articles on May 1st and 5th, respectively, and show how well each stood up under the pressure of adversary proceedings, rules of evidence, and the like.

The fifteenth article charged Strafford with billeting soldiers under arms and, hence, with levying war upon the subjects of Ireland. The managers of the prosecution for Commons called nine witnesses to testify but only one, Sergeant Savile, connected Strafford with the warrant for billeting.[9]

The twenty-third article charged that Strafford had gathered an army in Ireland to invade and subdue a near-rebellious England for King Charles. Of all the members of the Council, only Sir Harry Vane testified to the point and his testimony was ambiguous as to whether England or Scotland was meant to be invaded. Scotland was in open rebellion at the time. Vane testified that Strafford had said in Council to the King, "You have an army in Ireland. You may employ it to reduce this kingdom." Whether "this kingdom" referred to Scotland or England was not clear. Vane testified to the words not the interpretation.[10]

It is clear from the proceedings that the two articles of the indictment which were statutable as treason, were *each* testified to by a *single* witness. However, the admission of evidence to a treason trial was highly conditional and came under a special law: the statute *1 Eliz., cap. 6* enacted that no person should be indicted, convicted, or condemned of any offense of treason unless he be accused by two witnesses.

It was this rule of evidence, pressed *ad litteram* by Richard Lane, and not any particular loophole in treason law, which made ineffectual the statutory charges of the articles of impeachment, a difficulty which the managers solved by recasting the two articles as the centerpiece of a Bill of Attainder.

Subsequently, the Commons succeeded in establishing articles 15 and 23 as the primary questions for decision from among the particulars of the bill. The author of Harleian Manuscript 6424 reports that the bill's supporters in the upper house took article 15 to be treason by *25 Edw. 3*.[11] In the final vote of the Lords,[12] when most of the attainder bill had fallen by the wayside, articles 15 and 23 still survived. Indeed, it is quite clear from the votes of the Lords that it was almost entirely upon these two articles that the legality[13] of their adjudgment was rested. As Russell points out, both of these articles are outside the mainstream of the Commons' treason argument and completely bypass their keystone position that treason can be against the state as well as against the person of the sovereign.[14]

Both articles are reducible to the treason statute of Edward III and this was what the supporters of the bill intended. To be sure, in the bill a great show of non-statutory general charges was still made, devoting many high-sounding words to "subverting the fundamental laws of the kingdom," "exercising a tyrannous and exorbitant power against the laws," "slandering the House of Commons," and "being an incendiary against the Scots." Such accusations probably served to soothe the hotheads among the Commons and the Scots who had almost opened an irremediable breach between the two Houses. Be that as it may, articles 15 and 23 were placed at the point of the new thrust and their centrality is demonstrated by the postscript which follows each in the bill:[15]

1. Phrase following article 15, the charge of billeting: " . . . executed in a warlike manner . . . and in doing so he did levy war against the king's majesty and his liege people in that kingdom."

2. Phrase following article 23, the charge regarding the Irish army: " . . . for which he deserveth to undergo the pains and forfeitures of high treason."

Articles 15 and 23 had, then, the obvious attraction of being reducible to statute law. The articles held further advantages for the prosecution. They did not involve the question of whether the *21st Rich. 2, cap. 20* (which allowed parliament to declare treason) was still in force,[16] nor the difficult question of whether there were treasons at common law.[17] Finally, the two articles ignored the vague doctrine of constructive treason upon which so much labor had been spent by the managers, especially their counsel Oliver St. John.

The Lords' final judgment of the Strafford case and the basis of their decision will now be shown through an examination of the sequence and the subjects of their voting on the Bill of Attainder.

On May 5, 1641, their lordships

Resolved upon the [first] question: that going by way of Bill in the discussing of the matter of fact in this whole case, the rule shall be the persuasion of every man's conscience.

The key words in this resolution are "going by way of Bill in the discussing of *the matter of fact*." We have seen that articles 15 and 23 square with the treason statutes of three sovereigns: *25 Edw. 3, 6 Edw. 3, 1 Mary 1*, and *1 Eliz. 1*. Not because of any weakness in treason law, but because of *1 Eliz., cap. 6* was a Bill of Attainder enacted. With their strongest charges, the Commons were unable to make a case because their evidence was barred by the rules, but an act of attainder enabled these rules to be suspended.

The manuscript notes are quite clear on this point and, in three different places during the voting of May 5, 6, and 7, state that the peers were debating matters of fact, not of law, and were deciding by vote what had been proven, not what was illegal.

Another key phrase in the initial resolution above states that the matter of fact was to be decided not by rules of evidence but by the persuasion of every man's conscience.

I feel it necessary to cite now the entire text of the *Braye MSS* for May 5, 6, and 7, so that the questions of law and evidence may be fairly judged and answered and so as to lay at rest some of the longer-standing, historical problems which have surrounded the last days of Strafford's trial.[18]

May 5, 1641

1. Resolved upon the question: that going by way of Bill in the discussing of the matter of fact in this whole cause the rule shall only be the persuasion of every man's conscience.

2. Resolved etc. that the Earl of Strafford gave warrant for the sessing of soldiers upon men's lands in Ireland, and the same was executed accordingly.

3. Resolved etc. that the sessing of soldiers was done for the disobeying of the Earl of Strafford's orders made upon paper petitions between party and party against their consents.

4. Resolved etc. that the sessing of soldiers was with armies and an officier conducting them.

**[After this the house was resumed to debate the matter of fact of the 23 article.

E. Northumberland's deposition.

Sir Robert King's dep., who heard of S. Geo. Radcliff's speak.

Lord Ranelaugh's testimony.] **

May 6, 1641

6. Resolved etc. that the Earl of Strafford did counsel and advise his Majesty that he was absolved from rules of government.

7. Resolved etc. that the Earl of Strafford said unto his Majesty that in cases of necessity, and for the defence and safety of the

kingdom if the people did refuse to supply the king, the king is absolved from rules of government. And that everything is to be done for the preservation of the king and his people. And that his Majesty was acquitted before God and man.

   8. Resolved etc. that the Earl of Strafford used these words to his Majesty, that his Majesty having tried all ways, and refused in cases of this extreme necessity, and for the safety of the kingdom, you are absolved from all rules of government, and are acquitted before God and man, or words to that effect.

   9. Resolved etc. that the Earl of Strafford said to the king these words: you have an army in Ireland, which your Majesty may employ to reduce this kingdom, or words to that effect.

   10. Resolved etc. that these words (to reduce this kingdom) were spoken of the kingdom of England.

May 7, 1641

   **[House was resumed and took into consideration the matter of fact of those charges in the Bill which are charged as treason by the common law.] **

   11. Resolved etc. that the Earl of Strafford hath by his words counsels and actions endeavored to subvert the fundamental laws of the kingdoms of England and Ireland, and to introduce an arbitrary power.

   12. Resolved etc. that the Earl of Strafford hath exercised a tyrannous and exorbitant government above and against the laws, over the lives **[of his M's subjects of both kingdoms of England and Ireland.] **

   13. Resolved by vote that this question be put to the judges; that upon all the Lords have voted to be proved, that the Earl of Strafford doth deserve to undergo the pains and forfeitures of high treason by law.

   "We are of opinion upon all that your lordships have voted to be proved: that the Earl of Strafford doth deserve to undergo the pains and forfeitures of high treason by law."[19]

   **[Resolved by the majority that the B of A against the E of S should pass as a law.] **

The deliberations and the votes of the House of Lords show that C. V. Wedgwood, although her emphasis was slightly misplaced, has been substantially correct in her judgment that the Commons were unable to make a faultless case against Strafford and for this reason had recourse to legislative means to bring him down.

Where the managers had strong evidence, they found no law. And where they had the law, they lacked evidence. Conclusively, the most important law in the trial of Strafford was *1 Eliz., cap. 6* which mandated a minimum of two witnesses to make faith in a treason trial. Strafford and Lane's effective use of this law forced Commons to bring in a Bill of Attainder. The vote in the Lords was not upon the application of treason law to Strafford's case but rather upon the validity of trial evidence. The House of Commons did not piece out with the bill a want of legality but a want of evidence. If this is granted, surely the Commons did slaughter a man they could not convict.

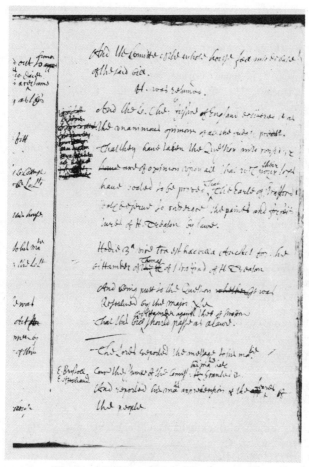

The Lords' Voting to Break the Rules of
Evidence (Braye MS)

NOTES

NOTES TO CHAPTER 1

1. For a fuller discussion of the early Stuart Parliaments, see Esme Wingfield-Stratford, *Charles, King of England, 1600-1637* (London, 1949), chap. ii, "The Basic Conflict," pp. 21-38.

2. Will Durant, *The Age of Reason Begins: A History of European Civilization, 1558-1648* (New York, 1961), p. 200.

3. H. R. Trevor-Roper, *Archbishop Laud, 1573-1645*, 2d ed. (Hamden, Conn., 1962), pp. 15-31.

4. Quoted by Godfrey Davies, *The Early Stuarts, 1603-1660*, Vol. IX of the *Oxford History of England*, ed. G. N. Clark, 14 vols. (Oxford, England, 1962), p. 33.

5. Sir John Eliot, *Negotium Posterorum*, ed. A. B. Grosart (London, 1881), I, p. 102. *Commons Journals*, I, pp. 801, 803.

6. William Knowler, ed., *The Earl of Strafford's Letters and Dispatches*, I, p. 34.

7. Quoted in Symonds D'Ewes, *Autobiography* ed. J. C. Halliwell (London, 1845), I, 293.

8. *Ibid*.

9. Knowler, *Strafford Letters*, I, 21.

10. Quoted in C. V. Wedgwood, *Thomas Wentworth, First Earl of Strafford, 1593-1641* (New York, 1962), p. 54.

11. *Calender of State Papers*, Domestic, 1625-1626, XVIII, 110.

12. *Harleian Mss*, 286, f. 297.

13. Knowler, *Strafford Letters*, I, 36.

14. *Strafford Mss*, XXII. Various letters relating to his imprisonment.

15. Davies, *Stuarts*, p. 34.

16. *Ibid*.

17. For the story of Buckingham and the French war, see Davies, *Early Stuarts*, pp. 62-67.

18. *Lords Journals*, III, 687.

19. Quoted in Wedgwood, *Strafford*, pp. 62-64.

20. *Ibid*., p. 64.

21. *Strafford Mss*, XXI, 48.

22. From this and similar positions consistently taken by Strafford throughout his career, I shall argue that he held a theory of "mixed government" (Weston) which antedated Charles' Answer to the Nineteen Articles by nearly two decades.

23. For Wentworth's work with this committee, see *Strafford Mss*, XXI, 48.

24. *Ibid.*, XXV.

25. For the Petition of Right, see Keith Feiling, *A History of England* (London, 1963), pp. 453-454.

26. Wedgwood, *Strafford*, p. 68.

27. *Historical Manuscript Commission*, IV, 90.

28. Wedgwood, *Strafford*, p. 69.

29. *Ibid.*, pp. 69-70.

30. *Tanner Mss*, LXXII, f. 300-303.

31. *Commentaries on the Laws of England*, ed. William C. Jones (San Francisco, 1915), Book I, 52.

32. *English Constitutional Theory and the House of Lords, 1556-1832* (New York and London, 1965), p. 3.

33. *Ibid.*, p. 5.

34. *Ibid.*, p. 8.

35. Wedgwood, *Strafford*, p. 91.

NOTES TO CHAPTER 2

1. Quoted in Leopold Von Ranke, *A History of England* (Oxford, 1875), II, 31.

2. For the Hampden case, see Edward, Earl of Clarendon, *History of the Rebellion and Civil Wars in England* (Oxford, 1826), I, 120-141. For the social, economic, and foreign policy of the personal rule, see Esme Wingfield-Stratford, *Charles, King of England* (London, 1949), pp. 302-318.

3. Winston S. Churchill, *The New World*, Vol II of *A History of the English Speaking Peoples* (New York, 1956), p. 196.

4. Thomas, Lord Fairfax, *Fairfax Correspondence*, ed. G. W. Johnson (London 1848), II, 237.

5. *Strafford Mss*, XXI, nos. 67, 72.

6. John Rushworth, *Historical Collections* (London, 1680), II, 205.

7. Wentworth to Carlisle, Oct. 24, 1631; in the Preface to *Calender of State Papers*, Domestic, 1631-1633.

8. William Knowler, ed., *The Earl of Strafford's Letters and Dispatches*

(London, 1739), I, 65.

   9. Knowler, *Strafford Letters*, I, 286.

   10. For Strafford's handling of the 1634-1635 Irish Parliaments, see Hugh F. Kearney, *Strafford in Ireland* (Manchester, 1959), chaps. 6, 7, and 8.

   11. Knowler, *Strafford Letters*, I, 301, 331.

   12. *Ibid.*, p. 345.

   13. Knowler, *Strafford Letters*, I, 448.

   14. *Strafford Mss*, XV, no. 175.

   15. For the fall of Mountnorris, see Kearney, *Strafford in Ireland*, pp. 70-74.

   16. H. R. Trevor-Roper, *Archbishop Laud, 1573-1645*, 2d ed. (Oxford, England and Hamden, Conn., 1963), p. 56.

   17. For Archbishop Laud's ecclesiastical policies after he assumed the primacy, see *Ibid.*, chap. v.

   18. *Ibid.*

   19. John Rushworth, *The Tryal of Thomas Earl of Strafford* (London, 1721), p. 775.

   20. Knowler, *Strafford Letters*, II, p. 374.

   21. Knowler, *Strafford Letters*, II, 398.

   22. Churchill, *New World*, p. 208.

   23. Rushworth, *Tryal of Strafford*, p. 544.

   24. Rushworth, *Collections*, II, 12.

   25. George Radcliffe, *Letters*, ed. by T. D. Whitaker (London, 1810), pp. 203-204.

NOTES TO CHAPTER 3

   1. Godfrey Davies, *The Early Stuarts* (Oxford, 1952), p. 97.

   2. C. V. Wedgwood, *The King's Peace* (London, 1955), p. 364.

   3. Strafford to Radcliffe, Nov. 5, 1640; quoted by Samuel R. Gardiner, *History of England* (London, 1894), IX, 221.

   4. C. V. Wedgwood, *The King's Peace* (London, 1955), p. 400.

   I lean heavily on Dame Veronica's work in this chapter, and it is right that I should. Inevitably, in two or three places I paraphrase her very words and fully acknowledge my debt. However, quotation marks are used only when I use her exact words.

   5. Quoted in C. V. Wedgwood, *Thomas Wentworth, First Earl of Strafford* (New York, 1962), p. 310.

   6. *Ibid.*

   7. H.M.C., *Egmont*, I, 129.

8. George Radcliffe, *Letters*, ed. T. D. Whitaker (London, 1810), pp. 222-223.

9. Hugh F. Kearney, *Strafford in Ireland* (Manchester, 1959), p. 199. See Mary L. Keeler, *The Long Parliament* (Philadelphia, 1954) for the election of members and their connections.

10. Esme Wingfield-Stratford, *King Charles and King Pym*, (London, 1949), p. 72.

11. Wedgwood, *Strafford*, p. 314.

12. Wingfield-Stratford, *Charles and Pym*, p. 72, Gardiner, *History*, IX, 231.

13. *Commons Journals*, II, 26.

14. *Ibid*.

15. Wedgwood, *Strafford*, p. 318.

16. Symonds D'Ewes, *Journal from the Beginning of the Long Parliament to the Opening of the Trial of the Earl of Strafford*, ed. Wallace Notestein (New Haven, Conn., 1923), p. 45.

17. *Commons Journals*, II, 27, 28, 30, 31.

18. *Lords Journals*, IV, 90.

19. *Commons Journal*, Ireland, 1640, p. 162. For the handling of the remonstrance, see Kearney, *Strafford in Ireland*, pp. 201-202.

20. *Lords Journals*, IV, 106.

21. *Commons Journals*, II, 38-42.

22. *Lords Journals*, IV, 100.

23. Wedgwood, *Strafford*, pp. 323-324.

24. John Nalson, *Impartial Collection of the Great Affairs of State* (London, 1682), I, 686-688.

25. *H.M.C.*, IV, 60.

26. *Commons Journals*, II, 63, 66.

27. *H.M.C.*, IV, 45.

28. *Lords Journals*, IV, 149.

29. Quoted in Wedgwood, *Strafford*, p. 326.

30. *Lords Journals*, IV, 139.

31. *Lords Journals*, IV, 105 ff.

32. *Ibid*., p. 171.

33. John Rushworth, *The Tryal of Thomas, Earl of Strafford* (London, 1680), p. 33. See also *Braye Mss*, March 5, 1641.

34. *Strafford*, p. 332.

35. *Lords Journals*, IV, 174.

36. Wedgwood, *Strafford*, p. 333.

37. Lord Clarendon, *The History of the Rebellion and Civil Wars in England* (London, 1826), III, 95.

38. H. M. C., *Cowper Mss*, II, 279.

NOTES TO CHAPTER 4

1. Sir Bulstrode Whitelocke, *Memorials of English Affairs from the Beginning of the Reign of Charles I to the Happy Restoration of King Charles II* (Oxford, 1682), I, 40.

2. Robert Baillie, *Letters and Journals* (Edinburgh, 1841), I, 314.

3. C. V. Wedgwood, *Thomas Wentworth, First Earl of Strafford* (New York, 1962), p. 338.

4. Rushworth, *Tryal*, p. 42.

5. The proceedings for the day are in *Braye Mss*, March 23, 1641. For the names of the Lords in attendance on this day, see the *House of Lords Daybook* also in the *Braye Mss*; hereafter referred to as the *Daybook*.

6. *Ibid*.

7. Terms such as "data," "warrant," "claim," *et al.* are used in their technical sense according to rhetorical theory. For a definition of all rhetorical terms used to explain the strategies and tactics of the trial, see the Appendix.

8. Rushworth, *Tryal*, pp. 108-109.

9. Rushworth, *Tryal*, p. 116.

10. *Ibid*., italicizing mine.

11. For the Lords in attendance, see the *Daybook* for March 24.

12. Rushworth, *Tryal*, p. 129 (My emphasis.)

13. *Ibid*., pp. 137-138. For the proceedings on the entire first article, see *Braye Mss*, Mar. 24, 1641. Since the articles in their entirety are not available outside of rare sources, I will quote all twenty-eight *verbatim*. The more general reader may omit reading them without losing the thread of development.

14. Rushworth, *Tryal*, p. 145.

15. Rushworth, *Tryal*, p. 149. For the proceedings on the entire article, see *Braye Mss*, Mar. 24, 1641.

16. Rushworth, *Tryal*, p. 152.

17. *Ibid*.

18. H.M.C., *Various*, II, 261.

19. Quoted in C. V. Wedgwood, *Thomas Wentworth, First Earl of Strafford* (New York, 1962), p. 342.

20. Rushworth, *Tryal*, pp. 155-156. For the proceedings on the entire article, see the *Braye Mss*, Mar. 25, 1641. For the Lords in attendance, see the *Daybook*.

21. Rushworth, *Tryal*, p. 164.

22. *Ibid*., p. 169.

23. *Ibid*., p. 173. For the proceedings on the entire article, see *Braye Mss*, March 25-26, 1641.

24. For the Lords in attendance, see the *Daybook* for Mar. 26, 1641.

25. Rushworth, *Tryal*, p. 182.

26. *Braye Mss*, Mar. 26, 1641.

27. Rushworth, *Tryal*, p. 186. For the proceedings on the entire article, see *Braye Mss*, Mar. 27, 1641. For the Lords in attendance, see the *Daybook* for Mar. 27, 1641.

28. Rushworth, *Tryal*, p. 205. For the proceedings on the entire article, see *Braye Mss*, Mar. 29, 1641. For the Lords in attendance, see the *Daybook* for Mar. 29, 1641.

29. Rushworth, *Tryal*, pp. 221-222. For the proceedings on the entire article, see *Braye Mss*, Mar. 30, 1641. For the Lords in attendance, see the *Daybook* for Mar. 30, 1641.

30. Lord Clarendon, *History of the Rebellion and Civil Wars in England* (Oxford, 1826), I, 390.

31. Rushworth, *Tryal*, p. 241. For the proceedings on the entire article, see *Braye Mss*, Mar. 30, 1641.

32. Rushworth, *Tryal*, p. 241. For the proceedings on the entire article, see *Braye Mss*, Mar. 31, 1641. For the Lords in attendance, see the *Daybook* for Mar. 31, 1641.

33. Rushworth, *Tryal*, p. 401. For the proceedings on the entire article, see *Braye Mss*, Mar. 31, 1641.

34. Rushworth, *Tryal*, p. 416. For the proceedings on the entire article, see *Braye Mss*, Apr. 1, 1641. For the Lords in attendance, see the *Daybook* for Apr. 1, 1641.

35. *Braye Mss*, Apr. 1, 1641.

36. Rushworth, *Tryal*, p. 426. For the proceedings on the entire article, see *Braye Mss*, Apr. 1, 1641.

37. To the point of levying war, Palmer could have cited *1 Eliz., cap. 6*, but he did not, probably because the same statute mandates that two witnesses are needed on a charge of treason, and the managers did not want to bring this rule of evidence to the attention of Strafford and Lane.

38. The Commons' tactic of attempting to force a vote on article fifteen is not recorded by Rushworth. However, Wedgwood discovered this detail in a fragmentary Parliamentary Diary from March 22 to April 26, 1641, compiled by an unknown writer who was evidently a friend or connection of Sir Philip Percival. See *Thomas Wentworth, First Earl of Strafford* (London, 1962), pp. 345, 356, n. 19. The proceedings of the *Braye Mss* for Apr. 1, 1641 confirm the diary evidence found by

Wedgwood.

39. Rushworth, *Tryal*, p. 460. For the proceedings on the entire article, see *Braye Mss*, Apr. 3, 1641. For the Lords in attendance, see the *Daybook* for Apr. 3, 1641.

40. For the text of the articles passed over, see the Appendix.

41. Rushworth, *Tryal*, p. 489. For the proceedings on the entire article, see *Braye Mss*, Apr. 3, 1641.

NOTES TO CHAPTER 5

1. John Rushworth, *The Tryal of Thomas, Earl of Strafford* (London, 1721), p. 515.

2. *Ibid.*, p. 516.

3. *Ibid.*, p. 517.

4. *Ibid.*, p. 518.

5. *Ibid.*, p. 519. For the entire proceedings on articles twenty through twenty-five, see *Braye Mss*, Apr. 5, 1641. For the Lords in attendance, see the *Daybook* for Apr. 5, 1641.

6. Rushworth, *Tryal*, p. 544.

7. Rushworth printed the word "England" here. Vane was to quote Strafford twice on the fateful phrase, and Rushworth puts down England in the first quote and Ireland in the second. However, the *Braye Mss*, Apr. 5, 1641, show that Rushworth slipped and that Vane actually used the word "Ireland" in both instances.

8. *Ibid.*

9. *Ibid.*

10. Northumberland's testimony, which was finally read, did not bear out Vane.

11. Rushworth, *Tryal*, p. 545.

12. *Braye Mss*, Apr. 5, 1641.

13. *Ibid.*

14. *Ibid.*

15. Rushworth, *Tryal*, p. 553.

16. The use of suggestion, or *insinuatio*, slowly and subtly prepares the minds of judges to receive a proposition without shock to any preconceived beliefs. Carroll Arnold describes the forensic use of suggestion in his monograph on the pleading of Lord Erskine. See "Lord Thomas Erskine: Modern Advocate," *QJS*, XLIV, no. 1 (Feb. 1958), 17-30.

17. Rushworth, *Tryal*, p. 561.

18. *Ibid.*, p. 562.

19. *Ibid.*, p. 564.

20. *Ibid.*

21. On May 1, 1641, King Charles himself, in a speech on Strafford's behalf to Parliament, declared upon his word as a king that the earl had never advocated the use of the Irish army in England. This made it unanimous against Vane.

22. *State Trials*, p. 1447.

23. *Ibid.*, p. 1448.

24. Symonds D'Ewes, *Autobiography*, ed. J. C. Halliwell (London, 1845), p. 9.

25. Rushworth, *Tryal*, p. 582. For the proceedings on the entire article, see *Braye Mss*, Apr. 7, 1641. For the Lords in attendance, see the *Daybook* for Apr. 7, 1641.

26. Rushworth, *Tryal*, p. 600. For the proceedings on the entire article, see *Braye Mss*, Apr. 7, 1641. For the Lords in attendance, see the *Daybook* for Apr. 7, 1641.

27. Rushworth, *Tryal*, p. 600. For the proceedings on the entire article, see *Braye Mss*, Apr. 7, 1641. For the Lords in attendance, see the *Daybook* for Apr. 7, 1641.

28. *Braye Mss*, Apr. 8, 1641.

29. *Ibid.*

30. *State Trials*, p. 1455, n. 1.

31. *Braye Mss*, Apr. 9, 1641.

32. *Ibid.* Strafford was ill from an attack of the stone.

33. C. V. Wedgwood, *Thomas Wentworth, First Earl of Strafford* (New York, 1962), p. 353.

34. *Braye Mss*, Apr. 10, 1641.

35. *Ibid.*

36. *Ibid.*

37. *Ibid.*

38. Wedgwood, *Strafford*, p. 355.

NOTES TO CHAPTER 6

1. In the *Rhetoric*, Aristotle discusses the unwritten law which takes cognizance of exceptional goodness or badness. This justice supplements the written law and offers remedies, when written law fails, on the basis of equity. However, the trial took place in England, not ancient Greece, and the Commons knew that any argument based on unwritten law would be thrown out of any English court. Hence, their attempt to make written law cover Strafford's case. In addition, an argument on unwritten law and

equity would be doubly weak, because only deliberate purpose constitutes crime. They were having trouble showing deliberate intent, showing motive, and properly describing some of the crimes.

2. C. V. Wedgwood, *Thomas Wentworth, First Earl of Strafford* (New York, 1962), p. 358.

3. *Ibid.*, p. 357.

4. This important conference was attended by Lords Bath, Saye, Savile, Roberts, Warwick and Southampton. The Commons agreed to waive new evidence if Strafford did the same. The conferees also agreed to hear the closing statements of Strafford and the managers the next day. The Lords then took along Pym's paper to their House. Obviously, the House of Lords expected the trial to continue and the bill to be dropped. For this important conference, see the *Braye Mss*, Apr. 12, 1641.

The *Braye Mss* here close the great gap in the data which was left by Rushworth when he unaccountably jumped from the 27th article to Strafford's last speech.

5. Wedgwood, *Strafford*, p. 359.

6. There are several, variant versions of Strafford's closing statement. I have depended mainly upon the text in the C.S.P.D., 1640-1641, pp. 540 ff. which is more extensive and detailed than Rushworth. Again the *Braye Mss* have been invaluable in setting straight important details, giving a more accurate picture of the maneuvers of both sides during these last days.

7. *Ibid.*

8. *Braye Mss*, Apr. 13, 1641.

9. *Braye Mss*, Apr. 13, 1641.

10. *Ibid.*

11. Bulstrode Whitelocke, *Memorials*.

12. Rushworth, *Tryal*, pp. 706-733. Rushworth erred and placed Pym's speech before Glyn's. The *Braye Mss* and a reading of both speeches show that Pym's was last. *Braye Mss*, Apr. 13, 1641.

13. *Ibid.*, p. 731.

14. *Ibid.*, p. 731.

15. *Ibid.*, pp. 732-733.

16. *Braye Mss*, Apr. 13, 1641.

17. Rushworth, *Tryal*, p. 669.

18. *Ibid.*, pp. 669-670.

19. Robert Baillie, *Letters and Journals* (Edinburgh, 1841), I, 348.

20. One account of the incident was: "It was sport to see how Master Pym in his speech was fearfully out, and constrained to pull out his papers, and read with a great deal of confusion and disorder, before he

could recollect himself; which failing of memory was no small advantage to the Lord-Lieutenant, because by this means the House perceived it was a premeditated flash, not grounded upon the Lieutenant's last answer, but resolved on before, whatsoever he should say for his own justification." *A Brief and Perfect Relation of the Answers of the Earl of Strafford* (London, 1646), p. 63.

21. Symonds D'Ewes, *Autobiography* (London, 1845), p. 45.

22. *Commons Journals*, 1641, II, 121.

23. *Braye Mss*, Apr. 14, 1641.

24. *Ibid.*, Apr. 15, 1641.

25. *Braye Mss*, Apr. 15, 16, 1641. Prior to the meeting with Commons, Bristol, Holland, and Essex met with the king on Apr. 15 to discuss the bill. Unfortunately, no details are given.

26. For Lanes' argument in Strafford's behalf, see *Braye Mss*, Apr. 17, 1641.

27. *Ibid.*

28. *Ibid.*

29. *Ibid.*

30. *Ibid.*

31. *Ibid.*

32. *Strafford*, p. 364.

33. *Ibid.*, p. 365.

34. *Commons Journals*, 1641, II, 123.

35. Lord Digby's speech is given in Rushworth, *Tryal*, pp. 50-53, and in Chauncey Goodrich, *Select British Eloquence* (New York, 1963), pp. 16-19.

36. Rushworth, *Tryal*, pp. 51-52.

37. *Ibid.*, p. 52.

38. *Ibid.*

39. *Ibid.*, pp. 52-53.

40. *Ibid.*, p. 53.

41. *Commons Journals*, 1641, II, 123-125.

42. Wedgwood, *Strafford*, pp. 368-369.

43. Leopold Von Ranke, *History of England* (Oxford, 1875), II, 255.

44. Clarendon, *History*, I, 426.

45. Von Ranke, *England*, II, 255.

46. Clarendon, *History of the Rebellion and Civil Wars in England* (London, 1826), I, 422-428.

47. Von Ranke, *History*, II, 254-259. Clarendon, *History*, I, 428-437.

48. Von Ranke, *History*, II, 259-260.

49. Rushworth, *Tryal*, pp. 748-750, 754-755.

50. *Ibid.*, pp. 58, 746-747.

51. *Ibid.*, pp. 56-57.

52. *Commons Journals*, 1641, II, 137, 158-159.

53. Rushworth, *Tryal*, p. 59.

54. William Knowler, ed., *The Earl of Strafford's Letters and Dispatches* (London, 1739), II, 416.

55. Gilbert Burnet, *Memoirs of the Lives and Actions of James and William, Dukes of Hamilton* (London, 1677) pp. 182-183.

56. Rushworth, *Tryal*, pp. 56-57.

57. *Braye Mss*, Apr. 22, 1641.

58. *Ibid.*, Apr. 26, 1641.

59. *Ibid.*

60. *Strafford*, p. 369.

61. Rushworth, *Tryal*, pp. 54-55.

62. *Braye Mss*, Apr. 27, 1641. "Brief Journal, March 1-May 3," *Calender of State Papers*, Domestic, CCCLXXX, 9.

63. *Brief and Perfect Relation*, p. 83.

64. *Braye Mss*, Apr. 28, 1641.

65. For the text of St. John's argument, see Rushworth, *Tryal*, pp. 675-705.

66. *Ibid.*, p. 703.

67. Rushworth, *Tryal*, p. 734.

68. Strafford to Charles, May 1; John Rushworth, *Historical Collections* (London, 1680), IV, 251.

69. See Rushworth, *Tryal*, p. 746, for Billingsley's examination on the subject by the House of Commons.

70. *Ibid.*, pp. 735-741.

71. Baillie, *Letters, Journals*, I, 352.

72. Baillie, *Journals*, I, 351. Rushworth, *Tryal*, p. 741. *Brief and Perfect Relation*, p. 85.

73. *Braye Mss*, May 3, 1641.

74. *Braye Mss*, May 3, 1641.

75. *Ibid.*

76. Rushworth, *Tryal*, p. 736.

77. *Braye Mss*, May 3, 1641.

78. Rushworth, *Tryal*, p. 742.

79. *Braye Mss*, May 4, 1641.

80. Rushworth, *Collections*, IV, 240.

81. *Lords Journals*, 1641, IV, 233.

82. Rushworth, *Tryal*, p. 744.

83. Quoted in Rushworth, *Tryal* p. 743 ff.

84. These were subverting the fundamental laws, and exercising a government against law.

85. These were article 15: levying war upon the subject; article 20: being incendiary of war between Scotland and England; article 23: desiring to use an Irish army against England; and article 24: slandering the House of Commons.

86. I intend here legality under the strict letter of treason statute. A Bill of Attainder was unquestionably legal but it was a specific legislative act. Despite their bill's legality, the Commons were at great pains to bring it under cover of one or another treason statutes. See Appendix D where I explain in detail the legal position of both sides and show the statute *1 Eliz. 1, cap. 6* to have been the basis of the Lords' decision in the Strafford case.

87. See pp. 219, 220-222.

88. See pp. 133-134.

89. See pp. 118, 133, 135.

90. During the reign of Richard II, Lord Chief Justice Thirning extended *21 Rich. 2, cap. 20* to this point. But *21 Rich., cap. 20* was specifically repealed by *1 Hen. 4.* See pp. 222, 241 n. 16, where I discuss the law on the question of the power of Parliament to declare treasons upon its authority alone.

91. *Braye Mss,* May 3, 1641.

92. *Ibid.,* May 4, 1641. See the list of Lords who signed the Protestation.

93. *Ibid.*

94. *Ibid.*

95. To be precise for the benefit of readers who are interested in the legal aspects of Strafford's case, articles 15 and 23 are statutable under *25 Edw. 3, 6 Edw. 3, 1 Mary 1,* and *1 Eliz. 1 cap. 6.* See below, pp. 220-222.

96. *Braye Mss,* May 5, 1641 (emphasis mine).

97. The law was *1 Eliz. 1, cap. 6.* See below, pp. 218-225. In short, the opposition Lords did not piece out want of treason *law* by way of bill. They were using the bill to piece out want of *evidence.*

98. The official recorders twice attribute the tactic to Arundel, once on May 3rd, when it was declared as policy, and again on the 10th, when it was "Ordered that the House did approve of the...Lo. Steward in his forming & managing of his plan at the trial of the E. of Strafford & gave him thanks for the same." The ultimate compromise between the two Houses was apparently worked out by a joint committee which met several times between April 29 and May 3 in Westminster Hall. The members from Lords were Lord Privy Seal, Lord Steward, Bath, Essex,

Bristol, Say, Warwick, Southampton, Roberts, and Seymour. *Braye Mss*, May 3 and 10, 1641.

99. *Braye Mss*, May 5, 1641.

100. *Ibid*.

101. *Ibid*.

102. *Braye Mss*, May 6, 1641.

103. *Ibid*.

104. *Ibid*.

105. This date is one of the more important corrections of the historical record made by the *Braye Mss*. Other scholars of the trial have given Saturday, May 8, as the date of the vote on the Attainder in Lords. The minutes of May 7th in the *Braye Mss* make it clear that Friday is the correct date.

It would have been nice if the Braye Papers also had shown which of the Lords were present and voting on the 7th. Unfortunately, the last roll given in the *Datebook* was for April 10; the rest of April and May is missing. Still, the *Datebook* up to the 10th, the signatures on the Protestation for May 4-8, and other evidence do allow an estimate to be made of who voted, and how they voted; a question I turn to in due course.

106. *Braye Mss*, May 6, 1641.

107. Rushworth, *Tryal*, p. 751.

108. *Ibid*.

109. Wedgwood, *Strafford*, p. 375.

110. *Braye Mss*, May 4, 1641.

111. Wedgwood, *Strafford*, p. 375.

112. *Braye Mss*, May 7, 1641. This was the first of four votes of the day on the bill.

113. *Ibid*.

114. *Ibid*.

115. *Ibid*. Observe the careful wording of the question and the reply: "upon all your lordships have *voted to be proved*." To have done otherwise would have been illegal.

116. *Ibid*. This was the last of four votes on May 7th.

117. *Memorials*, p. 43.

118. Wedgwood, *Strafford*, pp. 375-377.

119. *Ibid*., p. 376.

120. Rushworth, *Tryal*, p. 774.

121. *Braye Mss*, May 7, 1641.

122. John Hacket, *Scrinia Reserata* (London, 1693), p. 161.

123. Charles Louis, Elector Palatine to the Queen of Bohemia, May 18,

1641; quoted by John Forster, *British Statesmen* (London, 1840), IV, 71.
124. *Lords Journals*, IV, 245.
125. H. R. Trevor-Roper, *Archbishop Laud,* 2d ed. (London, 1963), p. 109.
  In a last bizarre gesture, the House of Lords appointed a delegation of the Lord Chamberlain, Essex (of all people), Cambridge, Holland, and Saye "to wait upon Lady Strafford and children." *Braye Mss,* May 11, 1641.
126. Wedgwood, *Strafford,* p. 387.

NOTES TO CHAPTER 7

1. Lawrence Stone, *The Crisis of the Aristocracy, 1558-1641* (Oxford, 1965), p. 749.
2. *Ibid.*
3. *Ibid.*, pp. 749-750.
4. The question is highly conjectural because at the Restoration, King Charles II ordered all proceedings relative to Strafford's impeachment and attainder to be expunged from the Journals of the House of Lords. Consequently, the position of individual Peers on the bill is unknown to history. None of Strafford's biographers has tried to reconstruct the vote, abstentions, and absenteeism of the Lords. However, the *Braye Mss*, the *Daybook*, and internal evidence give some pretty strong indications as to the probable action of individual Peers.
5. Many Lords may be eliminated from consideration of the final vote count because they did not attend the proceedings at all. The number in parentheses indicates the days a Peer attended the trial out of a random sampling of eleven days from March 22 to April 10, plus May 4—the day of the Protestation. An attendance polygraph (shown in Appendix C) shows the mean attendance from March 20 to April 10 to have been 89 Lords. Fifty-three Peers attended less than two sessions during this period.
6. Judging from later service to the parliamentary cause, it would have been plausible to infer that Bruce, Somerset, Salisbury, Kent, Rutland, Pembroke, Maynard, Mulgrave, Boteler, and Kingston voted against Strafford. However, the *Braye Mss* show that these nine were not attending the trial.
7. Actually there were 108 absentees, but six were minors, Gerard (Gerard), Petrie (Petrie), Vere (Oxford), Villiers (Buckingham), Villiers (Angelsea), West (de la Warr), so I have discounted them. Finch had fled. Bedford was dying.

8. Paul H. Hardacre, *The Royalists During the Puritan Revolution* (The Hague, 1956), p. 3.

9. Stone, *Crisis*, p. 752.

10. *Ibid*.

11. *Ibid*., p. 753.

12. C. V. Wedgwood, *Thomas Wentworth, First Earl of Strafford* (New York, 1962), p. 392.

13. Carroll C. Arnold, "Lord Thomas Erskine: Modern Advocate," *Quarterly Journal of Speech*, XLIV, No. 1 (Feb., 1958), 20.

14. In general, both ancient and modern rhetorical theory speak in terms of the doctrine of massive response, not in terms of flexible response. The *Rhetorica Ad Herennium* and Cicero both conceive of a single justifying motive and question for decision. Lew Sarett writes that "There is in the mind of the listener a single issue," and the problem is to find it and direct all persuasion thereto, "leaving the rest aside in surplusage." Such methods are exactly what put Strafford at his final disadvantage.

NOTES TO APPENDIX B

1. The concept of rhetorical feasibility was suggested by Williams' work on audience analysis. Williams wrote for the rhetorical theorist and speaker; I have adapted his ideas for the critic. See Kenneth R. Williams, "Audience Analysis: A Conceptual Clarification" (unpublished Ph. D. dissertation, the Pennsylvania State University, 1964), Ch. 3, 60-96.

2. *Ibid*., p. 105.

NOTES TO APPENDIX C

1. John Rushworth, *The Tryal of Thomas, Earl of Strafford* (London, 1721), p. 64.

2. *Ibid*., p. 66.

3. *Ibid*., p. 67.

4. *Ibid*., p. 69.

5. *Ibid*., pp. 69-70.

6. *Ibid*., pp. 74-75.

NOTES TO APPENDIX D

1. House of Lords, *Braye Mss*, fo. 142b, May 7, 1641.

2. *Ibid*.

3. For the text of the questions to the judges, see *Lords Mss*, May, 1641. For their answer, see *Braye Mss*, fo. 142b, May 7, 1641.

4. The best argument that I have seen in favor of a sound basis in law for the Lords' decision is Conrad Russell, *English Historical Review*, Vol. LXXX, No. CCCXIV (Jan., 1965), 30-50. In the end, however, Russell's excellent position is not statutable *ad litteram*.

5. For an excellent statement of this position, see C. V. Wedgwood, *Thomas Wentworth, First Earl of Strafford, 1593–1641: A Revaluation* (New York, 1962), pp. 357-378.

6. Refer to the Bibliographical Essay (pp. 243-251) for an account of the survival and utility of the *Braye Mss.*

7. See pp. 223-224, where I give *in toto* the proceedings in Lords during their votes on the bill.

8. I mean no strong criticism here. Given the earlier gaps in the record, Miss Wedgwood came very close to what actually happened and Mr. Russell has done an excellent job of showing how the making of a division between king and people might be interpreted as treason, if the law is extended and interpreted.

9. For the proceedings on the entire article, see John Rushworth, *The Tryal of Thomas, Earl of Strafford* (London, 1721), pp. 427-459.

10. Rushworth, *Tryal*, p. 546. For the proceedings on the entire article, see pp. 520-581.

11. fo. 62a.

12. See the proceedings for May 5, 6, and 7 given below.

13. I intend here legality under the strict letter of treason law by statute. A Bill of Attainder was unquestionably legal but it was a specific legislative act. It still is legal, of course, as a bill of pains and penalties.

14. "Theory of Treason," p. 50.

15. None of the other charges in the bill were so appended because they were not statutory offenses.

16. The best discussion of the question by a legal historian that I know is by J. F. Stephen, *History of the Common Law*, ii, 250-253. After a great deal of hesitation, he decides that the Commons' abandonment of the impeachment should be taken as a tacit admission that the salvo was no longer in force. Vaughan (*Verney's Notes*, p. 53) argues that *1 Mary 1, cap. 1* allows parliament to declare treasons but not to punish for them unless they are committed after the declaration. I don't understand this hesitation. *21 Rich. 2, cap. 20* was specifically repealed by *1 Hen. 4* and I find no ambiguity in the law. Further, the *1st Edw. 6, cap. 20* fixed treason to be *25 Edw. 3*, as did *1 Mary 1*. On this question, see also Elton, *The Tudor Constitution* and Rezneck, "The Parliamentary Declaration of

Treason," *Law Quart. Rev.,* XLVI (1930), 80.

17. The authority of Coke is against common law treasons. The House of Lords did consider treason at common law on May 7, 1641, but voted only that the matter of fact had been proved and not whether the general charges made treason. The question was then submitted to the judges, whose opinion simply held that Strafford was guilty of treason on the basis of what had been voted as proven. The judges did not divide the question and state which charges were to be taken under statute law and which under common law. Given the disposition of the questions, however, and the unmistakable centrality of articles 15 and 23, it seems clear that the main effort was to bring Strafford's under the sway of statute law.

Furthermore, the Lords on the morning of May 5 requested a committee conference with Commons to ask whether the general charge of subverting the fundamental laws was to be taken as standing alone or as relative to article 15. The Commons replied that the charge was made relative to the article. See *Braye Mss,* May, 1641. I take it then that the aim was to reduce the charges to statutable offenses.

18. The *E.H.R.* has already printed a partial text of the *Braye Mss* as an authentic record of the Lords' proceedings for May 5, 6, and 7, 1641. However, Mr. Russell inadvertently left out approximately one-hundred words which are important to both my argument and the historical record. I have set off these sentences with **[like this] ** and offer my reading of the *Braye Mss* as a slightly more authentic version of the proceedings.

19. Observe the careful wording of the question and the reply: "upon all your lordships have voted to be proved." To have done otherwise would have been illegal.

BIBLIOGRAPHICAL ESSAY

The standard books on the first half of the seventeenth century are S. R. Gardiner, *History of England, 1603-1642* (1884) and C. V. Wedgwood, *The King's Peace* (1955) and *The King's War* (1958). Gardiner lived in an epoch when moral certainty was natural; Wedgwood in an age when it was extremely difficult to decide about moral issues. Gardiner's prejudices and Wedgwood's point of view are quite evident, so that the reader must temper their positions with the interpretations of A. P. Newton, J. V. Nef, R. H. Tawney, H. R. Trevor-Roper, and several of the modern works listed below.

The bulk of the material available for writing a narrative account of events leading up to Strafford's trial is official correspondence either written by the earl or intended to be read by him. Subconsciously, therefore, the historian may come to look at all events through Strafford's eyes; thus the main problem is to lay hold of other sources.

The official viewpoint of events leading up to the trial is most fully documented in Strafford's own papers. Letters between him and the two secretaries of state, John Coke (1625-40) and Francis Windebank (1632-41), form a large part of the Strafford Mss, along with other members of the Privy Council and the king. With Francis Cottington, chancellor of the exchequer, and William Laud, archbishop of Canterbury, Strafford corresponded on a more informal plane than with the rest, and these letters provide insight into his unofficial views.

The largest and most important collection of the Strafford Mss is now housed in the Sheffield City Library, desposited there from Wentworth-Woodhouse by their owner Earl Fitz-William. They consist of eleven letter books, containing copies of Strafford's official correspondence. There are also eight books from 1627 to 1629. Many of the letters have been printed in W. Knowler (ed.) *The Letters and Dispatches of the Earl of Strafford* (1739). Other letters of Strafford are to be found in the *Works* of William Laud, ed. W. Scott and J. Bliss (1847-1860), vi-vii, and in *Camden Miscellany*, viii (1883) and ix (1895), which contains a few letters edited by S. R. Gardiner and C. H. Firth. The Harleian Mss, 4297, contain Strafford's Council Order Book, 1633-1635. The Mss of the House of

Lords, *New Series*, xi, 1514-1714 (1962) contain other letters and papers relating to Strafford.

Two of Strafford's biographers, Lady Burghclere (1931) and Lord Birkenhead (1938) had acess to the Strafford Mss while they were still at Woodhouse. Both biographers used the Mss with discrimination but it was impossible for any investigator to make full use of the papers while they remained in private hands. Hence, the basis of all work, until Wedgwood, remained Knowler's two folio volumes, which gave an incomplete picture of Strafford. The Strafford Mss taken as a whole reveal a complex and contradictory character, whose depth was not plumbed until the clear and perceptive estimate of C. V. Wedgwood. Wedgwood's is the definitive work on Strafford's life and the introductory chapters of my study of his trial are based on her 1962 revision.

Other evidence gives a point of view of events independent of Strafford. The attitude of the Earl of Cork is indicated in his diary printed by A. B. Grosart in *Linsmore Papers*, 1st series, i-v, and his letters, a selection of which were printed by Grosart, 2d series. The letters of Sir Arthur Ingram, who was involved in the Irish customs farm and other business, is partly calendared in H.M.C., *Var. Coll.*, viii, 1-191. The dispute between Strafford and Loftus is to be found in H.M.C. *Report*, ix, 293ff. The commissions of North Riding-Yorkshire illustrate the rivalries between Strafford and Sir John Savile, Sir David Foulis, Lord Eure, Henry Bellasis and his connections with Sir Arthur Ingram, William Pennyman, and Christopher Wandesford. The sentiments of Queen Henrietta Maria are given in part in her letters ed. by Mary A. E. Green (1857). The Masereene papers (P.R.O.N.I.) might have thrown light on John Clotworthy's activities prior to and during the trial, but they are of no value for this period.

One of the most valuable sources is the correspondence of Philip Percival to John Barry (Egmont Mss) and the Papers of the Ormonde, Bath, and Portland Mss, calendared H.M.C., Reports II, IV, VI, VII, IX, XI. They provide letters during the trial when the Irish and Scots agents were in England, seeking redress of their grievances, during the period of Strafford's trial.

The letters of George Radcliffe, edited by T. D. Whitaker (1810) and Christopher Wandesford, Add. Mss, Bodleian, 286, throw light upon Strafford's administration in Ireland and the North from the point of view of a trusted friend and lieutenant. Also of importance are the *Correspondence of the Earl of Carlisle*, Egerton Mss, Brit. Mus., 2592-7, and *Manchester's Memoirs*, Add. Mss, 567, Brit. Mus.

The sources cited in the references represent only a part of the works consulted. I am indebted to more modern scholars than I can name here either for the impersonal assistance of their writings or for personal help. The following biographies were especially informative in setting the stage for the trial: D. H. Willson on James I; H. R. Trevor-Roper on Laud; F. M. G. Higham and E. Wingfield-Stratford on Charles I; J. H. Hexner on Pym; Harold Hulme on Eliot; C. Bowen on Coke. Specialized studies that cast light on Pym's management of the parliament are G. F. Berquist, "The Parliamentary Speaking of John Pym," unpublished Ph. D. dissertation, Penn State University (1958) and L. Crowell, "The Speaking of John Pym," *S.M.*, xxxiii, no. 2 (June, 1960), 77-101.

Especially useful for understanding the relationship between Strafford and Ireland and the outcome of the trial is H. F. Kearney, *Strafford in Ireland, 1633-1641* (1959).

C. C. Weston's excellent *English Constitutional History and the House of Lords, 1556-1832* (1965) breaks new ground in the history of constitutional theory and shows the importance of Charles I (and, indirectly, Strafford) in the germination of the theory of the constitution which underlay the Glorious Revolution. For theoretical background on this issue, I owe much to Francis Wormuth's work *The Royal Prerogative* (1939). Lawrence Stone's monumental *The Crisis of the Aristocracy* (1965) is of fundamental importance for understanding the acquiescence of the peers in the Bill of Attainder.

For the economic background, I have learned much from the insight of R. H. Tawney, from the writings of Hugh Trevor-Roper, and the provocative stimulus of Christopher Hill. Two specialized works which give insight into Strafford's sources of wealth are J. P. Cooper, "The Fortune of Thomas Wentworth, Earl of Strafford," *Econ. Hist. Rev.*, 2d ser., xi (Dec. 1958) 227-248 and E. Klotz and Godfrey Davies, "The Wealth of Royalist Peers and Baronets During the Puritan Revolution," *Eng. Hist. Rev.*, lvii (1943), 218-221.

The whole question of the Civil Service under King Charles has been investigated by Dr. Aylmer, *The King's Servants* (1961) in which he notes Wentworth's pluralism unfavorably in view of his avowed disapproval of the accumulation of offices.

J. H. Gleason's *The Justices of the Peace in England, 1558-1640* (1969) is a careful, fully-documented study of politics and connections at the county level.

The primary documentary problem of Strafford's trial itself arises from the fact that, at the Restoration, Charles II ordered the proceedings on the attainder (and the proceedings on his father's trial) to be expunged from the *Lords' Journals*. Consequently, all historians of the Stuart period or of the trial have been forced to depend upon John Rushworth's account of the trial (1680). Fortunately, Rushworth was a trained stenographer and recorder, so that his account of the trial is very detailed and, moreover, contains important ancillary documents such as letters, petitions, proclamations, and the like which were issued during the trial by the king, Pym, Parliament, and other principals.

Despite the strengths of his work, Rushworth has two crucial shortcomings: (1) he cannot in any case be treated as an official source comparable to the *Lords' Journals*; (2) he was absent from the trial at its climax. The second shortcoming is extremely serious because Rushworth's account of Strafford's trial jumps unaccountably from the proceedings on the twenty-seventh article to the accused's final speech in his own behalf, a seriously broad omission during the most crucial phase of the trial. Wedgwood, in a *tour de force* of colligation and inference, tried to close the gap by using fragments and traces of the events which she found in diaries, speaker's notes, privately-printed separates of spectators and the *Memorials* of Whitelocke, chairman of the Commons' committee for the prosecution. Yet, each of these sources has definite weaknesses which make the basis of many of her conclusions shaky:

1. *Diaries*. None of the diarists was a professional stenographer. Their training in the taking of notes was, at best, that learned at the Inns of Court or the university. Moreover, their attendance at the trial was often irregular. Briefs of argument, rather than word-for-word accuracy, was generally the diarist's primary concern. Hence, the diaries are highly irregular accounts—detailed on one day, completely devoid of trial information on another.

2. *Speaker's notes*. Notes of the trial exist which were made by Baillie, Knyvett, and others. The coverage of these notes is very incomplete, their worth depending upon the individual's attendance at the trial and his skill as a recorder.

3. *Privately-Printed Separates*. Copies of speeches delivered at the trial by individuals appeared in print from 1641 onwards in great numbers. John Pym and Oliver St. John, for example, had their best efforts at the trial printed. The purpose of these printed speeches was not to preserve a faithful record of a speech for posterity, but rather to circulate the speaker's views or to demonstrate his eloquence for friends and admirers. Hence, the separates were literary works aimed at a reading audience and usually were carefully edited by the speaker himself. These are generally a fair record of the speaker's main ideas and arguments but cannot be taken as a precise report of what was actually said at the trial.

The discovery of new documents, the *Braye Manuscripts*, now allows

Wedgwood's inferences to be checked and the historical record to be corrected and extended. The Braye Mss are a nearly complete set of notes taken down at the trial by the *official* recorders and stenographers of the House of Lords. From these minutes the *Lords' Journals* were written. John Browne was the Clerk of the Parliaments, 1638-1691, and many of his papers, including official and semi-official records of the House of Lords, passed on his death to his daughter and from her ultimately to Lord Braye. The most important of these have been bought or photographed for the House. They include Draft Journals (1621-1690), original Manuscript Minutes of the Trial of Archbishop Laud (1644), Papers laid on the Table of the House, and Parliament Office Memoranda (1625-1691). Cf. the general description given in H.M.C., *10th Report*, Appendix, Part VI, pp. 104-106, the Record Office List of Braye Mss, the Record Office Memoranda, Nos. 7, 11, and 24, and the Addenda 1514-1714 volume of the Calendar. See also House of Lords Record Office Memorandum No. 24, *The Braye Manuscripts bought by the Record Office on 26th January, 1961* (1961). Thus we have the very source of the entries which Charles II had ordered to be blacked out of the *Lords' Journals*.

The Braye Mss allow several problems to be solved or, at least, intelligently attacked:

I. Wedgwood's structure of inference is found to be not only brilliant but also substantially correct, as far as she was able to go, given the sources with which she had to work. She is confirmed on nearly every point—from trivia like the order of speaking of Pym and Glynn in their closing statements, to substantial points like the breakdown of the managers' case on April 10th. Thus many important issues are laid to rest and the record may stand.

II. Because of Rushworth's lapse, and despite Wedgwood's excellent work, several substantial points during the final phase of the trial remained unknown, some of the most important of which were:

A. the sequence of events and relations between Lords and Commons—committees, conferences, petitions, and the like.

B. the events leading to the near-rupture between Lords and Commons.

C. the process of reading and voting the Bill of Attainder in the House of Lords.

It took me several months to sort out these problems and events. In the end, to protect the flow of narrative from a rash of foot and note disease and a jungle of detailed argument, I simply corrected the record where necessary or else filled what gaps I could, therewith indicating the source from which the information had been directly drawn.

A single detailed example will show the extent of what the Braye Mss allowed me to accomplish, as well as show the kind of significant *new* issues which they raise: When the proceedings on the attainder of Strafford were expunged at the Restoration from the *Lords' Journals*, the marginal rubrics were not obliterated. The marginal rubrics for May 5, 6, and 7 record four separate sets of votes on the bill, but the votes themselves have hitherto been unknown (*L.J.*, IV, 236-237). In the Braye Mss in the H.L.R.O. (vol. 2, fos. 142a-b) there are recorded a series of *thirteen* votes which, considering that the *L.J.* were taken from this source, are probably those taken by the Lords on these days. They are headed *Die Mercurii 5 Maii 1641*. The first five votes appear under this heading, the next five under the heading *Die Jovis 6 Maii*, and the last three under the heading *7 Maii*. The votes under 6 Maii concern the two parts of article 23, the charge of saying that the king was absolved from all rules of government, and the Irish army charge. On this day, the *Lords' Journals* record two sets of votes (nothing else is legible except the fact that two votes took place). Under May 5, on which day the *Journals* record one set of votes, are the votes on article 15; and under May 7, on which day one set of votes is recorded in the *Journals* are the final votes on alteration of the government, and the vote to refer the question of law to the judges. The accuracy of this record can be checked against Harleian Ms 6424 (fos. 62b-64a). It is impossible to check the dates in this manuscript, since the diarist has put all the proceeding on the Bill of Attainder together under the heading of May 4. It is, however, possible to check the matter. The text of the Braye Mss for May 5, 6, and 7 (detailed in Appendix D) provides an authentic record of the voting in the House of Lords on the Bill of Attainder against the Earl of Strafford.

The Braye Mss, by covering the gap in Rushworth, settle and raise many questions, from the slight to the very pertinent, *viz.*:

1. The final vote on the attainder took place on May 7th and not on May 8th, as Wedgwood gives it.

2. It appears from the Lords' vote that the House of Commons succeeded with their bill mainly through articles 15 and 23. Yet, both of these articles were outside the mainstream of their treason argument. They were both treasons by levying war and thus possibly reducible to the terms of the 1352 statute. Each article involved the assumption that levying war against the people was levying war against the king, but they did not involve the main body of argument which had been put forward by the Commons. Now that we know the point to adjudicate, which the Lords chose, the question between statute and common law treasons can

be more intelligently discussed by legal historians. The question, I believe, hinges on whether the salvo to the 1352 statute was still in force. (See my conclusion in Appendix D.) Vaughan (*Verney's Notes*, p. 53) argues that *1 Mary cap 1* allows parliaments to declare treasons, but not to punish for them unless they are committed after the declaration. The best discussion of the question by a legal historian is J. F. Stephen, *History of the Common Law*, ii, 250-253. After a great deal of hesitation, he decides that the Commons' abandonment of the impeachment should be taken as a tacit admission that the salvo was no longer in force. The question of common law treasons is even trickier, for the authority of Coke is against it. On the salvo, see Elton, *The Tudor Constitution* (1960), p. 86, for the Duke of Norfolk's admission that the salvo was in force, and also Rezneck, "The Parliamentary Declaration of Treason," *Law Quart. Rev.*, xlvi (1930), 80.

3. The first vote of May 5th shows that the Commons went by way of the Bill of Attainder on *matter of fact* as well as matter of law. This single point blows wide open whole legal theories of treason and fine points of law which legal historians have been arguing ever since the trial of Strafford. Heretofore, it was held that the House of Commons employed a Bill of Attainder because their *evidence* in support of the articles did not constitute treason under law. Now, we see that the evidence itself, the "*matter of fact*" was *declared to be true by a legislative act*. Can a legal basis be found for declaring evidence to be true facts? Perhaps. But despite the high caliber of Conrad Russell's reasoning "The Theory of Treason in the Trial of Strafford" (*Eng. Hist. Rev.*, lxxx (1965), it seems more and more clear that the Commons "slaughtered a man they could not convict," as I argue in my concluding chapter.

III. One of the most intriguing problems concerning Strafford's trial is the vote on the Bill of Attainder in the House of Lords. Who was present and voting? What was the exact vote? Who voted for or against the bill?

Brief and Perfect Relation states the vote to have been 26 to 19. Another figure is given in C.S.P.D., 1640-41, p. 571, 51 votes to 9. No roll is given in either source for the vote.

The Minute Book of the Braye Mss gives attendance (a roll *naming* those present or absent) of the Lords at Strafford's trial from Jan. 11 to Apr. 10, 1641 and the Journal Notes, no. 18, shows attendance on May 4, the day the Protestation was signed. These records of attendance show: (1) which Lords attended the trial and when and how often; (2) who did not attend at all and thus may be eliminated from consideration; (3) that the mean attendance from March 22 to April 10, plus May 4, was 86 Lords present; (4) that the attendance of a great many peers was sporadic; 53

attended two or less sessions; (5) that a "hard core" of 68 peers attended nearly every session of the trial; (6) that nearly all (seventeen) of the Roman Catholic peers feared to come.

This record of attendance provides, at last, a firm basis for inferring the vote of the House of Lords on the Bill of Attainder. (See pp. 176-178 and Appendix A.) Applying a "method of residues" (Mill) to the list of "Straffordians," Rushworth (on Newport and Clare), *Brief and Perfect Relation*, C.S.P.D., Baillie, Cork, D'Ewes, Nalson's *Collection*, and Whitelocke, I give the vote as 26 to 19.

Furthermore, the above sources taken in connection with the Braye Mss indicate, directly and indirectly, Strafford's supporters and adversaries, i.e. who might have been expected to vote one way or another. The Minute Books record attendance, which allows the expectation to be tested. For example, the list of Straffordians shows that Lord Bristol's son Lord Digby voted against the attainder in the House of Commons. But the Minute Book shows Bristol abstaining from voting as the trial moved to its climax. Again, Robert Sydney, Earl of Leicester was upon many occasions prior to 1640 a strong ally of Strafford and it would be plausible to assume his vote against the bill. However, the Braye Mss show positively that Leicester attended not a single session, March 22 to April 10, May 4. Again, Lord Coventry had served on the Council with Strafford and taught him many administrative skills. Coventry became so fond of Strafford that he married his daughter to Strafford's nephew, Sir William Savile. The Minute Book shows that Coventry faithfully attended the sessions, missing but one. When the first five votes on the bill appear under the heading *Die Mercurii 5 Maii 1641*, they are preceded by name after name of peers who are suddenly "excused for being sicke." The indications from such internal evidence were often very clear. Therefore, I felt justified in *naming* thirteen of the nineteen votes for Strafford, and nineteen of the twenty-six who voted against him, fourteen with a high level of confidence, four with a lesser level of confidence. This provides, so far as I know, the first and only estimate of the attendance and vote of the Lords on the bill in the three hundred years since Strafford's trial.

For other insights into the trial, the *Memorials* of Bulstrode Whitelocke are invaluable. Whitelocke was the manager of the committee of Commons which prosecuted Strafford. For the view on the proceedings of one of the Scots' Commissioners, see *Baillie's Letters and Correspondence*, edited by D. Laing (1841). Especially valuable for background and connections of the principals is the *Journal of Symonds D'Ewes*, edited by W. H. Coates (1942). Clarendon, Fairfax, and Knyvett also provide important information, as does Nalson's Collection (1682) and Verney's Papers.

For the gap in Rushworth, *A Brief and Perfect Relation of the Answers of the Earl of Strafford* (1647) is extremely helpful. On individual members of Parliament, see Keeler, *The Long Parliament* (1954) and Brunton and Pennington, *Members of the Long Parliament* (1954). These show that political divisions in Parliament did not follow any clearly defined lines of class, property, or social interest, yet allow important connections to be made between the two sides on the bill.

Harleian Mss 6424, to which one or two references are made, is a diary of the House of Lords during the Long Parliament compiled by an unknown bishop, wherein the part played by Williams in arranging the abstention of twenty-six votes on the bill is made explicit.

Howell's *State Trials* is sparsely used, since it is merely a brief of Rushworth.

The *Strozzi Transcripts* in the Folger Library are the reports of Rossetti, the agent of the Vatican, and are valuable in chronicling the shift of sentiment in Strafford's favor around April 10.

The best view contrary to mine on the status of the Strafford case under law is Conrad Russell, "The Theory of Treason in the Trial of Strafford," *Eng. Hist. Rev.,* lxxx, no. cccxiv (1965), 30-51.

England's Miraculous Preservation

BIBLIOGRAPHY

A. Original Sources

(1) Manuscript Material

Additional Mss. 15, 567, 1467. British Museum.
Additional Mss. 286, Letters of Christopher Wandesford. Bodleian Library.
Braye Mss. House of Lords Record Office. Manuscript notes of the stenographers of the House of Lords on Strafford's trial and from which the Lords Journal was written. These papers therefore fill the gap in the official record which was created when Charles II ordered all proceedings on Strafford's trial expunged from the Lords Journals.
————. *Minute Book, 1640-1641.* Official record of the Lords in attendance, of the motions made, and results of divisions. Missing after April 10, 1641.
Egerton Mss. 2592-7, Correspondence of James Hay, Earl of Carlisle, d. 1636, British Museum.
Harleian Mss. 4297, Wentworth: Council Order Book, 1633-1635, British Museum.
Manchester's Memoirs, Add. Mss. 567. British Museum.
Pym, John. *The Speech or Declaration of John Pym after the Summing Up of the Charge of High Treason against Thomas Earle of Strafford.* British Museum. Thomason Tracts, E. 160 (20).
————. *The Speech of John Pym to the Lords upon the delivery of the Articles of the Commons against William Laud.* British Museum. Thomason Tracts, E. 196 (33).
Strafford Mss. Sheffield Library.
Strozzi Transcripts. 103, Folger Library.
Tanner Mss. Oxford, Bodleian Library.
Thomason Tracts. British Museum.

(2) Printed and Calendared Material

Baillie, Robert. *Letters and Journals.* Vol. I. Ed. D. Laing. Edinburgh, 1841.
Camden Miscellanies. Papers Relating to Thomas Wentworth, First Earl of Strafford. Vol. IX. London, 1895.

Clarendon, Edward Hyde, Earl of. *State Papers Collected by Edward, Earl of Clarendon.* Ed. R. Scrope and T. Monkhouse. 3 vols. Oxford, 1767-1786.

──────. *Selections from Clarendon.* Ed. G. Huehns. London, 1955.

Cork, Earl of. *The Linsmore Papers*: Being the private diaries and papers of the Earl of Cork. Ed. A. B. Grosart. London, 1886-1888.

D'Ewes, Sir Symonds. *Journal: From the Beginning of the Long Parliament to the Opening of the Trial of the Earl of Strafford.* Ed. W. H. Coates. New Haven, Conn., 1942.

──────. *Autobiography.* Ed. J. C. Halliwell. London, 1845.

Fairfax, Lord. *The Fairfax Correspondence.* Ed. G. W. Johnson. London, 1848.

Historical Manuscript Commission (H.M.C.) Reports II, IV, VI (Appendix I), VII (Appendix II), IX, XI (Appendix VII) *Bath Mss, Ormonde Mss, Cowper Mss, Egmont Mss, Montague of Beaulieu Mss, Ormonde Mss, Portland Mss, Salisbury Mss, Hastings Mss, Mss from Various Collections,* II, III, VII, VIII, XII.

Hogan, J. ed. *Letters and Papers Relating to the Irish Rebellion, 1642-1646.* Dublin, 1936.

Knyvett, Sir Thomas. *The Knyvett Letters.* Ed. Bertram Schofield. London, 1949.

Laud, William Archbishop. *Works.* Ed. W. Scott and J. Bliss. Oxford, 1847-1860.

Nalson, John. *Impartial Collection of the Great Affairs of State.* London, 1682.

Pym, John. "Pym's Speech Against Strafford." *Old South Leaflets.* Vol. III, No. 61. Boston, 189?. Library of Congress, DA396. A5P9.

Radcliffe, Sir George. *Letters.* Ed. T. D. Whitaker. London, 1810.

Rushworth, John. *Historical Collections.* 8 vols. London, 1721.

Strafford, Thomas Wentworth, First Earl of. *Private Letters from the Earl of Strafford to his third wife.* Ed. R. Monckton Milnes. London, 1854.

──────. *The Earl of Strafford's Letters and Dispatches.* Ed. William Knowler. 2 Vols. London, 1739.

Stuart, Henrietta Maria. *Letters.* Ed. Mary A. E. Green. London, 1857.

Ussher, Bishop. *Works.* Ed. C. Elrington. Dublin, 1864.

Verney, Sir Ralph. *Verney Papers: Notes of Proceedings in the Long Parliament.* Ed. John Bruce. Vol. XXXI. Camden Society. London, 1845.

B. Parliamentary Debates and Public Documents

Cobbett, William, ed. *Parliamentary History of England.* Vol. II. London, 1807.

Great Britain. British Sessional Papers. *Commons Journals,* 1640-1641 (microprint edition).

——————. *Lords Journals*, 1640-1641 (microprint edition).

Great Britain. Public Record Office. *Calender of State Papers, Domestic Series* (1603-1643). Vols. VIII-XVII. London, 1857-1882.

——————. *Calender of State Papers, Ireland* (1509-1670), 24 vols. London, 1860-1911.

Great Britain. Public Record Office. *Calender of State Papers, Colonial Series* (1574-1660). London, 1860.

——————. *Calender of State Papers and Manuscripts Relating to English Affairs, Existing in the Archives and Collections of Venice, and in Other Libraries of Northern Italy*. Vol. XXV. London, 1925.

Lyle, J. V. ed. *Acts of the Privy Council of England*. London, 1905-1949.

The Manuscripts of the House of Lords. Papers Relating to Thomas Wentworth, First Earl of Strafford. Vol. XI. New Series. Addenda, 1514-1714. London, 1962.

Notestein, Wallace, *et al.*, eds. *Commons Debates, 1621*. 7 vols. New Haven, 1935.

——————. "Commons Debates for 1629." *University of Minnesota Studies in the Social Sciences*. Minneapolis, 1921.

Parliamentary or Constitutional History of England. 24 vols. London, 1761.

C. Contemporary and Nearly Contemporary Chronicles etc.

A Brief and Perfect Relation of the Answers . . . of the Earl of Strafford. London, 1647.

Anon. *A Complete Collection of State Trials and Proceedings for High Treason from the Reign of King Richard II to the End of the Reign of King George I*. 6 vols. London, 1730.

Burnet, Gilbert. *Memoirs of the Lives and Actions of James and William, Dukes of Hamilton*. London, 1677.

Clarendon, Edward Hyde, Earl of. *The History of the Rebellion and Civil Wars in England*. 8 vols. London, 1826.

Lestrange, Hamon. *The Reign of King Charles*. London, 1655.

Rushworth, John. *Historical Collections. The Third Part; in Two Volumes. Containing the Principal Matters which happened from the Meeting of the Parliament, November the third, 1640 to the end of the year 1644*. Vol. IV. London, 1692.

Rushworth, John. *The Tryal of Thomas, Earl of Strafford*. London, 1721.

Sanderson, William. *A Compleat History of the Life and Raigne of King Charles from his Cradle to his Grave*. London, 1658.

Steele, R. ed. *Tudor and Stuart Proclamations, 1485-1714*. 2 vols. Oxford, 1910.

Smith, Sir Thomas. *De Republica Anglorum: A Discourse on the Com-

monwealth of England. London, 1583.

Temple, Sir John. *The Irish Rebellion . . .* London, 1646.

Warwick, Sir Philip. *Memoires of the Reigne of King Charles I with a Continuation to the Happy Restauration of King Charles II.* London, 1701.

Whitelocke, Sir Bulstrode. *Memorials of English Affairs from the Beginning of the Reign of Charles I to the Happy Restoration of King Charles II.* Vol. I. Oxford, 1682.

D. Modern Works

Adams, Charles K. *Representative British Orations.* Vol. I. New York, 1844.

Arnold, Carroll, "Lord Thomas Erskine: Modern Advocate." *Quarterly Journal of Speech,* XLIV, No. 1 (February, 1958), 17-30.

Ashley, Maurice. *England in the Seventeenth Century.* Baltimore, 1962.

Aylmer, G. E. *The King's Servants: The Civil Service of Charles I, 1625-1642.* London, 1961.

Berquist, Goodwin F. "The Parliamentary Speaking of John Pym, 1621-1643." Unpublished Ph. D. dissertation, Department of Speech, The Pennsylvania State University, 1958.

Birch, Thomas. *The Court and Times of Charles the First.* 2 vols. London, 1848.

Birkenhead, 1st Earl of. *Famous Trials of History.* New York, 1926.

Birkenhead, 2nd Earl of. *Strafford.* London, 1938.

Bowen, Catherine. *The Lion and the Throne: The Life and Times of Sir Edward Coke: 1552-1634.* Boston, 1957.

Brett, S. Reed. *John Pym: 1583-1643: The Statesman of the Puritan Revolution.* London, 1940.

Brunton, D. and Pennington, D. H. *Members of the Long Parliament.* Cambridge, Mass., 1954.

Burghclere, Lady. *Strafford.* London, 1938.

Carte, Thomas. *The Life of James, Duke of Ormonde.* 6 vols. Oxford, 1851.

Cooper, J. P. "The Fortune of Thomas Wentworth, Earl of Strafford." Economic History Review, 2nd series, XI (December, 1958), 227-248.

Craig, Robert. *A History of Oratory in Parliament, 1213-1913.* London, 1913.

Crowell, Laura. "The Speaking of John Pym, English Parliamentarian." *Speech Monographs,* XXXIII, No. 2 (June, 1966), 77-101.

Davies, Godfrey. *The Early Stuarts, 1603-1660.* Vol. IX of *The Oxford History of England.* Ed. G. N. Clark. Oxford, 1937.

Durant, Will. *The Age of Reason Begins.* Vol. VII of *The Story of Civilization.* New York, 1961

Gardiner, Samuel R. *History of the Great Civil War.* 4 vols. London,

1893.

————————. *History of England from the Accession of James I to the Outbreak of the Civil War, 1603-1642.* Vol. IX, 1639-1641. London, 1894.

Goodrich, Chauncey. *Select British Eloquence.* New York, 1963.

Hardacre, Paul H. *The Royalists During the Puritan Revolution.* The Hague, 1956.

Hexner, J. H. *The Reign of King Pym.* "Harvard Historical Series." Cambridge, Mass., 1941.

Hill, Christopher. *Puritanism and Revolution: Studies in Interpretation of the English Revolution of the 17th Century.* London, 1958.

Howell, T. B., ed. *A Complete Collection of State Trials and Proceedings for High Treason and Other Crimes and Misdemeanors from the Earliest Period to the Year 1783.* Vol. III: *3-16 Charles I, 1627-1640.* London, 1816.

Hulme, Harold. *Sir John Eliot.* London, 1957.

Feiling, Keith. *A History of England from the Coming of the English to 1918.*

Forster, John. *Sir John Eliot: A Biography, 1592-1632.* 2 vols. London, 1864.

Keeler, Mary F. *The Long Parliament, 1640-1641: A Biographical Study of Its Members.* Philadelphia, 1954.

Kearney, Hugh F. *Strafford in Ireland, 1633-1641: A Study in Absolutism.* Manchester, 1959.

Klotz, Edith and Davies, Godfrey. "The Wealth of Royalist Peers and Baronets During the Puritan Revolution." *English Historical Review,* LVIII (1943), 218-221.

Newcastle, Margaret Duchess of. *The Life of William Cavendish, Duke of Newcastle.* London, 1849.

Moir, T. L. *The Addled Parliament of 1614.* Oxford, 1958.

O'Grady, Hugh. *Strafford and Ireland.* Dublin, 1923.

Pearl, Valerie. *London and the Outbreak of the Puritan Revolution.* Oxford, 1961.

Ranke, Leopold von. *A History of England.* 3 vols. Oxford, 1875.

Russell, Conrad. "The Theory of Treason in the Trial of Strafford." *English Historical Review,* LXXX, No. CCCXIV (1965), 30-50.

Stone, Lawrence. *The Crisis of the Aristocracy, 1558-1641.* Oxford, 1965.

Traill, H. D. *Lord Strafford.* London, 1925.

Trevelyan, George M. *England Under the Stuarts.* London, 1904.

Trevor-Roper, H. R. *Archbishop Laud, 1573-1645.* 2nd ed. Hamden, Conn., 1963.

Turner, Raymond. *The Privy Council of England.* 2 vols. London, 1927.

Wedgwood, C. V. *Thomas Wentworth, First Earl of Strafford.* New York, 1962.

————————. *The Great Rebellion.* Vol. I: *The King's Peace.* New

York, 1969.

Weston, Corrine C. *English Constitutional Theory and the House of Lords, 1556-1832.* New York, 1965.

Wormuth, Francis. *The Royal Prerogative, 1603-1649: A Study in English Political and Constitutional Ideas.* Ithaca, 1939.

Wingfield-Stratford, Esme. *King Charles and King Pym.* London, 1949.

————. *Charles, King of England.* London, 1949.

Passage of the Bill of Attainder (Braye MS)

INDEX

Charles I (Van Dyck)